ENDORSEMENTS

Heaven Stormed delivers a deeply fitting work for our times. Randy profoundly bridges the gap between the celestial and terrestrial realms, prompting us to gaze skyward for greater grounding and heightened insight into living. This work intricately refines his personal encounters where he offers us the knowledge that he acquired while harmonizing them into a symphonic guide for the challenges of the current era. His approach is pragmatic, yet he strikes resonant chords within our hearts while stirring visions of our ultimate destination. This is a must-read for those whose soul hungers for more eternal-mindedness.

Rabbi Felix Halpern
Author of *Dancing Past the Darkness, A Rabbi's Journey to Heaven,* and *Heaven's Soul Cleanse*

Heaven Stormed is a wonderfully detailed description of a journey that is crafted for each individual to understand how the Lord intervened in one's life for the ultimate story of God's glory. Randy has given readers the ultimate "behind the scenes" glimpse into his personal story for the purpose that God is revealed through the heart of a father. This book is a powerful insight into the before, present, and future of what God not only had in store for Randy but what is being revealed for you and me. This book will challenge and encourage everyone who takes the time to invest in the reality of the Kingdom of God!

Ryan Johnson
Ryan Johnson Ministries and Author of
How to Contend for Your Miracle

I have always been fascinated with near-death experiences (NDEs), and I've studied over 1,000 of them. These experiences happen outside of our human limitations of time and space. Given this, I've had the honor and pleasure of talking with Randy firsthand for hours about his encounter with Jesus and the wonders of Heaven he experienced when he clinically died for 30 minutes. Randy's newest book, *Heaven Stormed*, constitutes the most complete account of his NDE. This captivating book will leave you in awe of God's compassion, lovingkindness, and personal plan for each and every person, while at the same time preparing you to always be ready for His return.

John Burke
New York Times Bestselling Author of *Imagine Heaven* and *Imagine the God of Heaven*

There is a reason we are here. We are part of God's plan. And even more than that, we have a key role to play in what He is about to bring forth. I know this to be true. Which is why I was so excited to hear about Randy Kay's new book revealing God's plans for these times, what He is about to release, and how you and I can be a part of it! *Heaven Stormed* did not disappoint. Just the opposite. It is a profound read that will take you deeper into your knowledge and connection with Jesus, as well as help you understand what is coming and the part you have to play in it all.

Robert Hotchkin
Robert Hotchkin Ministries / Men on the Frontlines

Randy Kay weaves together an end-time revelation from what he saw in Heaven with a thorough comparison of Scripture and a study of Judaic history along with Randy's prophetic words. Randy Kay is a trusted board member of Messianic Vision, Inc. I have interviewed Randy on *It's Supernatural.* His story and analysis are compelling for several reasons: Randy died, met Jesus, experienced a series of life reviews that Jesus revealed to him, witnessed the triune

God within the throne room of Heaven, saw the unveiling of the end times from Heaven, and ties what he witnessed with the importance of Israel and the Jewish people. For these reasons, I endorse *Heaven Stormed* as a means to help usher forth the "greater glory" from a heavenly perspective.

Sid Roth
Founder and CEO, Messianic Vision, Inc.
TV Personality and Host of *It's Supernatural*
& CEO of ISN (It's Supernatural Network)
and METV (Middle East Television)
Author of *Heaven Is Beyond Your Wildest Expectations,*
It's Supernatural, and *There Must Be Something More!*

Near-death experiences change you. The revelations you learn are way beyond what mere words describe. Yet, Randy Kay uniquely unpacks a few of these: eternal time, things seen in reverse, the Joshua generation, and the time when Heaven storms! The anointing I felt while reading the last six chapters is amazing! *Heaven Stormed* is a worthy read and I highly recommend it. God bless and may this book stir a revival in you!

B.W. Melvin
Author of *A Land Unknown: Hell's Dominion*

Reading Randy Kay's newest book *Heaven Stormed* gives the reader a backstory of what Heaven will be like. The reassurance of knowing God has planned out our lives is a comfort that there is still hope even after death because of Jesus. I had so much revelation and confirmation as the heart of Jesus was revealed through the pages. How marvelous is our God that He is always watching and seeing every situation of our life? As believers, the urgent calling to be the hands and feet of Jesus was loud and clear in *Heaven Stormed*. I loved this book and thank Randy for his obedience to release it. His life, heart, and mission are woven so beautifully together in this book that you feel you have found a new friend!

Lisa Perna
Author of *Touching The Father's Heart Through Prayer* and Broadcaster

I am privileged to have known Randy Kay for many years, but it was at a very unexpected moment in time that I encountered the real Randy. I was interviewing him on the *God@Work* show on GodTV regarding his experience in business. Then, suddenly, without warning or notice, something happened. Randy's face and demeanor took on a new look and his voice became empowered with God's presence. Randy began to talk about Heaven in a way that was so powerful and personal that I knew we had entered into a new dimension.

Since then, Randy has been writing, talking, and impacting the world through his encounters with God, Jesus, and Heaven. His books are powerful and full of scriptural insights. His newest one, *Heaven Stormed*, is equally powerful but it adds a personal touch. We get to know Randy from childhood to college; from skeptic to Bible teacher; from C suite executive to financially broke to full of God's presence. Set aside some time, because once you start reading you won't be able to stop.

Rich Marshall
Author of *God@Work, God@Work II* and *God@Rest*

Heaven Stormed provides an eye-opening and revelatory look at the end times pertaining to the coming storm from a biblical and heavenly perspective. With grace and humility, Randy lays a solid biblical foundation for the spiritual truths he shares from his time in Heaven.

Heaven Stormed is a powerful challenge to believers today to keep our eyes focused on God and trust His plan as we step out into our heavenly assignment at this time. As you read this book, may the Lord fill you with a hopeful expectation and peace for what's to come and your important role in it

Debbie Kitterman

Founder of Dare2Hear Ministries; founder and Sound the Call, LLC International Speaker, Podcaster, Pastor and Blogger

Author of *Legacy: The Lost Art of Blessing, The Gift of Prophetic Encouragement: Hearing the Words of God for Others,* and more

Randy Kay is a man I've learned to trust and admire. Using valid biblical insights, he describes wonderful encounters with God and revelations of last-days world events which will help readers face the future with greater hope and confidence.

Capt. Dale Black

Airline Pilot Instructor (Retired)

Author of *Visiting Heaven, Flight to Heaven,* and *Life, Cancer, and God*

We live in unprecedented days. The world seems to be shaking and anxiety is rising, even in God's children all over the earth. For such a time as this, God has raised Randy Kay to be a clarion voice of hope in an unsettling culture. *Heaven Stormed* will not only help you find a high level of connection with what God is saying to the Church right now, but it will also help you bond with Him as your Father. Read this book, because faith rises when we have proper knowledge of what God and His Word say.

Dr. Chad Norris

Senior Pastor of The Garden Greenville

Author of *God Is Shaking His Temple* and *Your Mess Is Your Message*

In his book, *Heaven Stormed*, Randy Kay does a masterful job of combining his personal experiences in Heaven with an understanding of what God is doing on planet Earth in the last days. You will be greatly encouraged by the stories, experiences, and biblical insight God has given Randy. I highly recommend this book to all who are seeking a deeper relationship with the Lord and an understanding of God's supernatural glory being released on the earth in these last days.

Craig Hill
Author, Speaker, and Founder of Family
Foundations International

Heaven Stormed is an expedition into the glory of God and the profound mysteries of the end times This revelation, carefully couched in biblical truth, offers both a window into the afterlife and an urgent wake-up call to the world, highlighting the imminence of God's final act on the stage of human history.

I believe that this book has arrived at an essential moment in our history, a time when understanding Heaven, prophecy, and God's divine orchestration is paramount. For those yearning to grasp the mysteries of the end times or seeking reassurance of God's eternal promises, *Heaven Stormed* offers a profound and timely perspective.

Alan DiDio
Pastor of The Encounter Charlottem
Host of *Encounter Today*

After reading *Heaven Stormed*, I began to remember things that I had never been taught! Randy Kay has skillfully penned words of weight and wonder that will transport the teachable spirit into a supernatural realm of the ever-present NOW! The reader will learn that they are a potential candidate for experiencing these life-changing, heavenly encounters that transport the believer into the "habitat of holiness."

I know this book, like all of Randy's previous inspiring works, will open realms of the miraculous. It will help enable the reader to tune into the divine frequencies that are continuously broadcasting to the sensitive overcomer, with the invitation to become a gateway, a window, or an entrance into this realm.

After prayerfully reflecting on the supernatural content of this book, *Heaven Stormed*, I heard such an invitation from the Lord. "Come up here, see what I see, be what I be, learn! My best is a people at rest! Be seated at my right hand and learn to administrate My Kingdom. Learn of the finished work of Christ from the revelation of your life being hidden in Christ!"

Read the book!

Dr. Clarice Fluitt
President of Clarice Fluitt Ministries

I am delighted and honored to endorse Randy Kay's newest book, *Heaven Stormed.* This is a work of incredible detail and prophetic explanation that will answer many questions and, dare I say, change lives. Randy's open and honest style of writing regarding his personal health challenges and courage in the face of many issues is an encouragement to us all.

Jim Woodford
Author of *Heaven, An Unexpected Journey*

HEAVEN STORMED

A HEAVENLY ENCOUNTER REVEALS YOUR ASSIGNMENT IN THE END-TIME OUTPOURING AND TRIBULATION

RANDY KAY

DESTINY IMAGE® PUBLISHERS, INC.
P.O. Box 310, Shippensburg, PA 17257-0310

"Publishing cutting-edge prophetic resources to supernaturally empower the body of Christ"

This book and all other Destiny Image and Destiny Image Fiction books are available at Christian bookstores and distributors worldwide.

For more information on foreign distributors, call 717-532-3040.
Reach us on the Internet: www.destinyimage.com.

ISBN 13 TP: 978-0-7684-7330-8
ISBN 13 eBook: 978-0-7684-7331-5

For Worldwide Distribution, Printed in the U.S.A.
4 5 6 7 8 / 28 27 26 25 24

DEDICATION

This book is dedicated to those who have been involved in Randy Kay Ministries as guests, supporters, partners, workers, prayer partners, and participants. One day you will see all the countless people in Heaven who have benefitted from your contributions—and it will be beyond amazing.

Thank you!

ACKNOWLEDGMENTS

Thank you foremost to God, whose inspiration challenged me to write about experiences and discoveries that exceeded my abilities. Lord, You saved my life, and then Your grace allowed me to see into your heavenly realm so that You could bless others.

Also, thanks to my supportive family and friends; primarily my wife, Renee, who encouraged me during the hundreds of hours I was authoring this book. To my editor and friend Paula Langhoff, you took my words and anointed them with your inspiring talent. Shaun Tabatt, you honored my story and believed in me enough to help launch something that began as a book but progressed into a ministry.

John Burke, I will never forget that first luncheon with you and your son, Justin, when I first shared my story while gushing forth tears—thank you for your encouragement. My spiritual mentors Rich Marshall and Sid Roth believed in me enough to become my friends. The ministry team at Messianic Vision Inc., have also become my friends—thank you for spreading the greater Glory of God to the Jews and to a hungering world.

Finally, to my fellow afterlife survivors who have honored Jesus with your testimonies on our shows. You too, have become my friends as we share an unparalleled experience that truly, only God, His angels, and we can fully comprehend.

The list could go on and on and my apologies if I have missed you. A final acknowledgment to my readers; may you allow the words in this book to seep into your soul and I pray an everlasting blessing over you and those you love.

May Love, who is God, shower you all with His Glory, forever.

CONTENTS

FOREWORD

Were it not for my role in Christian publishing, Randy Kay and I might never have crossed paths. In God's providence, we connected around six years ago when he was working on his book *Dying to Meet Jesus*. I still remember being somewhat skeptical of the project when it came up for discussion in our publishing board meeting. Although I was open to supernatural moves of God, at that time, I was quite uncomfortable with near-death experiences. In fact, Randy's book *Dying to Meet Jesus* was one of the first books I read in the afterlife genre.

Fast-forward six years and Randy and I have launched a podcast heavily focused on NDE testimonies, co-authored three books under our *Real Near Death Experience* Stories brand, and with this book, *Heaven Stormed,* I will have been a part of bringing to life Randy's three books that explore his time in Heaven.

While books and interviews about Heaven, hell, and the afterlife have been around for a long time, Randy and I began to see a new move of God taking shape following our first interview in late 2020. As more and more of our content went viral, we began to receive numerous e-mails and comments about lives being radically transformed as people watched our interviews. Some viewers accepted Jesus as their Lord and Savior for the first time. Others told us how God radically healed them. As the concrete evidence that God was uniquely breathing on this afterlife content continued to mount, we couldn't help but go all in on being a part of what God was doing through these powerful testimonies.

Between our podcasts and traveling together for media interviews, I've heard Randy talk about his experiences in Heaven over 50 times. The one thing I've noticed is that every time Randy shares his testimony, the Holy Spirit breathes upon it anew and there is a fresh anointing to dramatically impact the viewers and listeners who encounter it. Randy's new book *Heaven Stormed* is no exception.

In the first part of the book, you are going to experience in vivid detail the many ways God was showing up supernaturally in Randy's life prior to his NDE. On the one hand, God was trying to get his attention, and on the other, He was preparing the ground for what would be sowed into Randy's life during his time in Heaven.

In the second part of the book, Randy goes into great detail about what he experienced on the other side of the veil. Even if you've read all of Randy's previous books and watched all of his previous interviews, you are going to encounter something fresh and new here. I know Randy's testimony very well and I was dramatically impacted and ministered to as I made my way through this middle part of the book.

Finally, we come to the third part of the book where Randy has saved the best for last. On average, it takes a near-death experiencer seven years to initially come to terms with and have a level of understanding about what they experienced during their NDE. It's almost like the human brain lacks the capacity to hold what was downloaded during their time on the other side. Most NDE-ers experience a sort of ongoing revelation about what they saw and experienced in Heaven or hell. For Randy, it was 16 years after his NDE that God gave him insight into what the storm he saw in Heaven foretold. Pay close attention to what unfolds in this latter part of the book so you can understand and be ready for the things God is about to unleash in the earth and your specific assignment during these end times.

Shaun Tabatt

Publishing Executive, Destiny Image Publishers

INTRODUCTION

Many, including me, have shared their afterlife experience in Heaven and even hell, but this event I am about to share with you is different. Only recently did God's Holy Spirit explain to me the fullness of what He revealed to me in Heaven. In Heaven, I witnessed the last days of earth and the fulfillment of the ancient prophecies of the Bible, after I died and journeyed with Jesus in Heaven and in God's Throne Room.

At first, I struggled with how to write this storyline. Then God's Holy Spirit inspired me to portray in a meaningful way, what believers in Jesus may expect in the afterlife, as well as the revelations of the last days I beheld in Heaven. My story begins with several of my life events on earth that were later revealed in a series of heavenly life reviews (and the reasons Jesus chose them for review). Most of what you will read in this book will be found in Heaven, including a portrayal that could only have been expressed under God's divine inspiration and guidance. I certainly could not have painted any picture of what I experienced, without His direct influence.

Less than a year before writing this book, the Holy Spirit directed me to describe what I previously thought would be forbidden to be publicly revealed. What I am about to share with you speaks to what God created in the heavenlies, and will release onto this world with a force and influence never before seen in the history of humankind. I will share the beginning of the *end of times* (or end times) with you, as I witnessed the scenes as they formed in Heaven.

Know that the forthcoming "Storm" of God will bring not only destruction in the last days but a cleansing that restores God's Greater Glory in the world. God's Glory is arriving right now. The Glory of God is the Holy Spirit's presence, God's presence. The Bible explains in Nahum 1:3 (NIV) that the Lord's *way is in the whirlwind and the storm."* He spoke to the prophet Job out of the whirlwind, and He descended on Mount Sinai in a storm and a tempest.

Oftentimes, we think of God's wrath as compared to a whirlwind and a storm that is suddenly executed upon humanity. For example, when the Babylonians came against the Jews in Jeremiah 4:13 (ESV), the Lord came up *"like clouds; his chariots like the whirlwind."* At the head of this Storm was the Lord Himself; ordering, directing, and succeeding such that no one could stand against it.

I beheld "God's Storm" in Heaven. It was preceded by a review of my life and the meaning of the events that I will describe in detail, in the beginning of this book. I learned in Heaven that for God, every person's life events hold meaning. I also knew as an agnostic and as a believer that demons swirl in this world and anxiously await opportunities to torment us with their manifestations; and that angels do not manifest whimsically as demons do, but with the intention and direction of God.

My story begins with my life as it was eventually revealed to me in Heaven, and crescendos with my witness of God's Storm forming in the heavenly Throne Room—a Storm that is soon to be released upon the earth. Toward the end, I will explain how God uniquely revealed the Season of the Storm on this earth to me and what this means for all people during these last days.

My friend, I saw this Heaven-shaking event with my spiritual eyes. At the time, my dead body lay on a hospital bed, while my spirit body stood in Heaven alongside Jesus. I observed all of Heaven shifting before my spiritual eyes. I viewed the heavenlies much like the way the biblical prophet Elijah's servant saw into the spirit realm. While in his physical body, he viewed the chariots of fire all around himself and young prophet Elisha, as in 2 Kings 6:17. What I beheld while I was a spirit being, flowed from the brilliantly lighted Throne Room of God. However, unlike Elijah's servant, I was entirely in the spirit.

Millions of towering angels (called cherubim in the Bible) stood around God at full attention, with wings folded as they repeatedly sang in unison, "Holy is the Lamb," and other names for the Almighty. Thousands of humans in white robes also shouted praises of all kinds to the Father. God the Father's frame appeared in size as that of a massive building. God then decreed the beginning of the end of the world as we know it.

At the time of this appearance, my physical body no longer existed. I was dead. Several blood clots had blocked blood flow to my lungs. A drug-resistant bacterium had spread throughout my body causing sepsis, which resulted in a severe drop in blood pressure, blood cells clotting throughout my body, and my subsequent death. In a period that seemed like eternity, a light pulled me out of my body to behold warring spirits off in the distance within a space that was darker than a starless night.

At the time that I beheld Heaven's Storm, I was "Godsmacked." I coined that word as a derivation of the word *gobsmacked*, meaning utterly astonished. However, that word understates what really happened. I do not even know if a word exists to properly describe the moment when all of Heaven shifted from the pleasantry of paradise, to the seriousness of what Almighty God had just executed. Events rolled in obedience to a reverberating roar that stilled everything in Heaven with the alarming importance of the moment.

Suddenly, a breath-like, soft wind I innately knew as the Holy Spirit, turned into a spiraling whirlwind. Blossoming flowers stopped blooming. Trees stopped growing. Towering angels bowed like little children. All of Heaven ceased being a wonderland as the wind rolled with a somber gravity. History would mark this moment as the culmination of God's redemptive plan, and it was good.

After I died and journeyed with Jesus throughout Heaven, I was in the middle of the feeling of being encased within a rolling Storm. I heard the sound like a declarative roar, roll its way along until it crashed with a noise mightier than the breaking of a ten-thousand-foot tidal wave. At the sound, all of Heaven quaked and angels bowed in absolute reverence.

What did this dramatic shift in Heaven mean? I did not know—until sixteen years later, when God's Holy Spirit began revealing the secret of the Storm I had witnessed in Heaven. Only now do I understand what the Storm foretold, and also that it is rapidly approaching.

Life as we know it is about to change. Nothing will ever be the same. Heaven's Storm is being poured forth even now, and it will rain on every nation. When it does, look up because the only rescuer will be God. Anyone not covered by the saving blood of Jesus will be—well, I will tell you about that part later. Suffice it to say that nothing and no one will remain untouched by God's Storm.

With love in Christ,

Randy Kay

PART ONE

LIFE REVIEW PREQUEL: DYING TO GOD AND OTHER GHOSTLY THINGS

1

FINDING GOD THROUGH THE DARKNESS

Heaven Storms because the Spirit desires to be known. He oftentimes is preceded by the darkness, until the darkness is exposed by the light of life.
—INSPIRED BY JOHN 1:4-9

As a seven-year-old, I viewed the side profile of my Uncle Carlyle's face as his body lay in the open coffin at Greaves Mortuary in Keokuk, Iowa. Greased black hair and a relaxed grin belied his rigid condition. Outside sat a skylight blue 1964 Mustang. Weeks earlier, my aunt Margaret took mom and me for a spin in the hardtop that had that "new car" smell. Now it served as car number three in the funeral procession of a stormy day soon clouded over with darkness.

On the way to Oakland Cemetery, Mom pointed to a square, red brick building on her right with a gray, peeling-paint garage door below and two windows above that were boarded up with plywood.

"We lived in the upstairs apartment when we were children," Mom commented, as we followed the hearse to the cemetery.

"How many lived there?" I asked.

"Your four aunts and your uncle, my mom (who died of blood clots before I was born), your Grandpa Renard, and me," she said.

"All in that tiny apartment?" I asked.

"Yep. It was the Depression and there wasn't much to go around."

"But they were rich, compared to my family," my dad chimed in.

"Why?" I asked.

"Because they had food; they sold food in the grocery store," my dad explained. "We just had the shoe repair shop, and not too many people were shining their shoes back then." (This was during the Great Depression, in the late 1930s.)

"See that garage?" Mom pointed to the peeling gray door below the apartment.

"Yeah."

"That was the storefront. Grandpa Renard sold most of the food for the poorer, south side of Keokuk. A nickel for bread and ten cents for a box of cereal," said Mom.

My mom and dad met as children, in that small town of Keokuk. Grandpa Edward Renard had owned the garage-sized grocery store in the early 1900s. It was just three blocks south of the Oakland Cemetery, where his bones now rested in an otherwise empty plot, once meant for the entire estranged family. Grandpa Renard frequently binged on alcohol; often flying into a rage, like the evening when my mom, her mother, four sisters, and one brother snuck out of the house to catch the premier of *Gone with the Wind* at the Keokuk Theater.

Returning home, they all had to be rushed into a closet by my grandmother, to escape Grandpa Renard's drunken fury for having secretly escaped the apartment without his permission. His abusive curses imparted a lifelong effect that would plague each member of the family (including my incessantly worrisome mom) with some kind of emotional scarring, long after the store was a discarded relic.

Following the burial of Uncle Carlyle's body, my parents visited relatives, after dropping me off at Grandma and Grandpa's shoe repair shop on Main Street. About the only redeeming aspect of sitting in the shop and inhaling shoe polish vapors occurred on a hot, muggy day when I inserted a dime into the vending machine and received a bottled Coca-Cola *straight from Heaven*.

River towns were just beginning to die in the 1960s, after trains and planes replaced the commerce and trade along American rivers. A statue of Native American Chief Keokuk stood in the park peering across the Mississippi River, as a quasi-mascot of the many long-forgotten people who withered into obscurity and dust, like my once-successful Uncle Carlyle.

That night, while sleeping in my grandmother's musty bungalow, I awoke around midnight, to a badly-timed, howling wind, after dreaming about the corpse I had viewed the day before. Somehow, the fragrance of the carnations that were placed around the coffin had seeped into my nostrils. I smelled them throughout the day and into the night. Thank God we would be leaving Keokuk in the morning, because that town seemed only to consist of old people, old buildings, the aging, and the dead. Death stuck with me for a long time after that, and seemed to portend my own death, decades later.

We packed the car for our trip back to Chicago. Dad drove across the bridge above the Mississippi as its murky waters swirled below. I always thought the mighty Mississippi looked scary, and silently feared that our car might swerve off the bridge, due to the screeching noise the tires made as soon as we entered the bridgeway.

I rolled down the window, only to breathe in the pungent aroma of burnt corn. Its origin was the Hubinger Electric Starch Factory, located on the nearby riverbank. After seeing my first dead body, I would associate "the smell of death" not with burnt corn, but with the sickening-sweet smell of carnations that had dotted my uncle's coffin. As we drove, macabre thoughts kept swirling in my head—along with the lingering profile of Uncle Carlyle.

"You okay?" Mom asked, while my head turned to the back window to see the fading outline of Keokuk.

"Is Uncle Carlyle in the ground now?" I asked.

"He's in Heaven," Mom offered, as she fiddled with the radio knob, probably in search of a Glen Campbell song.

"Does everybody go to Heaven?" I asked.

"Only God knows," she said. That was pretty much the end of our conversation for the rest of the four-hour drive.

Thoughts kept pouring through my young brain. Before then, the dead had only appeared in my life in entertaining Frankenstein and Dracula movies. The only funeral I ever saw on TV was that of John F. Kennedy, the year before Uncle Carlyle's comparatively discreet affair. We drove by cemeteries here and there, but up to that point, death existed as a theoretical possibility, not an actual observed fact.

Whenever a hearse passed by our midnight blue Plymouth, we religiously sang a one-liner: "Oh my, oh my, the hearse drove by. Who will be the next one to die?" But after seeing that dead body of my middle-aged uncle in the coffin, I no longer joked about dead people. I think his death instilled within me, a perpetual fear that my own parents might one day "bite the dust" (as they say).

After arriving home, life resumed in an altered state of normal. I say "altered" because as a sickly kid living in a three-bedroom ranch-style home in Arlington Heights, Illinois, the thought had crossed my mind that I was unlike other "normal" kids. Most children could play and not run out of breath. My signature sound was a bubbling wheeze that proved a little embarrassing at the school cafeteria, not to mention unappetizing to would-be friends. Almost nightly, Mom would pound my back to loosen the congestion caused by asthma, while my high school-aged sister and brother tried to sleep.

As a kid, it just seemed normal to me, despite occasional trips to the hospital from collapsed lungs. "Normal" is a very relative term and often interpreted from a rather biased viewpoint. I tried living like any normal kid, despite an inability to run without provoking an asthma attack. Naturally, a cat lived next door, and of course my friend Patti and I "needed" to hold the cat. Then my eyes would itch and I would wheeze. The next thing I would remember was Mom waking me up from the shaggy floor of our home, as she shook me and pounded my back as if I had done something wrong—and you guessed it, another trip to the hospital. That was normal life for me.

Dad got promoted to a sales manager position after selling dry ice and CO_2 gas. Moving to the suburbs of Philadelphia in Cherry Hill, New Jersey, as a first grader, introduced me to another facet of death. One night, as my older brother's teenage friend sat on our white, quilted living room sofa, I looked through the picture window to see an ambulance flash its lights across the street.

The teen cupped his head in his hands for a while, then lifted his head when my mom offered him a hot chocolate. As he looked up, I could see his reddened eyes and tear-stained cheeks. My dad happened to be home after a long day managing a dry ice sales team. He stood next to me, so I asked him why Tony was crying. My dad bent down and whispered into my ear, "His dad died."

"How?" I asked.

A long pause followed as my dad looked out the window. He wore his satiny silver suit with his oiled hair that normally made him appear regal. But now because he slumped and some hairs were unusually out of place, he seemed different. I looked closely and saw something in his eyes that resembled a tear. He and Tony's dad were about the same age, and they played couples bridge together. His eyes stared at those flashing ambulance lights, then at Tony—back and forth, like a tennis match. It seemed like forever before my dad's eyes finally turned toward me.

"Probably a heart attack, I'm not sure, but it was too late when the ambulance got there."

"Did Tony find him there?" My thinking was that if Tony found him dead, then somehow he was now contaminated with some kind of "death cooties." I didn't want to be around Tony anymore. I figured that just being around someone who lost someone, automatically contaminated them and possibly invited the effects of death to come after them. (A child's mind can go to the strangest places.)

Even stranger to me than death, was God. I had seen death, but God remained a mystery rarely considered. As a boy, I believed that God primarily resided at St. Andrew's Methodist Church, in Cherry Hill, New Jersey. That was because the only time God came up in discussion, was on Sunday morning at 10:00 a.m., and darn it if the church folks didn't place those wretched-smelling carnations at the front.

Once services began, hell always seemed more real than Heaven. For me, the only thing worse than learning about Noah, Moses, and all the other ancients, was the hell of being sandwiched in those unforgiving wooden pews and listening to a droning pastor turn words into sounds worse than fingernails scratching a chalkboard. At least the chalkboard scratching didn't bore me to death.

Then, something life-changing happened. It was another death, of sorts—the death of whatever faith one was supposed to believe as a so-called Christian. One day, a letter arrived in the mail, after which we stopped going to church. I saw the letter on my dad's desk sit there for weeks, which sparked my curiosity. After school one day, I read that letter, removing it from atop my dad's desk. The desk's presence alone was significant, as Mom and me had spent weeks sanding and staining it after retrieving the "two thousand pound" 1930s office castaway from a junkyard.

Now that desk served as the only place I could see my dad; albeit buried in papers on weeknights, if he wasn't traveling for work. At least occasionally I could watch him *tap-tap-tap* his foot in sync with some performer on the *Lawrence Welk* TV show as he sat at the desk.

I turned my attention to the letterhead that I held in my hands and that said *St. Andrew's Methodist Church* at the top. The body of the letter said something to the effect of:

"Dear Mr. Kay, We regret to inform you that since you have not honored your tithing commitment to this church for ("x amount of time"), you have been excommunicated from our church."

At the time, I didn't understand the word "excommunicated," but Mom later explained that we wouldn't be attending that church anymore. I knew after looking that word up in the dictionary, that the church had kicked my dad out because *he didn't pay them.*

I thought about how my dad had served as a hero in the Pacific Fleet during World War II, saving lives after a Kamikaze attack. Now the church made him out to be a loser. I think that was the point when I rejected the church. I never thought very highly of it in the first place; now this confirming offense against my heroic dad was the proverbial "last straw." If the church didn't want my dad, then I didn't want the church; and because the church represented God, I didn't think very much of God.

Later on, I believed that the key to the so-called "Greatest Generation" had much to do with their fortitude in following through with commitments, even when others did not. They also worked very hard in those days, for very little pay. Ironically, the church did not seem to demonstrate that same kind of fortitude, or as they said back then, "stick-to-it-tiveness."

I entered puberty at Brainerd Junior High School, where life reinforced my "God is irrelevant" tacit belief (if I had any beliefs at all). As a budding teen, I ballooned to be one of the heaviest "fat kids" in school. A cadre of student terrorists often reminded me of this fact as they spread their conviction that I was the "nerd fat boy" who gave them all "cooties." In grade school, I had attended speech therapy to correct my stuttering. During that training, I learned to speak more slowly and deliberately, but the stress caused me to stutter again, thus providing more fodder for the bullies.

Being in homeroom with the three chief terrorists—Joel, Vincent, and Jeffrey—was akin to being trapped in a prison cell with three adolescent stranglers who smelled bad. Mom bought me some trendy, checkered bell-bottom pants and a contrasting striped shirt to wear to school which, when worn, lit me up with a neon arrow that screamed "kick me" to the devourers. The bullies scorched me with their taunts. Naturally, most of the students joined in the chants, while a few (along with our homeroom teacher Mrs. Pfeiffer) tried to ignore them. It was perhaps the first time most of the students actually dug their heads into any school textbook.

Further confirming God's absence, one harrowing day, I escaped to the library in search of an isolated nook where I placed my books and three-ring binder that was full of notes, on a small table. After that, I went to the bookshelves in search of the title *Chicago,* and found a book to bury my head inside. I read about Chicago history, hoping to one day return to that beloved city.

The pictures showed Mrs. O'Leary's cow kicking over a lantern in an 1871 barn, which started the Great Chicago Fire, burning an area roughly four miles long and a mile wide, in the Windy City (including its business district). *Now, there's a woman with bad luck,* I thought. *Why couldn't that have been my school?* I mused. After returning the book to its shelf, I walked back to my desk, only to find all my notebook papers scattered throughout the library. My textbooks had somehow managed to find themselves lodged within the swing door of the library's metal trash can.

Not once did I experience a day of peace during class or at recess. Even gym class salted my wounds. I often caved to the ground heaving for breath, confirming perceptions that I was a vulnerable weakling. My only reprieves from sneers and taunts came when I got sick, allowing me the luxury of staying home to enjoy reruns of *Leave it to Beaver* and *Dennis the Menace.* On wintry snow days, I recall intently listening to the radio as the broadcaster announced each and every school closure. When he would finally call out the name "Brainerd," Christmas would come early that year.

I did have one friend though, Jimmy. On weekends we played catch. He hailed from Alabama, with a thick Southern drawl and a buzz cut identical to his ex-Marine dad. Jimmy and I would stand together each school day at the corner, awaiting our bus. One day, I stayed home from school because I had "caught a cold." (I commonly caught colds because of my damaged lungs.) That day, as Jimmy stood alone at the bus stop, a gang from nearby Camden happened along, looking for trouble. Soon, they discovered a kid with straight pants that stopped an inch above his ankles, standing vulnerable and alone at the corner.

Later, police discovered that the gang from neighboring Camden had heard Jimmy's thick, Southern accent and immediately identified him as a Southern segregationist or "racist pig," even though Jimmy probably didn't understand the word. Back then, race was a term children heard only on the news, as when Martin Luther King Jr. marched in the streets. Regardless, the gang decided to bash Jimmy's head into a tree, which broke open his skull. It took weeks for Jimmy to recover once he left the hospital. During that time, Mr. Hobby placed a "for sale" sign on their front lawn. Jimmy never returned to school. My only friend moved back to Alabama.

I was alone, except for my little Rat Terrier, Casey—and Mom, since my dad worked most days and nights on the few occasions he wasn't traveling. When I returned from school after a long day of harassments, Casey would climb onto my lap and feverishly lick my face. He maintained an uncanny ability to sense the darkest of my moods. Each time, his cure was a free lick-facial.

On days when the sun shined, I would link Casey to a long chain so he could roam the yard freely and sit under the large oak tree for shade. Most afternoons I would look through the back picture window to watch the silliest battles. A squirrel would casually wait for Casey to notice him and then race to the outer limit of Casey's chain. Then the squirrel would perch just beyond Casey's reach and purposely taunt him as it munched on a nut. *Maybe one day Casey would catch the squirrel and then—no more squirrel,* I thought to myself.

Well, that day came. When Casey ran to the end of the chain, it snapped and the squirrel froze. Casey and that squirrel were suddenly face-to-face in a furry stand-off. I rushed out the back door to save my little friend from a fight, but when I reached the scene, Casey just stared at the frozen squirrel that had suddenly "up and died." Perhaps it had a heart attack from the shock. I will never know, but the event would be retold countless times by my father and me as a kind of humorous bond between us.

The stand-off had finally happened and little Casey had won. If not for my dog and his various escapades, life as a scorned adolescent might have been unbearable. The thought of whether dogs existed in Heaven never even crossed my mind, although more than three decades later, I would be fortunate to discover the answer.

2

THINGS I WOULD
SEE IN HEAVEN

Life can only be understood backwards;
but it must be lived forwards.
—SOREN KIERKEGAARD

D ad's transfer back to the Chicago area after my graduation from junior high school, felt like being released from solitary confinement. Finally, I could escape from the bullies of Brainerd prison. I entered as a freshman at Hinsdale South High School in Darien, Illinois, to begin a new era. Academics became my refuge as I buried my head in books for four straight years, earning no less than an A on every test except one: typing class. Playing football reduced my weight from obese to a shy, thin young man, who never dated because of scaly facial skin caused by severe eczema and extreme insecurities.

Hinsdale Hospital provided an ideal venue for an introvert interested in medicine, through their weekend youth program. I could bag groceries at the local food store after school, bury my head in homework after that, watch *Star Trek* or some other series posted on my calendar of shows that I taped to my bedroom wall, and serve as an orderly at the hospital on weekends; all part of my self-imposed social isolation program.

One morning, I nearly dropped my food tray after entering the hospital room of a sickly boy. His eyes were deeply set in their sockets, and his facial skin draped over his cheek bones to reveal more skull than flesh. It appeared as though someone had dropped a wet sheet of skin over his bones, since no muscle remained in his arms and legs. He spoke to me through blue, peeling lips.

"I'm going to Heaven," he said.

"Oh, okay," I responded, with some apprehension.

I fully extended my arms in order to gingerly place the food tray on his bedstand, before quickly pulling them back to avoid touching anything.

"Do you know Jesus?" he asked.

"I know about Him," I said, "but I'm not a Christian."

"You believe in Heaven?"

"Not really, but if there's one, I'm sure you'll be there someday."

"I'll pray for you," he said. "You'll be in Heaven someday, too."

I could not help but be impressed with the deep serenity reflected in the boy's placid expressions. Though my young mind could not fully describe it then, his personhood imbued a serenity that defied his condition. Although the word "spiritual" made my skin crawl at the time, the word fit the boy. Up to that point, no one had ever prayed for me (at least to my knowledge). It sounded strange to hear such an offer from this suffering little stranger, of all people. I thought that only able-bodied churchgoers prayed. One day, I would discover the full impact of that little boy's prayers, and why God chose him to do so. He was the first person to prophetically pray for me, and I would indeed see him again—but not on this earth.

A few days later, I returned to the boy's room just to say "Hello." His bed was now topped with neatly-folded sheets. The balloons and teddy bears were gone.

"He died yesterday," the floor nurse said.

I hoped he was right and I was wrong but I thought, *If God is real, why would He take the life of such an innocent one as him?*

Not long after the boy died, I quit my job at the hospital. I was too busy pursuing academic success and too worldly to ponder the reality of death any longer, much less the afterlife that the boy's empty room imposed upon my thinking. When Princeton and Northwestern Universities accepted my college applications, I chose Northwestern University (NU) for two reasons. First, my dad's dream was to attend NU, but in no way could my young dad afford it, much less buy the necessary clothing. Second, Northwestern offered me a financial grant.

Northwestern University presented fertile ground for practicing my form of militant agnosticism. As a student activist, I lobbied to force the Christian group off our campus because "it violated freedom from religious indoctrination." I took theology classes more to *disprove* religion than to discover the truth. A group of fellow agnostics and I joined together to work on a thesis project, with the intent of disproving all religions. We received permission to use the computer system that was housed in a large building at the school, to program various dates, documents, and historical facts, in order to statistically analyze the probabilities of each major religion.

Because of a prophetic accuracy of less than 10 percent, we could invalidate all of the religions, except for one. The Bible maintained 1,000 percent accuracy in prophecies from multiple writers, spanning thousands of years. Even that could not convince me that Christianity was real, because of the Christian hypocrisy I had observed for much of my life. I could conceptualize Christ as good, but I hated Christians because I believed (and often quoted) Mahatma Gandhi, who said, "Your Christians are so unlike your Christ."

I contended before the university's provost that the Christian group on campus actively proselytized students. I used my room-mate's girlfriend as an example since she continually preached to me about Jesus—all the while covering my roommate's neck in purple hickeys, forcing him to wear turtlenecks while she boasted of their "sexcapades." I told my roommate that my name for his girlfriend would hereafter be "Dracula," because she lusted to pierce his neck with her teeth. One evening, I discovered a note on my desk that said: "Randy, Jesus loves you." It was signed "Dracula."

Shortly thereafter, the provost asked the Christian group to meet somewhere off-campus.

During one of many fraternity parties, I engaged in an argument over abortion rights, with a drunk, self-professing Christian fra-ternity brother. After our skirmish, one of my other non-religious fraternity brothers, named Brad, swung open my door to tell me that one of our classmates committed suicide at the Foster Walker Complex, which had only single rooms.

Brad and I decided to commiserate over this shock while jogging southward from Northwestern's Evanston campus, as the pungent septic odor of Lake Michigan to our left, wafted through the air.

We rounded the bend along Lake Shore Drive, between pumps of my asthma inhaler, to catch a glimpse of the lights of Chicago's skyline as darkness settled. An eerie sound suddenly erupted on our right. It was coming from the old Calvary Catholic Cemetery. Centuries had eroded the carved names on the moss-covered headstones. Somewhere beyond the high gates, amidst the weathered mausoleums, and through the murky darkness, a voice echoed, "I hate you for killing me." The vexed voice repeated the same diatribe over and over. Brad and I jerked our heads toward one another.

"You heard that?" Brad asked.

"Yeah—'I hate you for killing me.'"

Our jog instantly turned into a sprint. We stopped at the nearby Loyola University campus to recount what had just happened.

"No way could someone have jumped over that high fence," I said.

"You didn't see anyone?"

"No one. It came from behind one of those crypts, I think."

"Or from inside the tomb," Brad said.

"No way could anyone climb over those locked gates with those spears at the top."

"Yeah," Brad concurred, "No way, and it wasn't like a normal voice. It was like a growl."

We ramped up our sprint for about two miles, until I dropped. I plummeted headfirst onto the pavement in front of a condominium along Lake Shore Drive, heaving for breath and thinking that maybe something or someone from that cemetery was killing *me*.

"You okay?" Brad asked, as my body lay prostrate on the cement sidewalk.

"Asthma." I managed to eke out the word as blood dripped from my nose onto the pavement.

Cell phones were at least five years into the future, so the best I could hope for was not to pass out before my twenty or more shots of albuterol provided blessed relief. I sat and began taking full breaths as my heart thumped away like a mad drummer.

Brad made it to a gas station to call a fraternity friend, so we did not need to walk to the fraternity or (perhaps even more importantly) pass by the cemetery a second time. Not since Uncle Carlyle's wake and our neighbor's death in New Jersey, had death felt so alarmingly real. This time, I dwelt on the spirit realm as a real and eerie possibility. The question of immortality or God now crossed my young mind with the seriousness of an astronomer looking for answers to the Big Bang Theory. I had just been exposed to the supernatural.

That night, I stood in front of the lone window of my room and stared into the darkened sky. The night was laced with clouds illuminated by flashes of lightning and accompanied by thunder claps that cracked the air in pulsating snaps seemingly directed at me. If ever a sound evoked the power of some god-like presence, it was then. Not only did the Storm foretell of my soon-to-be future, but it would also foretell of the future of the world—one I could see once I entered a place far grander than the faded outline of the Northwestern campus ahead of me.

"If You're real, God, I need to know You as more than pages in a book. Show Yourself to me as someone as real as the people around me or else You're just a story,w" I said to the sky outside my apartment window, with its metal bars that testified an ominous warning I chose not to see.

I waited, but nothing happened.

3

OLD ENDINGS, NEW BEGINNINGS

The Lord has made everything for its purpose,
even the wicked for the day of trouble.
—PROVERBS 16:4 ESV

That Friday, I asked my mom to pick me up so I could ruminate at home and visit with my old buddy Casey. Normally, Casey would greet me at the foyer with his bobbed tail wagging at warp speed. Instead, I found Casey cowering inside the sliding glass coat closet and shivering.

"He doesn't have control over his bladder. He's afraid he'll pee," my mom said.

I bent down and began stroking my childhood friend as his frail body shivered uncontrollably.

"It's okay, buddy. It's okay. I'm here for you buddy."

He was now twelve years old and had survived being hit by a car after straying in the neighborhood years before. I bent down and Casey addressed my face with his lollipop licks as he did so many times before when he comforted my traumatized adolescent years.

"It's okay. I love you, Casey. You've been the best friend anyone could ask for. You're the best and you got me through it." My teardrops fell onto Casey's fur, which he licked as if they were treasures to be remembered forever.

Casey looked at me with those endearing little eyes. I will never forget his look of total adoration. I was everything to him and I felt remorseful that I had not been with him during my college stay. That was the last occasion that I saw Casey. A few weeks later, my dad called me at the fraternity to ask if I wanted to go with him to the veterinarian's office as they "put down" Casey. I said no. I felt like a coward, but I just couldn't say goodbye. My best friend was already gone.

After graduating from Northwestern with a double major, I was financially broke. I held two jobs through college: as a waiter at the sorority house and as a clerk in the Human Resources Department. That, plus three summers working at a factory making electrodes for hospital monitors covered my expenses but little more, so I worked part-time while completing business school on campus. Afterward, the official full-time job search commenced.

Procter & Gamble issued me an IQ test as part of their qualifying process.

"You answered all of the questions correctly," the Chicago recruiter said. "We want to fly you to our headquarters in Cincinnati."

I became part of the company's new healthcare division, selling adult undergarments, which on the surface, seemed less than appealing. But altruistically, I felt that working in healthcare would be a noble endeavor, as it was about helping sick people. My boss called me his "superstar," which made my head swell. It swelled even more the day I traveled to a hospital on a three-lane highway after a station wagon drove through a barricade. The vehicle crashed into the car's side and flew over me, thrusting my unbuckled body forward and forcing my head through the windshield. The momentum catapulted my car over an embankment and into a flagpole—preventing my car from rolling over a steep hill and saving me from certain death.

I lost consciousness until I heard sirens off in the distance. A woman appeared at my door.

"You're going to be fine, son," she said. "God is with you."

Later, I discovered that she wasn't really a woman—or a human, for that matter. She only appeared for a moment before the fire department showed up with the Jaws of Life. I never saw her again. In the Emergency Room, one of the nurses told me that I was lucky to be alive. The news broadcast first reported one fatality—me, but later amended the report to "a man in critical condition."

For weeks, I recovered while staring at the ceiling, in braces, casts, and bandages, with no cogent memory of the accident except for the woman. She was about thirty, with sandy blonde hair, hazel eyes, and a melodic voice that assured me I would be fine. Her disappearance could be attributed to my jumbled brain's imagination, if not for the vividness of that one memory contrasting the blurry reality of everything else. After recovering enough to walk, I visited the junkyard where my car was stored. The attendant assured me that the car had not gone through a car crusher. When I told him that I was the driver, he stared at me for who-knows-how-long, as if he had seen a ghost.

I would stare at the ceiling for hours on end, in the foggy depression that follows a severe concussion. My neighbor across the hall from me occasionally knocked at my apartment door to check on me. Every once in a while, I responded. She taught a one-room class for first-through-sixth graders, at the Fairfield, Ohio, Lutheran Church. I presumed that the dress code demanded dresses no shorter than calf-length since I never observed her dress otherwise.

Most likely, a sixty-year-old schoolmarm lived inside her mid-twenties body, lending her a mature wisdom and an unflappable demeanor. She carried the stout frame of an older woman and had hair down to her buttocks, which she often tied in a bun or two—sometimes one bun over each ear, like Princess Leia of *Star Wars* fame. I never witnessed her cuss, drink too much, or speak negatively about someone. I would purposely offer her too much wine at restaurants, just to test her Christian resolve, but she refused. When I would tempt her with gossip, she would never engage me. I even bribed her with money to say one cuss word, to no avail.

For once in my life, I could find no hypocrisy in a professing Christian. Roxanne walked the Christian talk. For a devout agnostic bent on exposing the hypocrisy of Christians (whom I assumed were all actors playing the part of puritans), it seemed as if I had discovered an alien being from some unknown galaxy.

"You don't go out anymore," she said to me after turning on my entry light. I had drawn the curtains in order to block the midday sun.

"Just getting out of bed's a major undertaking," I said.

"What about your work?"

I had been working 60-hour weeks before the accident, but darkness spread inside of me that was reflected in my self-imposed isolation. I felt I had fallen into a pitch-black well, without hope of ever escaping this pit, and I lacked any motivation to even try.

"Let's go for an ice cream," she said, hopefully.

"No," I replied, "I'm not that person, Goochie." It seemed like the most driven part of me had disappeared into a vacuum of emptiness and I had somehow become lost within my own body and mind. I called Roxanne "Goochie," short for "coochie-coochie-coo," because of her round baby face, plump cheeks, and the innocence to match. Only a childlike faith like Goochie's could think that her prayers could convert an anti-religious zealot like me.

After the accident and despite Goochie's promptings to help me escape my apartment, I could not motivate myself to do much of anything. As a result, one afternoon, my boss called me over to his house to fire me. I had gone from being the so-called new "superstar" to a "super dud," in fewer than six months.

"He was never the same after the accident," my boss said to one of my co-workers, who later confided the comment to me. Indeed, I would never be the same again.

4

My Introduction to the Netherworld

They are "impure spirits" (Mark 1:27 NIV), *"deceiving spirit"* (1 Kings 22:23 NIV), *"the powers of this dark world," and "the spiritual forces of evil"* (Ephesians 6:12 NIV), *and "Satan's angels"* (Revelation 12:9 NIV).

With consternation, I moved back into my parents' home in Darien, Illinois, to fully recover and plan for a restart. Mom washed my sheets weekly, neatly tucking the folds of the covers while asking me how I felt—seemingly 10,000 times a day. Finally, the fog clouding my thoughts began to clear, and I could exercise again.

My job search placed me with Johnson & Johnson, the largest healthcare company in the world, in one of the most remote cities: Rockford, Illinois. Nearly seven months post-accident, I could walk and function normally.

That meant working 60- to 80-hour weeks traveling to hospitals to market in-service surgical devices in the operating rooms and critical care areas of hospitals. At a hospital in Freeport, Illinois, I trialed new vital signs monitors in the Intensive Care Unit (ICU). In one room, a man lay dying as his gray-haired wife stood by his side. With tears flowing, two middle-aged women were hugged by their respective male partners. Flowers adorned the room, and I watched as the man's vital signs fell. A surreal peace filled the room that was palpable, as if one could feel the dying man's serenity.

"He was such a wonderful man," his wife said, as everyone surrounding the dying man nodded in agreement. In the adjoining room, a man with a full head of brown hair and deep-set wrinkles lay in bed. A young lady sat at his side, presumably his daughter, although she looked more intent on reading her teen magazine. This man's vital signs fell as precipitously as the man's next door, but by contrast, this room felt heavy and smelled of decay. I looked for flowers or cards but found none.

Next, I walked outside to the nurse's station to inform them of the quickened demise of their patients. As I began to walk back to each room, a nosey housekeeper stopped me.

"Couldn't be more opposite men," she said.

"You know them?" I asked.

"Small town, people know people," she said. "The man with the family was a churchgoer who ran a hardware store and always treated me right. The other guy drank himself to death and slept with every woman he could find. Ain't no one who could say a (bleeped) nice thing about him."

Both men died that night—one with loved ones by his side, the other alone since the girl who had been with him, left before he died. What struck me was the feeling I gained in each of their rooms. As someone not prone to fanciful thinking, I dared not attribute it to some spiritual awareness. But nothing else could explain away the ethereal sense that resonated the diametrically contrasting impressions I felt in each room—one of oppression and one of peace.

A few weeks later, I checked into a hotel at night so I could rise early in the morning for a surgical case in Davenport, Iowa. Next door were remnants of a dilapidated drive-in theater, with speaker boxes that hung resolutely from their holders and a big screen that was torn. In bed and half-asleep, a vision of Mark Hoff, one of my former fraternity brothers, appeared from within a murky underground that seemed to be beneath me.

If this was a nightmare, it certainly felt real enough, as I physically felt his hand dig into my forearm as he attempted to pull me into the foggy abyss below. Startled, I jerked my arm upward and darted out of bed. Not wanting to return to bed after hearing a multitude of people outside, I got up to check out the film that was playing next door to the hotel, only to find a darkened drive-in theater and not a single soul in sight.

"Where were the voices I heard," I murmured to myself as I crossed the vacant parking lot. *And that thing—Mark who looked like a zombie pulling me, what was that about?!*

I finally crashed in bed well after midnight, from a steady diet of late-night TV shows.

Weeks later, I attended an alumni reunion party at Triangle fraternity on the Northwestern University campus. I sat down at the dining room table with some of my closer fraternity brothers while our cook, "Johnny G.," finished roasting our chicken.

"I had the strangest dream about Mark Hoff a few weeks ago," I said.

"The Bible-thumper who was always telling us that we needed to get saved," said Omar.

"Yeah, always in our face about his religion," I said.

Darrell's eyes opened wide while sitting across the table. "He died recently."

"How?"

"Car crash" said Darrell, "driving his parents' sports car in Arizona. He drove over a cliff."

"When?"

"Four weeks ago."

"Four weeks!" My nightmare of him was four weeks earlier. *Why of all the guys I know, did I dream of Mark?* I learned that he died sometime around the hour I had my vision of him. I did not want to think badly of him, but Mark seemed to be another of those Christian hypocrites who talked to me about the Bible and other Christian stuff, while lying. I learned of this fact when I served as the fraternity president and was made privy to everyone's grades. In order to remain a member, one needed to maintain a 3.0 grade average or more. Sadly, Mark had consistently lied when asked to tell us his grade point average.

That ghostly visage of Mark on the day he died stuck with me for years, as a conundrum. *Was he trying to lure me into a dead place or was this a warning of sorts?* Since I played on the opposing team against the Christians, I supposed that Mark, my poster boy for Christian hypocrisy, confirmed my belief that if there was a hell, then Christians were the ideal candidates to live there.

On the other hand, if God existed and was who Mark claimed, then why did Mark reach to pull me into a place of shadows, with fire burning below him, on the day that he died? This was all too uncanny to ignore and too bizarrely real to be imagined. Someone or something was calling my number.

As children, we dream of fairy tale and make-believe things in a world consumed with reality, but for those who don't know Him, God lives within that space of imagination. For those like me who, as a child and a youth never tasted of God's reality, unbelief was an open door to the spirit realm that invited evil spirits to toy with me. And I willingly let them play, even as God watched from a distance, knowing full well what lay ahead—the Storm. I was headed for the Storm.

5

EVEN SAINTS SIN

For all have sinned and fall short of the glory of God.
—ROMANS 3:23 NIV

I felt perplexed at this point in my life. I was too practically minded to believe in the bizarre as otherworldly, and too shaken with the series of bizarre events that evoked the netherworld, to deny a reality apart from the one I could see and hear. When an administrative assistant at a Rockford hospital where I worked asked me if I knew about the First Assembly of God Church, I said no (of course) but I still offered her the courtesy of proselytizing me as so many hopefuls had done in the past. Besides, her surgery department was one of our customers.

"You'll experience the Spirit of God in a way that will positively amaze you," she said. "Would you like to go with me (to service) this Sunday?"

I liked this woman because she had helped introduce me to the surgeons in the hospital. Furthermore, I had recently been introduced to the dark side of the spiritual world, and figured I might as well balance my experience with the "other side." Little would I confess to my prideful self that deep inside was a yearning to know this God that Goochie seemed to know personally—and not just as pages in a book. I called Goochie to tell her that I would be attending a church in Rockford, and she shouted "YES!" back to me, like a cheerleader rooting for her team that was poised to score on the two-yard line.

That Sunday I stepped into the packed church, feeling the vibration of a thunderous chorus and band pounding out unfamiliar songs of praise. Obviously, those raising their hands felt aligned to the words of praise that were projected onto a screen. It felt to me like a crazed rock concert full of people high on wishful thinking. Then someone stood up after the worship music and began speaking in a language that seemed part Arabic and part mumbo-jumbo. After she finished, she took a seat. Right after that, a man stood up and began speaking a message in English that said something like:

"The rivers of life flow throughout Heaven and they are being poured forth on earth as refreshment, but on the horizon, a Storm will come to bring about a cleansing, and all will be made right…"

Was he speaking to me? Years later, I came to understand that the words were indeed for me.

To this day, I remember the gist of what the man had spoken. After the service, a thirtyish-looking man ran up to me and said that the administrative assistant who invited me had asked him to introduce himself. I asked him about the strange ritual I just observed in his church. He explained it as "tongues" and the "interpretation of tongues," which sounded to me like something one might find at an African tribal ceremony. Then he scribbled the words of the so-called prophecy onto a piece of paper that he gave to me (and which remained in my closet drawer for years).

"We're starting a College and Career group now, and I'd love to take you there," he said.

Might meet some cute girls there, I thought, so I said, "Yes."

Sitting next to the fellow who invited me, I looked around to assess the young ladies scattered around the room and qualified only those who did not raise their hands in worship, thinking they were the less fanatical ones of the bunch. As the speaker stood at the podium and taught about how God answers prayer, I'm not sure when it happened, but my attention focused less on potential dates and more on what the pastor was teaching.

He talked about how sin is like the hidden specks on a lampshade that appeared clean, until the light was turned on to expose its imperfections. He explained that the light of Jesus is like the light bulb that exposes darkness. We were the lampshade and the imperfections were specks or sins that corrupted our body, our cover, or something to that effect. Oddly enough, it made sense to me. I now felt like a spectator as I thought about the stranger who now wanted to emerge from within my agnostic armor. *Was my prayer from years ago being answered, when I prayed to an unknown God and asked Him to reveal Himself to me as more than pages in a book?*

I never witnessed an altar call, but at the end of the message, the speaker asked by a show of hands if anyone wanted to give their life to Jesus. My hand immediately jerked into the air, in an uncontrollable spastic response by this someone or something that now possessed me. After being called to the front of the room, I prayed the so-called "Sinner's Prayer," without any noticeable effect. However, that night in my apartment, I fell to the floor and entered into a trance-like state, as though I was drunk and hallucinating.

Instantly, my mind traveled to an ethereal space of absolute peace and joy, in what I can best describe as a dream-like celebration—a birthday party of sorts. There were what seemed to be imaginary fireworks, an impression of obscure figures dancing, and an awareness of a faded face that smiled at me. I also had a feeling of being hugged inside of my body, in some kind of a spiritual realm that was apart from any cogent understanding. I even danced with those surreal figures, knowing in my heart of hearts that this was not just my imagination. It was more real than earthly reality ever was.

An unfamiliar feeling of joy consumed me as though I had never known joy before, only moments of happiness conditioned by my situations. This feeling of joy represented a complete immersion of unrestricted pleasure. Every part of me became satiated, loved, and known, and every feeling centered on the people in my midst. He was real. He was good. He was Jesus. He was God!

"Who are you?" asked a close friend from Northwestern, in response to my enthusiastic telephone call that I had "met God." My expectation that John would be happy for me would suddenly turn to disappointment.

"It's like I don't know you," another friend stated, when I told them the same thing. They felt as if I had suddenly turned into an alien.

My atheist and agnostic friends frowned upon my newfound relationship with Jesus and no longer wanted to be friends. I had crossed from this world into a spiritual realm that was as distasteful to them as it was treasonous. They believed (as I had) that Christians were hypocritical bigots. The irony that I had become the person I once disdained, now contrasted my fervent belief that I could not possibly have been so stupid as to have denied Jesus for all those years, despite a childhood laced with struggles. Now I understood that Jesus is real and that my unbelief was contrived.

Another irony struck me. The dark underworld seemed more real to me as an agnostic, than the heavenly world of God. Now the powers and principalities of darkness became unfamiliar spirits, as the Spirit of Christ eased into my soul like a missing body part I never even knew existed.

For months, it felt like a natural high or a supernatural buzz, as evidenced by my "Bless You's" to random cashiers, trash collectors, mail carriers, and just about anyone who made eye contact with me. Such a dramatic transformation for an introvert like me could not be explained as happiness since happiness is conditioned upon a situation.

No, this sense of joy came from the heart. It transcended even the most challenging situations, like staying at a hotel on Michigan Avenue in Chicago and waking up at 3 a.m. gasping for air because of an asthma attack. It remained even as I staggered down the street in search of an open drug store to buy an inhaler, only to cave onto the pavement before a policeman rescued me and delivered me to Northwestern University Hospital's Emergency Room. All the while I kept praising my Lord. That represents a truly dramatic change of heart.

It dawned on me that during my "BC" (Before Christ) days, spiritualism reared its head through external influences such as the woman or angel who spoke life to me through the broken window of my crushed car. It was also there in the demonic voice that resonated from the old cemetery as I jogged by with Brad, and in the ghastly visitation of a recently deceased fraternity brother.

Then of course, there was the eerie feeling that death had imposed upon my thinking at the wake of Uncle Carlyle or after the death of our neighbor in Cherry Hill. My spirit had been awakened by an internal presence that spoke to me in gentle promptings and undeniable whispers—one I came to know as the Holy Spirit. I became interested in the "still small voice" so often spoken about in Christian circles. To me, it wasn't a still voice at all. It was a feeling, a sense, a goodness that resonated within my mind as absolute conviction.

I began learning about this new language, the language of the Spirit. Once during a Bible study group, I blurted out to a young lady that God had healed her of lactose intolerance. Why I did that only God knows, but apparently it rang true because she later informed me that she began drinking several quarts of milk without side effects. In another instance, I uncharacteristically declared to a young man that his dream of becoming a pastor was "not just a dream but a calling by God." The man replied that he had prayed for a confirmation from someone that his desire to become a pastor was real and not imagined.

These brash declarations frightened me at first, due to my propensity to be a silent observer. Suddenly, I was drafted into active service and quickly morphed from church pew warmer to active participant. Words of knowledge and prophetic utterances described by the apostle Paul, now grew in frequency as I trusted more and more on my internal promptings—that persistent hunch, a first impression that conveyed a sense of urgency (1 Corinthians 12:8). The words seemed correct because they ushered forth peace and understanding. I simply trusted that it all came from the Holy Spirit because of a newfound belief that God speaks in the quietness of our soul, not in the brash conviction of needing to be proven correct.

I regressed a bit in my spiritual development when a church friend asked if I wanted to go with her and two others to an abandoned house on Blood Point Road.

"You've got to be kidding," I said. "An abandoned house literally located on a road called Blood Point?"

"Yep, it's haunted," she said.

"Yeah, right."

"No really. Lots of my friends have gone there and seen things or heard things."

"Ghosts?"

"There's only one way to find out," she said.

So, off we drove one weekend, to Blood Point Road.

The long dirt road seemed to lead nowhere except to another cornfield among endless rows of tall corn stalks. As if a mirage, a gated property appeared to the right, bordered by dead grass. It was a looming, deserted relic that glared at us through its broken windows. The Victorian-style house brooded with its decaying gray façade, ornate pillars, four-sided roof gables, and a corner tower that leaned as it pointed skyward, undoubtedly housing a secret bone pile.

"This is too much like a scripted scene," I said to the car's occupants.

"That's the house on Blood Point Road," replied the driver, who had invited me.

As sundown approached, the sky turned gray.

"Did you see that?" one of the backseat riders asked, rather pensively.

"What?" I quickly replied.

"The curtains in the top right window pulled back."

"No way," the driver said. "The house is deserted."

"Turn the car and put your bright lights on the house," I said to the driver.

As she turned the car to flash the light against the face of the house, the curtains indeed seemed to pull back.

"Did you see what I saw?" I spoke.

"Yeah...we're getting out of here," the driver said.

I suppose that someone more mature in the faith would avoid the scintillating effects of visiting a haunted or demon-possessed house. Yet, our Christian group would revisit that decrepit house on multiple occasions. Each time, the demons entertained us with manifestations such as a roar that sounded as we drove past the house; a light that floated at sunset down the dirt road—minus the person, car, or bicycle that might have beamed it; or the shadowy figure in the upstairs window in a room no one could access because the interior stairway had crumbled long ago.

To this day, I remember the most unsettling experience from the netherworld. It happened at dusk in the cornfield across from the ghoulish house. As the front screen door flapped in the wind with the sound of someone smacking their lips, the upstairs windows glared at us with their blackened eyes. With the windows rolled down, I could hear a faint whimpering in the cornfield that struck me as would the cry of a frightened child.

"Stop the car," I said to our driver.

"Why?"

"I hear a child crying in the cornfield, I think."

"A what?"

"A child, like a lost child or something, crying out there!"

My friend stopped the car. If not for the fear that a child was indeed crying in the field, I would never have set foot in that cornfield. But I found myself pushing cornstalks away and shining my flashlight in every direction, not knowing if I might see a ghost or a body. Each time I walked forward or sideways, the whimpering sound moved in another direction. A once-faded sunset now turned into the darkness of night.

Oh Lord, I know I don't deserve this but please save that child or me, if this is a demon. I prayed both silently and openly with every step as I frantically cast the flashlight beam in every direction.

"Jesus, whatever this is, take it away," I cried. "If it's a child, let me find it and if it's a spirit, stop it from haunting me, Jesus!"

The whimper settled into a spot about ten feet in front of me and at least a hundred feet beyond the car. I slowly moved forward as I shined the flashlight on the ground. No dead body appeared but a sulfuric smell wafted through the air. Suddenly, the whimpering stopped and only the sound of chirping crickets remained. I rushed back to the car, got in, slammed the door, and said, "Get out of here, quick!"

I arrived back at my ranch-style home in Rockford, and exited my car after the trip to the house on Blood Point Road. The car's antenna kept swaying back and forth in a rapid manner as if a hand had pulled it back just to release it. This back and forth motion continued even after my car was parked in the garage for several minutes.

I finally lay in bed and listened to the storm outside but its rolling thunder felt more ominous than usual. I sensed an oppressive presence in my room and fear rose inside of me as if some demonic spirit had hitchhiked a ride in my car to follow me home. A new heaviness pressed against my chest and I began heaving for breath as though experiencing an asthma attack. After several inhaler puffs, I felt relief. I eventually fell asleep listening to the crackling sounds of a thunderstorm.

A glutton for punishment, the very next day I drove alone to that horrid house—this time in the light of day. As I neared the address, I did not see the house's gothic turrets, so I drove closer to park in front. What used to be the ghastly structure now lay in ruins; with pieces of splintered panels and broken glass strewn about charred ground. Apparently, lightning struck the house the night before and leveled it to the ground. The storm must have included a tornado because only rubble remained. I felt scorned by God for tempting Him time and again and for returning to that house. To His credit, God ensured that I would never return to that house again, with its addictive, evil allure.

I learned an important lesson that day. God will not tolerate the source of sin because that source hurts His children with its deceptive attraction. Even if we are weak, God is a strong guardian of our soul who will even use the elements He created to rid us of the cause of our sin. In this case, an earthly storm cleared the evil that resided within and about that house on Blood Point Road.

Years later, I would bear witness to a different type of storm—a spiritual Storm. That Storm would tear down the demonic strongholds of the world the way God destroyed the spirits that inhabited or surrounded the house on Blood Point Road. This coming Storm that I would first behold in Heaven is of an intensity that would forever change this world and reveal God's will on a much grander scale than any natural storm ever could. This Storm would not only destroy demonic strongholds but it would usher forth the greatest revival in the history of humanity.

6

RELATIONSHIP
VERSUS RELIGION

Now this is eternal life: that they know you, the only
true God, and Jesus Christ, whom you have sent.
—JOHN 17:3 NIV

I know that God speaks to each of us privately, but sometimes He asks us to speak about Him publicly. I was not a public speaker, but apparently God likes choosing people to do the opposite of their natural inclinations. I have learned that God best uses our weaknesses to magnify and manifest His strength. He pours Himself into us the way one might fill an empty bag. As it relates to my introverted nature, my capacity for speaking boldly was truly as that of an empty vessel.

The first time I declared a "Thus saith the Lord" statement to someone, I felt like I was naked in front of the church. A man came up for prayer during the service. Afterward, he meandered toward the back hallway. I was compelled to follow him and felt my palms perspire. I was thinking that God wanted this man to take a new job, and that this new job would be working with a Christian supervisor who would introduce him to a new ministry opportunity. It was strange that I would think that, but my palms had never sweated before and the compulsion to talk to the man pulled at me like a rubber band so I could offload the message now nagging me. Before he exited the door, I mustered the courage to walk up to him and ask if I could share something. His back straightened as he said:

"Sure."

"Hi," I said. "My name is Randy Kay."

"Ted Schroeder," he said. "Have we met before?"

"No."

Now came the hard part. I said, "I just felt like God wanted me to share something with you," and waited for a response.

"Oh…okay."

"I think I heard God say that you're supposed to take a new position and that your new supervisor will be a Christian and that he would lead you into the ministry calling that God wants for you."

At that release, I was fully prepared to race out the door and never return to the church again, but the man's eyes opened so wide that they looked as if they would pop out of their sockets. "I was just given a job offer and the guy I would report to is a Christian. I was working under someone who was cussing and not really a good guy, and I've been praying that God would lead me to some way that I could serve Him more fully!"

Now I felt *my* eyeballs pop. I had never spoken so boldly about something I literally knew nothing about. Once or twice I had heard Christians mention the "still small voice," but I could never identify with the quiet prompting of God's Spirit, until I delivered this message. It felt a bit like what I had imagined someone with Tourette's syndrome might experience, like an involuntary compulsion to utter words. But unlike Tourette's, where people blurt out obscenities, the words I had spoken uplifted the man. He thanked me profusely and left the church with a brand-new spring in his step.

The floodgates opened to this newfound gifting, which poured out more frequently as I learned to trust the Holy Spirit's promptings to speak God's inspirations at my small group and during impromptu church meetings. On a few occasions, my declarations were met with blind stares. But as I became more in tune with God's voice, the accuracy of the "feels right" hunch that inspired an unnatural confidence to speak divine Words to others—words that spoke volumes to strangers—dramatically improved. I learned that my introverted personality contrasted with my extroverted spirit, who wanted to simply honor God by walking the plank into the deep waters of His anointing.

I considered how God uses the most unlikely people to convey His messages, such as Paul, the Christian persecutor who evangelized the known world; or Moses, the stutterer who declared God's Ten Commandments; or Mary Magdalene, a prostitute—all of whom teach us about pure devotion to Christ. All of these biblical examples helped me understand why God would use a formerly devout agnostic and practically minded person who died, to journey with Jesus in Heaven. For now, I was learning to walk in the Spirit, without realizing that God wanted me to sprint. Little did I know that a forthcoming Storm would compel me to declare a Word that would change everything.

Some people are eased into their charismatic giftings by first attending a more liturgical church. But my introduction to Christianity included witnessing a fire hose of miracles. Every Sunday, at least one person got healed or prophesied over. Later on, I learned that my first church had been experiencing what many call a "revival." A classic definition of a Christian revival refers to *a spiritual reawakening from a state of dormancy in the life of a believer, and the awakening of evangelism for the unbeliever.* A revival causes large numbers of people to confess Jesus as their Lord and Savior.

I have experienced both. My conversion from militant agnostic to fervent believer stirred up a revival in my spirit to experience the gifts of prophecy (defined in Greek translations as truth-telling and/or foretelling) and words of knowledge (the ability to know what God is doing or intends to do in another's life). Later, healing miracles would occur, and I learned that God could release giftings for different seasons of a person's walk with Christ.

Early on, I felt that clergy represented God's primary voice and that church attendees could be appropriated gifts that could only occasionally be used during Sunday service. More likely, they would be practiced if an opportunity presented itself outside of the church, although I rarely saw that happen. The inability to exercise my new gifts felt frustrating to me. It was as if I was only a part-time Christian.

For a season, I joined the vast army of God's pew warmers. Like most Christians, I looked for nooks and crannies where I could share my joy in Christ with the secular world but found only scattered opportunities. For example, when a hospital nurse lost her mother to cancer, I told her, "I will pray for you." Sadly, this is a common mantra in the Christian community that is more cliché than commitment.

The fact remains that even today, practicing one's faith is limited to small groups, church positions, ministry volunteerism, and so-called "open doors" to practice a Good Samaritan form of Christianity such as when someone in our midst suffers a crisis. But things are about to change. The Storm in Heaven has taught me this.

Meanwhile, I devoted my "youngish" life to career advancement, in lieu of an established ministry position. After interning at a public relations firm, I wrote tidbits for the *Chicago Tribune*. I also free-lanced as a writer of articles for *Forbes* and other business publications, while completing post-graduate business classes at Northwestern's Business School. At age twenty-six, I became the youngest manager within a medical device division at Johnson & Johnson.

By the time I was in my thirties, I had bought a house in the San Francisco Bay Area, was promoted several times, and relocated to Texas to help develop a large merger within Johnson & Johnson. After that, I returned to San Francisco to help a newly acquired Johnson & Johnson company, before attending a large church where I taught several classes, including during the main service.

A young lady approached me at one of the church fair booth displays for a small group I was leading. She noticed me in my baby-blue slacks that were pulled waist-high, with a matching plaid blue shirt and slicked-back hair. Apparently my "nerdy" fashion style didn't repel her, because she came to my booth under the auspices of seeking a small group. Her golden hair and infectious smile instantly turned my attention from a holy endeavor to a physical attraction. Her name was Renee Vanderbilt.

On Tuesday nights, Renee and about eight others joined me to study the Bible, but all this time we were really studying each other—so much so, that after only a few weeks, Renee and I could nearly finish one another's sentences. One momentous day at church, I asked Renee for a date, promising to take her to Angel Island in the San Francisco Bay, where I would serve her a home-made lunch on the grassy knoll overlooking the city.

"You'd better pack me a big lunch because I eat a lot," said my slender girlfriend, who looked like she barely finished a meal.

I meticulously packed four sandwiches, coleslaw, pickles, sliced fruits, and chocolate truffles into a basket, and off we traveled by ferry to Angel Island, the largest island in the Bay. After dining in a field next to an old civil war fort, we walked around the island that was littered with historic relics from World War I. We also had a sobering visit to the island's detention barracks, where immigrants from over eighty countries (mostly Chinese and Japanese) were once processed, detained, and/or incarcerated.[1]

Renee stayed behind to take in the sights while I journeyed around the bend to behold the sailboat-dotted Bay, against a back-drop of the Golden Gate Bridge. A soft ocean wind billowed through the tall grass of the island that was guarded by the undulating peaks of the Golden Gate Bridge. As the surrounding cliffs funneled white-crested waves as they rolled into the Bay, I stood and praised God. As the wind blew through the air, I heard God's voice resound within my innermost knowing. He said:

"Renee is to be your wife."

To this day, if I were completely honest, I wonder if the voice had been audible. Not prone to fanciful thinking, I could only accept the sound as an awareness of a very pronounced echo that may have been formed by the wind into syllables. I suppose this was the first time God had spoken to me in a heavenly voice, although at the time, I dared not consider it as such. Of course, years later I would have no choice but to hear that voice again, and in an undeniable way.

Up to then, I never heard anything with such heartfelt conviction that imbedded itself so deeply into my soul. God's words blended within the warm wind of an otherwise brisk afternoon. I did not say a word about this to Renee, until a couple of weeks later when I proposed to her aboard the *Hornblower* yacht. There, we dined during a night cruise on the San Francisco Bay, as we looked at the Golden Gate Bridge dressed in its distant sparkling lights. Despite the uncertainty of her answer, I had spent a large portion of my bank account on a diamond ring for the occasion. Thankfully, Renee said "Yes" to me, as I knelt on the floor before her.

Six months later, we stood at the foot of Bridal Falls in Yosemite National Park and exchanged our wedding vows outside of the Ahwahnee Hotel, amidst about a hundred guests. According to conventional dating standards, it happened suddenly, but I had learned to listen to the subtle prompts of God's Spirit. When God spoke to me through the wind, I understood that He needed to ensure that I knew *His* choice for my wife; because I had stubbornly held onto my single life until I was thirty-five. Not until my visit to Heaven would I again hear such a pronouncement from God. I firmly believe that God's divine instruction at this time was meant to help prepare me for the miraculous events yet to come.

Many lessons of the miraculous emerged during our early marriage, especially after we learned of Renee's pregnancy, our "honeymoon baby" conceived during our travels abroad. We visited Greece, Corinth, the island of Patmos, Ephesus (in Turkey), and Egypt, Jerusalem, and Bethlehem as our "biblical tour." I often think back on my time lying in the cave where the apostle John received his revelation from God, as a reminder to me that Heaven is only a divine inspiration away (as I would later discover).

We needed the foundation we gleaned from the Holy Land, especially after the news from Renee's obstetrician that a gap in our baby's spine would mean a diagnosis of spina bifida.

That Friday afternoon and throughout the weekend, Renee and I prayed almost unceasingly, imploring God to heal our baby. On Sunday, that same conviction came upon my spirit heart—that knowing beyond a shadow of a doubt—only this time, God declared to me that our son had been healed. The following day, we returned to the hospital for another ultrasound. The doctor entered our room, shaking his head.

"I checked and then rechecked both scans, and there was a gap, but now there's no gap in the spine," he said.

Renee and I looked at each other with a smile. Seven months later, our son Ryan was born a healthy baby. This confirmed to me that indeed, miracles do happen.

During my travel working in the healthcare field, I kept journals detailing Ryan's birth through each momentous event of his life. Renee and I tried to conceive another child to no avail. We kept our faith that God would bless us with another baby because we had learned the power of prayer and intercession. When Pastor Rich Marshall at Springs of Life Church in San Jose, California, called "couples wanting to get pregnant" to the front for prayer, we immediately approached the altar.

As Pastor Rich laid his hands on Renee's head, she immediately fell to the ground. I caught her, but I too collapsed to the floor. There I beheld a blinding, golden light that shined before me. After about twenty minutes on the floor, we returned to our seats. Less than a month later, Renee announced a positive pregnancy test. Our darling daughter arrived eight months later.

Although we experienced miracles, I still bemoaned the fact that I could not routinely serve God with my giftings outside of the church. The pastor of a church near our home learned of my desire to serve more fully and invited me to teach classes at his church. There, I taught about the spiritual gifts and a course about practicing one's faith in the workplace. If I could not be a pastor at church, I thought I could at least try to evangelize and pastor people at my workplace.

I began Christian fellowship groups at each of my company's offices, where we met during lunchtime and occasionally, after work. At one division in San Jose, California, the Vice President of Human Resources called me into her office.

"You run a Christian group that meets on campus?" she asked.

"Yes."

Her reddened skin signaled a demonic campfire burning within her slight frame.

"One of your members was passing around a flyer announcing your after-work meeting in one of our conference rooms, and she shared it with one of our VP's, who was very offended. He felt like he was being proselytized."

"I'm sorry he was offended," I said. "I'm sure it was just a kind gesture."

"No." She pushed her chair away from her desk and puffed out her chest. "It was not acceptable, Randy. You know we have a company policy against religious organizations meeting on campus."

"No, I didn't know that, because I requested a room from the Director of Facilities, and he said 'Yes.'"

Her eyes appeared pitch-black as she smiled through clenched teeth. "Then let me be very clear, Randy. Our corporate policy prohibits religious meetings on campus. And because you're the leader of this group, I am holding you responsible. We'll be investigating any violations made on your behalf."

After my dismissal from the "principal's" office, an investigation commenced. On numerous occasions, a Human Resource representative quizzed me about various things, seeking egregious offenses such as, "Whose copy machine did you use?" and "Did you use any company paper for printing your flyers?" I answered each question, confirming that no company equipment or paper was used for any of the planning. I had footed the bill for everything. Obviously, the VP of Human Resources was looking for any reason to fire me.

A Christian friend on the Board of Directors said that the issue became a topic during a Board meeting, as to whether I could be terminated for my "behavior."

"It went all the way to the Board?!" I asked, in disbelief.

Upon further review of the company policy, no one could find any statement prohibiting after-hour meetings of religious organizations in any of the company's facilities. I learned from a friend that a wine club hosted their meetings on campus, a clear violation of company policy that prohibited the consumption of alcohol on campus grounds. The Christian group I founded did nothing wrong. Still, the Board of Directors would take a vote as to whether I would be fired from the company.

One night, the Holy Spirit woke me with a clear impression that God would "clean house" at the company. When I arrived at the office in the morning, one of the members of our Christian group raced into my office and said, "I had the strangest dream last night that God was cleaning house." At the time, I didn't understand what a housecleaning meant, but a week later, every member of the Board of Directors left the company for various reasons. One died. Two resigned. Two retired, including the Vice President of Human Resources who initially condemned me, and the President. Only one Board member remained. It was my Christian friend who assumed the CEO role in the company, and who assured me that our Christian group could meet on campus, anywhere and anytime.

"And by the way," he said. "I authorize you to use our copiers and paper to print your flyers, if you would like to do so."

The investigation intended to terminate my employment ceased, not just because there was no evidence that merited my dismissal. It ended because God cleaned house at the company and replaced the Board members with those who were friendly to our Christian group. That is the power of God's Storm—it cleans house and clears the air. After this experience, I realized that God cleans house because people tend to sully His plans. Every house needs cleaning.

The housecleaning I saw in the physical world would one day be witnessed by me on a much grander scale—the world. But the events at the company introduced me to the dynamics of how God works. First, when the Holy Spirit declares a shift, it comes with a message that only our spirit can comprehend, such as impressing me with the term "housecleaning." Second, the declaration of a shift often comes with a confirmation such as another person (i.e., a prophet), like the fellow employee who told me she had heard the same term in her dream. Third, judgment removes the unjust and God then replaces the enemy's authority figure(s) with His own people.

Not only did our Christian group grow to be the largest extracurricular group on campus, but we also started multiple Christian groups in companies around the San Francisco Bay Area. I also helped numerous Christians in other workplaces around the nation start in-house Christian groups. I began to understand that "doing church" did not require *being* in church. The Bible says: *"For where two or three gather in my* [Jesus's] *name, there am I* [Jesus] *with them"* (Matthew 18:20 NIV). All I needed was a quorum of two or three and Jesus would bless our assembly with His presence.

This small example of God's housecleaning foretold a future housecleaning in the world that I would behold after dying. Today, I wonder at the ways in which God uses the seemingly "weak" things in the world to "shame" the strong (see 1 Corinthians 1:27).

Note

1.   Angel Island Immigration Station; Britannica.com; https://www .britannica.com/topic/Angel-Island-Immigration-Station; accessed May 16, 2023.

7

GIVING UP ON RELIGION

A religion that is small enough for us to understand
would not be large enough for our needs.
—GRENVILLE KLEISER

As I learned various facets of God's Storm, from eliminating evil to an outpouring of God's newness, it seemed as though God was preparing me for something. But I didn't know how that "something" would manifest in my life or in the lives of others. I certainly didn't feel special, although I earnestly wanted to do more, not unlike many people.

I sometimes think about how God overcame the apostle Paul with a flash of heavenly light. While blinded, Paul was led to Damascus, where Christ instructed him to wait. At times, I felt like I was in a waiting stage, blinded from the future yet knowing that God wanted something more from me than the part-time relationship offered by the confines of organized religion.

I started researching the history of the Christian Church, knowing that the Western Church looked much different from the first church I read about in the book of Acts. We now lived in our 1,800-square-foot home in Pleasanton, California, about forty miles east of San Francisco, where I worked on a white IBM desktop computer in my less than 300-square-foot office. In 1993, the Internet and the World Wide Web were still in their infancy. I could only glean limited insights about early church history from the Web and from my occasional trips to the library.

I discovered that the first Christian mother church existed in Jerusalem, under the supervision of James, the brother of Jesus. That gathering consisted only of Jews. While the authoritative apostles lived, they served as the elders or priests, as a movement within Judaism, where meetings were held in the synagogues. Paul lobbied to grant recognition to his Gentile converts, but by the end of the first century, believers in Christ largely separated from the synagogue.

Since believers did not have church buildings where they could meet, they gathered mostly in homes. The first house church is recorded in Acts 1:13, where the disciples of Jesus met in Antioch (northwestern Syria) in the "upper room," as the so-called Gentile Church.

Beyond that period, believers met mostly in homes as an interdependent community. The first church building appeared in the early 200s, but it took almost a century before Emperor Constantine created the Christian Church generally seen in the Western world today.

Constantine appeared on the scene during the so-called Great Persecution that began in the year 303 under Roman Emperor Diocletian. By 305, more than six different generals would fight to succeed Diocletian. Constantine distinguished himself from the others because he became a Christian and boldly declared Jesus as the patron of his army. By 313, only two contenders remained: Constantine and Licinius. The two jointly issued the *Edict of Milan*, which made Christianity a legal religion and officially ended the persecution. But it was not until 324 that Constantine finally became the sole ruler of the Roman Empire.

Constantine saw Christianity's belief in one God as a plan to unify an empire that had been grossly divided for two decades, and he saw that Christianity itself was not unified. He called the Council of Nicaea in 325 to bring together the 1,800 bishops from around the empire and work out an official doctrine providing the basis for a unified Church. Constantine employed the entire council and paid for all of their expenses, even giving bishops the right of free transportation on the imperial postal system.

Thus, the council laid the foundation of Orthodox (Catholic) theology while declaring several differing theologies "heretical." Constantine's support initially gave Orthodoxy the ability to require Christians to adopt their doctrinal formulation. But during the next few decades, the Church's fortunes struggled. Within a century, Christianity had been declared the official religion of the Roman Empire, while non-Christian religions steeply declined.

Christian religion in developed or emerging countries basically followed the same original Church doctrine, except for a few modifications such as those declared by Martin Luther, the seminal figure in the Protestant Reformation, and Lady Jane Grey, who became Queen of England for nine days, but was beheaded in 1554 for defying the Church of England. She had declared that one could hear from God apart from exclusively hearing a word spoken by a priest from the pulpit. Lady Jane rested during her times of ridicule and persecution by "resting in the presence and sustaining power" of Christ, and by fervently reading the Scriptures and praying.

Imagine my delight when my father, an avid genealogist, mentioned to me one day that he had traced our family's lineage to Lady Jane Grey. This fit nicely with my thinking at that period of my life (in the 1990s), that God served as the Head—not the church. Therefore, the church model needed to change from a "spectator sport" to active engagement of the entire church body.

At this time, the church where I taught classes asked me to serve on its Board of Directors. I suggested a change at a breakfast meeting with the senior pastor. "I've been teaching people about the gifts of the Spirit and we've determined through testing and affirmations, the specific gifts that the Holy Spirit has given to those who are in our class," I said. "But the problem is that once we've identified someone with a gift of pastoring, say, or a gift of healing or teaching, there's usually no place for the people to practice their gifts in the church."

"Sure there is," he responded. "If someone has a gift of teaching, then that person can teach people in small groups. And if someone has the gift of healing, that person can pray for people."

"But for the miraculous gifts, a person practicing them may feel uncomfortable at first, like praying for healing or speaking out prophecy," I said. "I think you need to encourage the congregation from the pulpit…you know, just explain the gift of prophecy and other miraculous gifts."

"I think that the Holy Spirit will make that happen, not me."

"Well, you're the leader and pastor of the church, so I think you need to at least say something about it."

"I feel like God will make that happen, without me pushing it."

"What about the gift of pastoring?" I asked. "You have several people in this church of about 3,000 who have the gift of pastoring, but only you and the staff can officially pastor the flock."

At this point, the pastor stopped eating and tilted his head downward, while staring at me across the top of his glasses.

"So, how would you suggest I engage people with the gift of pastoring?" he asked.

"Designate a team of volunteer pastors in the church," I said. "I'll give you their names, but you can see who they are in the church.

They're the ones who are consistently checking in with people and making sure they are taken care of. They are your nurturers, the ones who take the time to call someone at home, just to check in on them."

The pastor pushed away his plate. "So, you want me to designate a team of pastors?"

"Sure, why not? You and the three other pastors are paid staff. Then you have an unpaid volunteer staff of several pastors; not just your small group leaders, but people who follow-up with people at home and at work, or who invite them to lunch, or maybe go to their workplaces and help the congregation as needed. Make pastoring decentralized and widespread, to minister to people on a routine basis."

"That's the small group leader," he said. "You're pastoring a small group now, right?"

"I'm talking about a designated team of pastors in the church, who can help you and the staff shepherd people—not just small group leaders but co-pastors."

The pastor checked his watch. "I've got a meeting in ten, but I'll think and pray about it. Thanks for the idea." With that, our exchange ended as the pastor stood up and double-timed through the restaurant's front doors.

Ideally, I wished for a book of Acts kind of church that was based on fellowship instead of church events, but nothing happened after that meeting with the pastor. When conventional religion takes root, it is hard to change it. Yet, God's attention always remains focused on His beloved children—and sometimes He uses a different model from the norm. I agreed with small groups being the foundation of relationship within the church, but I also knew that God always challenges our comfort zone to usher in a new wave of

His outpouring. Later, Heaven's Storm would teach me the fullness of this truth.

Many people who were taught in our classes left our mega-church, either desiring a deeper relationship than what the church offered, or because they had failed to develop lasting relationships within the church. I became frustrated with the lack of engagement in church, so like many "laypeople," my attention returned to work and family.

I left Johnson & Johnson to join what eventually became the fast-est-growing pharmaceutical company in the world, then called Elan Pharmaceuticals. Discovery of a new drug to prevent Alzheimer's disease had catapulted the company to an expansion and an acqui-sition of three other companies, including one based in San Diego, California. A series of talent assessments ensued as we combined four companies into one. I became the Corporate Operations Director for the new biopharmaceutical company. Renee, our chil-dren Annie (now five), Ryan (now almost seven), and I relocated to San Diego, and we purchased a nearly 5,000 square foot house close to the ocean.

Time magazine featured our new drug on its front cover. I flew to Washington, DC, to help introduce the much-anticipated possi-ble "cure" for Alzheimer's to the world. All the major news networks featured interviews with our chief scientist.

The Holy Spirit inspired me with a tagline to introduce our new drug: "Making Alzheimer's History." After we returned from DC, I learned some devastating news. Nine patients out of nearly

300 patients in our final stage of three clinical trials had developed encephalitis, a swelling of the brain. The Food and Drug Administration (FDA) forced a recall of our drug, which meant that we could no longer proceed with plans to bring the drug to the market.

Our company stock dropped from a near market high to an almost penny stock. I lost over one million dollars overnight. More importantly, I lamented the many suffering Alzheimer's victims who would eventually die of this horrid disease, including my mother, several years later. After laying off my entire department, I too became a victim of layoffs. As with all companies with whom I had worked, I had started a Christian fellowship group in this company.

My last day at this pharmaceutical company ended with a prayer meeting in one of the conference rooms. When our prayer meeting concluded, I exited the doors to masses of employees lining the railways above, who were clapping for me. I teared up in response and held my hand over my chest as I waved goodbye and left the building for the last time.

Not long after, our daughter began experiencing seizures at night and Tourette's syndrome, which manifested as uncontrollable jerking head motions after she ate food. Just entering her adolescence as an eleven-year-old, Annie often refused to eat with friends in the cafeteria at school or at social occasions, to allay fears of embarrassing herself. On several occasions, Renee or I would enter Annie's room after midnight, in response to violent screams. We would try to comfort her with head rubs, to no avail. I recall sitting at her bedside, silently praying in the dead of night. Out of frustration, I shouted at the air, demanding that God heal or deliver Annie as she writhed in torment.

Several visits with a specialist failed to diagnose the problem. Then Renee found a child neurologist who diagnosed Annie with hemiplegic migraine disorder, a rare cause of mini-strokes that cause weakness on one side of the body (hemiplegia) and painful night terrors. The specialist prescribed medications to suppress Annie's traumatic events, but she still suffered from Tourette's—although the medications reduced the events.

At one point, I spent nearly $1,000 per day in treatment centers to help Annie. We were quickly going broke. For Renee and I, tears welled up and sometimes spilled out during the quietness of our nightly prayers. Our dearest daughter "with a heart of gold" and a smile that spread joy no matter the situation, gradually fell into deep bouts of depression. It seemed as if God did not like us anymore.

For a brief period, I served as a CEO of a biotech company, but the company was eventually divested, as is common to biotech companies. After needing to raise $80 million to keep the company afloat, I resigned, even after investing much of our personal finances there. That, coupled with hundreds of thousands of dollars of medical bills, brought us to a point of financial despair. One memory had fixed itself in my mind like a weight, further pulling me into the depths of depression. It was when in our bedroom, I looked over to the other side of the bed and Renee was sobbing.

"What's wrong?" I asked.

"We don't have any money left," she said.

We had lost millions of dollars, including our personal investments in the biotech company, due to the stock plunge fueled by the withdrawn Alzheimer's drug. Combined with the mounting medical bills, we were broke and broken.

"God, You need to show up this time," I cried one night, while staring at the ceiling of our empty bedroom.

I needed to find a job, so I flew to New Jersey to interview for a position with my alma mater, Johnson & Johnson, in New

Brunswick. The person who would fill the open position would direct a cardiovascular team that focused on minimally invasive surgery. Given my clinical training and business experience, I felt well-suited for the job. After a long series of interviews with no time for even a sip of water, I caught a return flight to San Diego and fell asleep aboard the plane.

During this time, I was dying but I didn't know it. In truth, I would be dead in a matter of hours. As I slept, I was blissfully unaware that God wanted a face-to-face meeting with me.

PART TWO

MEETING JESUS
IN HEAVEN

8

DEATH AND THE SECOND HEAVEN

We are confident, I say, and would prefer to be
away from the body and at home with the Lord.
—2 CORINTHIANS 5:8 NIV

After landing in San Diego, I was driven home by Renee, and I greeted Ryan, Annie, and our two little dogs, and went straight to bed. Around four in the morning, I awoke to use the bathroom. I felt heaviness in the calf of my right leg, as if someone had tied a weight to my lower leg. Unable to sleep again, I walked downstairs to the kitchen. Each step sent shooting pains up my leg.

At first, I assumed I had leg cramps from a lack of movement the previous day. I walked to the garage to retrieve my bicycle, hoping that a little exercise up the coastline of Route 101 would relieve my soreness. Normally, the ocean waves washing ashore with their glassy surface kissed by the sunrise would relax my soul. However, this time I labored to breathe on a straight road as my lower leg throbbed with each downward pedal stroke.

Along the mile trek home, I noticed that my calf appeared swollen. Immediately after opening the front door of our house, I hopped over to the kitchen counter to retrieve my inhaler from one of the drawers, thinking my increased wheezing stemmed from an asthma attack. I began to prepare some eggs and bacon for breakfast, stopping periodically for additional puffs on the inhaler, without relief.

I heard a knock at the door and saw that two friends had come for a visit, so I hopped upstairs on my left leg, to wake Renee. As the four of us sat at our dining room table to chitchat, I kept rubbing my leg, hoping to reduce the swelling from what I assumed was a muscle strain. Once the couple left, I proceeded to make breakfast. After that, I tried emptying the garbage but abandoned the idea midway between the kitchen and the side yard. Defeated, I hopped toward the family room, only to fall into a chair as I gasped for air.

"You need to get that checked," said Renee.

Since we had planned a trip to the mountains as a family getaway that weekend, I decided that the quickest solution was to obtain an anti-inflammatory for my leg, and possibly a painkiller, so I called the orthopedic surgeon's office, on a Friday, to explain my situation. Thankfully, a cancelled appointment appeared, allowing a visit later that same day. The phone in my home office now rang.

"Hello," I said, between breaths.

"Hello Randy. This is Kathy from Johnson & Johnson."

"Hi Kathy," I said, pausing to take a breath. "Nice to hear from you."

"I would like to offer you the Director position," she said. It was the cardiovascular position I had interviewed for. She reviewed the details of my employment offer and I quickly responded "Yes" to her offer. It was all I could do to finish our conversation before I felt lightheaded and unable to speak for more than a few seconds.

Renee was finishing breakfast but offered to drive me to the doctor's office. I bullishly insisted on driving to the nearby Oceanside office myself, and huffed and puffed during the entire short drive.

After hobbling from the waiting room into the doctor's office, I explained my dilemma.

"How long has it been swollen like this?" he asked.

"It started swelling last night," I said.

"Press the ball of your foot to the floor for me," he said.

"Do you feel pain?"

"Not really."

"Now press your heal against the floor."

After I did that, I dropped to the floor in pain, as I was unable to stand. Moments later, I passed out and was rushed to the Emergency Room for blood tests, an ultrasound of my right leg, and a CAT scan of my chest. After a while, the doctor came into my room with the results.

"You have six blood clots occluding your pulmonary artery, Mr. Kay," he said.

"What…does…that mean?" I whispered in exhaustion.

"It means quite frankly, that you are a walking dead man," he said. "My first inclination is to rush you to UCSD (University of California at San Diego) Hospital to open your chest so that a specialist there can remove the clots, but you wouldn't make it."

Men and women in white hospital gear now rushed their equipment into my room, including a ventilator and bags of solutions, anticoagulants. I don't remember anything after that except waking in a room with my heart racing as though it would leap out of my chest.

The man next to me was suddenly rushed out of the room and placed in isolation, due to the discovery of his highly contagious, drug-resistant bacterial infection. I later learned that the infection was transferred to me, contributing to further clotting issues. Sepsis soon surged throughout my body and caused a traffic jam of red blood corpuscles that prevented the doctor from drawing any blood from my arm.

Uncontrollable spasms now caused my body to jump on the bed, like a fish out of water. For those seconds, I fought not to let go. At the same time, I wanted to let go. Then, in sharp contrast to the anxiety of my rapid heartbeat, heaviness in my chest, and numbness—my struggle ceased.

I was left in a place of stillness after a soft pull from my chest. The tug allowed my spirit to somehow settle over my motionless body now lying near me on the table. A light from above suddenly enveloped me and gently pulled me upward. I felt perfect peace in a space of darkness that was slightly illuminated by the light now coming from above. I was dead.

For an instant, I looked down to see my body, not thinking it at all strange that just moments before, I was convulsing on a hospital bed. Oddly enough, a perfect calm now possessed me. My practically inclined mind no longer needed to reason about my condition or my surroundings, wanting only to absorb every facet of my experience. Clearly, I had no control over the situation. I only wanted to relinquish my all to whatever or whoever tugged at my body from above; this dark space was gradually illuminated by the light. Below, my body lay strangely still as I peered down at it as an onlooker thinking, *That body isn't me anymore.*

My second thought was, *I'm not in the world anymore.* It seems odd now, but I remembered a scene from the movie *The Wizard of Oz*, where Dorothy found herself in the Land of Oz and said, "I'm not in Kansas anymore." I had been partly exposed to the spiritual realm but had never fully lived in it as I now did—apart from any semblance of the world, existing in some unknown space.

Instantly, I could see a rush of galaxies as I was pulled rapidly upward by the light. The base of my body or my feet shot like a streak of lightning. I watched as sparkling trails broke off of my body, the way one might see a rocket ship's vapor trails break through the atmosphere. I felt like a surreal version of myself, a foreigner with no grounded identify other than some semblance of who I had become in a body comprised of a foreign substance tangible and penetrable and wonderfully made. Moreover, my sense of existence felt more defined by the Light that pulled me rather than the stuff that formed my body. My mind became consumed in the moment with no thought of the future—unencumbered for the first time even though I fully remembered only the pleasantries of my life on earth.

Next, I could see planets or giant rocks trail past as I ascended. After this rapid flight that seemed to last but a nanosecond, my feet settled on the ground of an ethereal space entirely different from the spiral galaxy I had passed. The atmosphere appeared surreal, as if imparting a faded effect onto a dynamic background. I looked outward in response to a faint clashing sound that seemed to come from somewhere off in the distance.

Whether miles or only a few hundred yards away, space and time appeared irrelevant, two groups of figures battled in what seemed to be a mixture of medieval and *Star Wars* garb and weaponry. On the right side, Heaven's warrior angels—figures roughly twice the height of my six-foot frame glistened in the same light that had pulled me from above. That light now beamed upon their silver shields and reflected a laser-like beam onto similarly-sized demonic figures that warred against them in the darkness on the left.

As the figures fought, the light beam burned through the tattered gray robes covering the demons. Although the light beam pierced their flesh, it did not bleed—at least it looked like flesh, or another composition I could not discern due to the murky smoke that infiltrated the scene.

On the left, the wounds of the demonic figures wept pus as they spread their multiple wings in response to the light that pierced their bodies. In sharp contrast to the heavenly warriors on the right, the demons appeared with monstrous, reptilian heads—black, beady eyes; sharp, bulbous skulls with rotting teeth; flattened, flared nostrils; an absence of ear openings, and bodies covered with decaying cloth. Some demons fell to the burnt floor that was faintly comprised of debris.

Once felled, the demons gnawed upon their own limbs or the bodies of other fallen demons. Their mummified faces did not appear even remotely human, and withered hide overlaid their bones. They had elongated, goat-like snouts with bloated, human-shaped foreheads and slits for eyes. Their disproportionately-sized arms dangled forward, perhaps six feet from their bodies. Legs exaggerated in length protruded from their shredded robes to reveal sinew and what appeared to be muscle tissue—like frayed, interwoven ropes in a perpetual state of decay.

The figures battled with rusty swords or spears that shed something like blackened snowflakes through the air. Figures from either side intermittently crossed into the opposite side to plunge their weapons into the gargantuan bodies of their enemies. As soon as a figure became wounded, it fell to the ground. As the decaying demons fell to the scorched ground, I detected a faint, sulfurous odor that fumed outwardly from their bodies. Thankfully, on the right, the heavenly warriors emitted a rather pleasant perfume that bathed everyone who was surrounded by the mysterious light, including me.

The decayed appearance of the demons on the left contrasted with the brilliance of the angels on the right. These humanlike beings wore full armor that hugged their muscular bodies like a wetsuit. Their silver helmets were conformed to their heads and glistened in the golden light that surrounded them. Their dimensions appeared comparable in size to the demons, except that the angels appeared toned and healthy. I marveled at their appearance and shiny silver armor.

Although their helmets wrapped around their heads, I could see the outline of their faces, which appeared proportionately human—although their eyes resembled flames of fire. Their wings, which were several feet long, flapped in response as they attacked the demons. The angels wielded swords the length of their bodies, which reflected the light rays, to penetrate the demon bodies. I think the light rays and not the swords toppled the demons, because demons fell from the reflective rays alone.

I don't know if the angels and the fallen demons lying on the ground died outright, because the figures would disintegrate into something dust-like. The dust of the stricken angels floated upward into the light, but the dust from the fallen demons descended into a pitch-black abyss below—a pit that appeared darker than black. At the base of the pit, I noticed a glowing orange cast like that of an active volcano. Even peering into the abyss elicited a sense of hopelessness stronger than anything I ever felt before. I dared not look above me because the light rays poured down with a force greater than sunlight. Even so, I realized that the light did not burn me.

At this point, I neither feared nor felt confused by this otherworldly theater. I simply assimilated all that I beheld as a spectator of a sporting event. Somehow, I knew that the angels represented my team, if only because a few had given me a confident nod. Only one of the demons tried to look at me, but instantly darted away while shielding his burning red eyes from the light that scorched it like a consuming flame of fire.

The same light glistened within and around the angels in crystalline sparkles. It seemed clear to me that the light from above emitted the angels' life source but scorched and destroyed the demons. Din from the clanging of swords and the thumping of fists on arms extending the length of bodies left me wondering why I perceived this fearsome match. Yet I remained at peace, as if the outcome had been predetermined.

I noticed a difference as the angels felled more demons than vice versa. I watched the angels begin to recover territory from the demons, including a scorched knoll that had faded mountains in the distance. A faint whisper blew feelings of encouragement into my ear, not as audible words but as feelings or impressions. Each time one of the demons fell, a word echoed not so much in my ears but in my soul. This gave me a sense of knowing that good triumphed—as testified to by an infinite calm.

Conversely, when an angel fell, only thumping and screaming resonated within me; a sound eliciting fear and anxiety. Before entering this space and even before entering the hospital, I had often felt abandoned by God because of my losses and the sufferings of my wife and family. Shortly before I died, I had even stopped praying and going to church. Before my heart stopped, I had wrongly assumed that God didn't care. I didn't pray for God's help, even while I was suffering in the hospital.

As the whispery feelings from the angels echoed within me, I found a renewed thankfulness for God. I would later learn that the victory of the angels over the demons had opened a space through which the angels could impute the Holy Spirit's impressions upon my soul. I supposed that it worked the way a storm clears the air, so that broadcasting waves could be heard more clearly after the din. Only later would I understand the fullness of God's Storm. Those "broadcasting waves" happened to be the Holy Spirit's unfettered communications with me.

Somehow, the victory of the angels over the demons had opened an impartation in my soul which emboldened me to cry out the name of Jesus, in praise of Him. Years later, I would understand that the battle I had witnessed was over the legal right to speak to my tormented soul.

Months before I left my body on that hospital bed, I had suffered under demonic oppression. Now I cried out with a new freedom and fervor unlike any emotion I had ever felt in my life.

"Jesus!" My declaration spoke more than just a name. I cried out with absolute surrender as one might cave to sleep after being thoroughly drained from the cares of the world—and yet, I felt more alive than ever.

At that moment, a figure stood to my right and gently rested His bearded cheek onto mine as He embraced my side with His left arm. My first thought was, *So this is Love.* Even now as I write this account, I must admit that I am weeping because of the intense emotions I felt at that first encounter. No words can adequately explain my full immersion in the perfect peace, comfort, and assurance I experienced for the first time in my life. I implicitly knew the figure as Jesus, and felt as if all of my yearnings were consummated at that first meeting. I was home. I was at perfect peace, knowing that my journey in life was complete.

More important was the overwhelming, singular feeling of being in the presence of Love Himself. This was not "love" as an emotion or sense. It was the feeling of being penetrated with an awareness of God's love for me and an assimilation of that love, filling me with immense gratitude and a desire to love God and everyone in return. I would give you an analogy, but no analogies exist for meeting the person of love. Suffice it to say that "love" no longer existed as a word or an understanding. Love, as we know it in this world, fails to approximate any experience associated with worldly living.

In Heaven, the ever-evading definition of "love" that many struggle with in this world, no longer meant anything. That's because love—Jesus—comprises the very definition of *existence* in Heaven. Indeed, *love's true source is Jesus,* and the full composition of Heaven is imbued with love.

I dropped to my knees. A dam of emotions broke forth into an effusive outpouring of devotion.

"My God!" I cried out.

"My Lord!"

"Almighty…Jesus…glory be…Your name!"

"Hail…" (A flood of tears flow from my eyes, even now as I recall the moment I first met Love.)

Jesus wrapped His arms under my armpits and pulled my saggy body upward until I mustered the strength to stand. Then He turned me to face His face. At first, I felt like turning away. I did not feel worthy to behold His face, but He cupped my chin to turn my head squarely in front of His face, as I looked into the eyes of Love. They appeared as the colors of the ocean—blues, grays, browns, and greens. A brilliant light emanated from Him that reflected in His eyes the way sunlight breaks forth upon the ocean surface in waves of color.

It was the depth of those eyes that struck me the most. The light of His eyes tunneled into me with the warmth of a cup of soothing elixir, infusing me with a feeling of protection and the trust of a newborn babe. Not a word was spoken at this point, although I sensed His feelings toward me. I knew He could sense my thoughts and feelings toward Him. We shared a common understanding in the love that Jesus absolutely had for me and I loved Him with a devotion I had never felt toward anyone before that moment.

A brilliant light now overlaid Jesus's body and projected outward from Him, with the intensity of what I would imagine was greater than the rays of the sun. Perhaps because I was only a spirit at this point, I could see through the rays emitting from Jesus to behold His figure. I noticed His almost shoulder-length brown, slightly wavy hair, but His face impressed me more. I was struck not only by the Middle Eastern features of His curved nose and square jaw, but He had the expression of someone who knew me the way a loving parent regards a child, only infinitely greater. I never realized that Love was a Person—a love pure, penetrating, and unending. Every facet of Him emanated love.

The light that shined from Jesus provided not only comforting rays, but I could also smell a sweet fragrance that was more spectacular than any I inhaled in the world—and that is impossible to describe. Jesus flared His nostrils and seemed to inhale a scent I emitted, as though I wore cologne He thoroughly enjoyed. He smiled, causing me to smile inside for evermore.

At this point, I understood things from more than mere observation. I could feel an intimate spiritual communion between us. Tears that had initially flooded from me in adoration of God, now sank deep within my innermost being. I would eventually come to understand this flow of waters as the living waters of Jesus that flow through my translucent spirit body—one that felt airy, light, and devoid of any earthly maladies.

Jesus leaned His head over my right ear and whispered.

"Trust Me."

I suppose one might consider that statement to be obvious, considering my position, but those two words said everything about what I lacked in the world, yet innately understood in Heaven. I knew I dwelt in Heaven because Jesus imparted that understanding to me. And I knew that He loved me because He imbued me with love. But trust—trust in God was the one thing I could give Him that He could never give to me, unless I willed it back to Him. I realized in Heaven that I was never fully trusting God while I was on earth, unlike the implicit trust in Jesus I now felt in Heaven.

"I surrender my all," I said.

9

My Life in Review

The Life Review is a preview of
Heaven's Awards Ceremony.
—John Burke

I entered through a series of opaque, concentric circles that narrowed and ended in a place where I stood, amid what seemed to be a kind of stage that morphed into different places. At the first place I found myself, I was a child looking at my Uncle Carlyle in his coffin, but what I perceived was not from a child's perspective. I now viewed his corpse from God's perspective—one filtered through my own understanding, even as I stood in the same place I had as a child being introduced to death for the very first time.

What I am about to share with you are not verbal insights imparted to me from Jesus. Rather, they were the Holy Spirit's thoughts, as conveyed to me for each moment I was shown, along with my inspired responses. These life reviews taught me the meaning behind the moments of my life. They also confirm to me that life is not a series of random events. Instead, they form a pattern known only to God. Jesus also revealed some of the reasons behind these moments, while I visited Heaven.

(Our spiritual conversations are italicized.)

What do you see, My beloved? Jesus asked.

I see my uncle, and I remember how scared I was because I didn't understand how lifeless he had become, I said.

You lost your innocence in believing that you would live forever, Jesus said. But you did not sin, beloved—you were introduced to your immortality.

I didn't turn to You then, I said.

No, you turned to your parents, beloved, but My eyes were always upon you. Each of My beloved children must learn the cost of death before they can realize the cost of life I paid.

You paid that cost to live forever in the Spirit, my Lord, but I had to learn that this life in the flesh would end, before seeking the answers to what exists after death, I said.

Jesus nodded, affirming my words.

Another series of concentric circles appeared within a vacuum, which "whooshed" me to another place. Now the stage turned to my childhood home in Arlington Heights, Illinois, when I played with a cat with my friend Patti, and I was rushed to the hospital hours later. All of these appearances were not visions, because visions are surreal or distant. I was actually there. I was in the hospital again, with my collapsed lungs, looking through the bars that kept me from falling out of the bed.

You were with me and I didn't even know it, I said.

Always, My beloved. You suffered as a child and I knew even then, how I would use your suffering.

I didn't blame You then, Lord, but I wanted someone to help me. I knew in that moment, that my compassion for those who suffer had come from my own understanding of suffering.

You only knew Me as a name and not as a Companion, beloved. But I knew you during all of your life.

I felt Jesus tear up as I lay in that bed, and during the flood of times when I had gasped for breath. He viewed me as though I was the only person in the world. I felt Jesus's absolute devotion as though He cared only for me and nothing else. I also knew that He sees every person He has created, as though nothing else matters.

"Whoosh"—a wind blew to clear the clouds or vapors and reveal another setting. In the next scene, I was sitting on the quilted, white satin sofa in the living room of 116 Covered Bridge Road, in Cherry Hill, New Jersey. It was 1965 and I was looking at Tony's red eyes. Then I was peering through the picture window all over again, as ambulance lights flashed red across the street, before attendants wheeled Tony's dead father into the ambulance.

Why did these episodes witnessing death strike me so much as a child, Lord?

Because you needed to find Me on the other side of death, My child. Wisdom cannot be earned; it finds itself through darkness, in seeking after My light.

I was losing my innocence.

No, beloved, you were awakening to the sadness that death causes so that you would seek after life, which only I could give you.

Were you sad?

Yes, beloved, because no one turned to Me during that time. Many mourn death without seeking after My life, so they busy themselves with the things of the world to entertain themselves. But I am always seeking after My children.

The next scene found me reading a letter that was left on my father's desk. Again, I saw the word "excommunicated" printed below the church letterhead—a word that struck me to my soul.

It was wrong, I said to God. At the time, I blamed You for that. I think that I lost my faith then.

But I did not blame you, beloved. Always, I loved you. Always, I wanted you to know Me, He said.

You're showing me this now, to show me how I turned against You, Lord? I asked.

Beloved, I am showing you this now so that you can know that My love for you was never hindered by your inability to love Me. My love is not conditioned by another's ability to love Me.

Oh Lord, if only I would have known. If only I could have known how much You loved me, even when I didn't even know You. How great is Your patience and mercy, but I was at fault for ignoring You.

Jesus pressed me tightly into Him. No words were needed since each episode revealed its deeper meaning to me. Here, I was freed from my physical body and brain. My spirit mind was consumed with the ways of Jesus as though I saw things through His eyes. What an amazing revelation—that in Heaven, I could see through the eyes of Jesus! This perspective eliminated all fear, sadness, and confusion. Now I could see the depth of meaning in every person and living being.

In my next vignette, I sat in a wooden chair, with my math and science books stacked upon my desk, in homeroom class at Brainerd Junior High. I saw on my notebook where I had scribbled: *I hate school.* Joel, Vincent, and Jeffrey now hovered over me as Vincent spoke aloud, "Awe, Randy hates school. Poor Randy." He said this loudly so the whole class would hear. Mrs. Pfeiffer kept her face hidden behind an open book. The students around the bullies chuckled, and the unusually tall Joel mockingly patted me on the head over and over until I swatted his arm away, like a fly that kept pestering me.

You were there, but it didn't seem like it at all, I said.

I was not even a passing thought to you then beloved, but yes, I was there.

Why? Why did that happen, Lord? It was like a living hell to me then.

I see not only what is, but what is to come. I knew that the boy who was bullied would grow into the man who would be tenderhearted to the broken of this world. Was it worth it, My beloved?

Yes, Lord. It was more than worth it, as I see it now. I had forgotten that painful time in my life until You showed it to me here. I don't remember any of the painful things that happened. But I'm glad that You are showing them to me because I see how You turned my wasteland into paradise and even purpose. Thank You for not abandoning me, Lord, even when I had abandoned You.

Beloved, I knew your heart. I always turn that which is bad for good, for those who turn to Me, even if it takes a lifetime.

The next moment, I found myself watching the program *Lost in Space,* on the new, tin-framed color television set, when my mom entered the downstairs family room and flicked off the TV.

"Jimmy's in the hospital, love," she said.

"How, why?"

"He was attacked at the bus stop." On that day, I did not go to school because I had felt sick—but I had actually *faked* being sick.

"Is he okay?" I asked, concerned.

"He's in serious condition," she said. "I hope he'll be okay."

Lord, his family went to church. They seemed like model Christians, but You allowed my best friend to be attacked for a reason?

Beloved, I redeemed it. Evil reigns only for a season. I have made life through dry bones, so I will turn good from evil for those who know Me. Beloved, I knew yours and Jimmy's futures, because I could see into your hearts and your hearts determined who you would become.

My physical death led to the purest joy beyond imagination in Heaven, because God redeems His children from brokenness and death. The Holy Spirit also imparted another epiphany to me:

Invariably my heart desired God because His Kingdom resided in me, but that Kingdom resided not in the flesh but the spirit. Jesus tucked it inside of my spirit in a divine connection between Heaven and earth, between the person I discovered myself to be in Heaven, and the person I could be on earth, if not for the mistrust of God that Jesus elucidated to me when we first met in Heaven.

The truest connection with God could only occur in the absence of any obtrusion caused by our physical body and brain. I knew then that our futures are all in God's past. Then it struck me. I realized that all this time of "knowing" came from the Holy Spirit, the One who indwelled me when I opened my heart to Jesus. Jesus normally spoke to my heart through the Spirit. When He spoke audibly, that voice came from Jesus Himself. The Holy Spirit always spoke to me through impressions. I understood then that Jesus walked with me as my kindred Friend, but the Holy Spirit indwelled me as my closest Companion on earth, and both seemed equally close to me in Heaven.

Just then, as though confirming my understanding, a warm wind washed through me as a signifier of my closest Companion, the Holy Spirit. He instantly informed me that what I had concluded was true. I didn't need an explanation from Jesus as to why bad things happened under His watch. I knew without any doubt that in the scheme of eternity, even the worst sufferings are nothing in Heaven. I also knew that the blessings of turning evil to good, far outweigh the pain of the world, for all who place their trust in God. Trust—it was all about trusting God.

In Heaven, I remembered nothing of my sufferings in the world. Even watching my trials in the world during my life reviews, did not evoke any sorrow. They spoke of the purpose and sometimes the joy that God created for me through those storms of life.

This epiphany manifested before my spiritual eyes as the Holy Spirit now blew forth a strong wind to wash through all of the vignettes I had viewed. He was cleansing them of all of the wrongs and restoring them to the fullness of what God intended in Heaven, turning them all for good, through a type of spiritual cleansing.

As Jesus revealed my life, I realized His complete redemption of everything in my life, such that the afterglow of Jesus's redemption, in tandem with the Holy Spirit's purifying breath, left me with a new appreciation of my earthly sufferings. I could see the spiritual rain as it poured forth from the Holy Spirit onto the earth, and from which He produces life from death, joy from suffering, and beauty from ashes.

In my next series of reviews, I found myself playing tug of war with my childhood dog, Casey. We were in the backyard beneath the same oak tree where weeks before a squirrel froze in horror when Casey broke his chain. I could smell the freshly cut grass I mowed, as Casey jumped up and down trying to snatch the short rope.

My setting suddenly changed. I was now in paradise standing beside Jesus, surrounded by rolling vineyards with flowers and trees growing in front of my eyes. Iridescent flowers instantly sprouted forth from their buds, in myriads of colorful shades and varieties. It dawned on me that the perpetual growth of flora appeared not because time accelerated in Heaven. Rather, the circadian rhythms were not predicated on the sun, because no sun existed. They thrived in the presence of Jesus's light, in a perpetual state of renewal, where nothing died.

The wonders of Heaven consumed me until Jesus motioned for me to look behind me. There in Heaven—not in the vignette I just beheld but in Heaven at the present time—I could see radiant and variably colored stones that pulsed with life. My eyes beheld vistas of mountaintops gleaming not from the sun—because again, no sun appeared—but that glistened from the brilliance of Jesus's own light. I peered with my spiritual eyes over the pinnacles of the mountains. At the same time, I saw the veins in the leaves below as if I was examining them through a microscope.

Worshipful choruses from angels with folded wings echoed throughout Heaven, their joyous songs of praise, thanksgiving, and triumph. Their pristine tones held a soft, yet reverberating resonance of a thousand choruses or more. Within the glorious sounds, Jesus somehow stilled my ears, to focus solely upon the "now" in Heaven's paradise.

We were surrounded by a meadow that burst forth with purple flowers, my favorite color. Jesus swung His arm to motion me toward my left. My little dog Casey jumped up and down, just as we did in play when I was a child. I picked him up and hugged him tightly, thanking God while snuggling my little dog. I didn't sneeze as I often had on earth. He licked my face up and down with the same veracity of his greetings when I returned home from school. Oh how I thoroughly enjoyed being with little Casey again in Heaven. I had missed him so much in the world. To see him again in Heaven inspired me with God's loving-kindness.

"See beloved, I give you the desires of your heart," Jesus said audibly. "You will see him again when you return here," He said.

"Thank You, Lord!" I said. Casey barked thrice as if saying, "See you again, my friend." I seemed to understand his barks as words. Then he ran into a greener-than-green field of grass before disappearing over the crest of a hill that had trees that waved elegantly due to what I thought was the breath of the Holy Spirit—a breath that orchestrated everything in Heaven.

That breath of life would bring another shift to my surroundings—one that was dark and that only God could make right.

10

HATING GOD

Everyone who does evil hates the light....
—JOHN 3:20 NIV

My viewpoint left Heaven in an instant. Once again, I found myself a spectator of my past. God had plopped me back in time into my "theater of life." Now I existed in real time as God juxtaposed two realities. I was in the spirit but I found myself in a hospital room with the boy who was dying of cancer. Unlike the dismay I felt as a teen when I saw his hollowed face, protruding cheekbones, and bony arms and legs, I now felt thankful to see him. The boy, a stranger, was praying for me, an orderly who had brought him his food. Now I saw the day he prayed for me after I had already left his room. He said:

"Jesus, save that man. Help him to know You."

Moments earlier, the boy had told me that one day I would be in Heaven. Sure enough, I was revisiting the scene while I was indeed in Heaven, thanks to the prayers of that little boy.

Oh Lord, I said to Jesus, You heard that boy's prayers even though he was a stranger to me.

But he wasn't a stranger to Me beloved, Jesus or the Holy Spirit said, or perhaps both. Yes, I heard his prayers, and what he declared in faith then, was established.

89

I was in Heaven witnessing that little boy say that I would be there "someday," and that "someday" was now.

I always hear the prayers of My children and I bring them to the Throne Room and we do that which is good, the Holy Spirit said.

"The Throne Room?" I asked audibly. Jesus answered me audibly.

"Yes, beloved, we will go there soon and some of what you will see you will understand and some of what you see is for later."

"Later?"

"Yes beloved. I will show you when you are to share that which you will see, but what you will see cannot be shared with anyone until My appointed time. A Storm shall arise and that which is good shall be made full, and that which is evil shall be destroyed."

I did not think to further question what Jesus meant, because in Heaven I felt implicit trust in God. Though Jesus's mention of a Storm did perplex me, I knew to trust Him with the unknown.

My thoughts returned to that little boy who had prayed for me.

A stranger, Lord. I stood in awe that a strange boy's prayers could have had that deep of an impact on the plan for my eternity.

"But I became an agnostic. I hated Christians," I said. Our conversations turned back to the Holy Spirit's impartation of knowing.

You hated Me, beloved.

"No, really, I hated You?"

If you hated even one of My children, you hated Me.

The realization that I offended God every time I called a Christian a "hypocrite, fool," or some other disparagement, caused a deep conviction in my spirit. I saw these vignettes not through the eyes of a child or youth or whatever stage I beheld them during my physical life. I saw them through the eyes of my spirit, and felt my experiences not just as I had felt them in the moments they were revealed to me. I perceived them through the eyes of Jesus, exactly as He saw them. I could see as a third party to my experiences, yet I fully understood those times in my life. Now in Heaven, I could clearly see and feel the grace of Jesus Christ throughout the moments of my life.

"You even forgave my hatred for You, Lord?" I asked.

"Yes," He responded. "Never has My love for you changed. I have always believed in you, even when you did not believe in Me."

"But I failed You, more often than not. How could You forgive me when I didn't know You and didn't ask for Your forgiveness, Lord?" Then I realized that I had asked Jesus for forgiveness—eventually.

"I searched your heart, My beloved, and when you came to know Me as your Lord, I gave you life. Having no relationship with Me left you without life, and your sins spoke death to you. I gave you life by imparting My righteousness to you."

I remembered when Jesus said to have life we must *"eat the flesh of the Son of Man and drink his blood"* (John 6:53 NIV). Jesus said that on earth we have no life in ourselves. The apostle Paul also wrote that *"God made him who had no sin to be sin for us, so that in him we might become the righteousness of God"* (2 Corinthians 5:21 NIV). This made perfect sense to me in Heaven. At that revelation, I felt Jesus's blood coursing through my transcendent body.

As I moved my right hand to touch the left side of my chest, I could feel the oscillating flow of Jesus's lifeblood as my hand pressed through my exterior to the interior of my body. Jesus's warmth entered my hand and traveled throughout my body as the soothing flow of His lifeblood filled my frame. It felt like I was being immersed in a warm bath, only better, because I was enlivened and relaxed at the same time. It was as if someone had injected me with a soothing sedative while I received an invigorating massage. This was the first time I truly understood the difference between life and death. Life to me now is quite simply, Jesus.

"And all this time I was dead to You?" I asked.

"Beloved, there is no life without Me," Jesus said.

"Because my spirit had no life?"

Jesus smiled, knowing I knew the answer was "yes," without Him having to speak.

Every failure or sin I committed during my vignettes did not serve to convict me. Instead, they reflected the grace of Jesus in each situation. As I understood from the Holy Spirit's impartation, this grace was applied because I eventually accepted Jesus as my Lord and Savior. Thereafter, I felt true remorse for my sins and asked Jesus to forgive me. Even if I did not ask for forgiveness verbally, God still knew my heart—I wanted to please Him and deeply regretted my offenses against Him. I also realized that our merciful God extended my life, knowing that in my heart of hearts, I would eventually come to a place of sincere repentance.

"The car accident, Lord, I was going to die if not for You, wasn't I?" Jesus smiled in response as the Holy Spirit confirmed my question.

Yes.

I looked at the towering angel who stood beside me all the time that I traveled with Jesus. He looked at me with eyes of fire; his bulging, bronzed arms appeared ready to attack any opposing force at any moment. Then it struck me that this was my guardian angel.

Was that my guardian angel—this guy who appeared as a plain woman at the mangled car door as my broken body lay inside? Was that the one who assured me I would be okay as I sat in shock after the accident?

Again, the Holy Spirit answered with that same sense of knowing.

Yes.

My guardian angel had somehow morphed into an innocent-looking woman who told me I would be fine. The Holy Spirit also communicated that this same fearsome-looking angel had prevented my car from rolling over the embankment, which surely would have caused my instant death.

Because I had seen the demons and angels battling as I rose toward Jesus after dying, I imagined the same warfare with demons and angels battling over my life, following the car accident. Then the Holy Spirit opened my mind to the outcome of that battle as I lay crushed inside my vehicle, during my final days as an agnostic. Had I died, I would have gone to hell. God saved me from certain death so that my spirit could be saved. The warfare over my life had ended in defeat of the demons: Angels-1, Demons-0. Now "Randy Kay" was destined for salvation because shortly after the accident, I was drawn by the Holy Spirit to learn more about God.

"I spoke life over you then," Jesus said. I knew at the very moment of Jesus's declaration, that my guardian angel had braced the car from rolling into the ditch.

My next vignette within the "theater of life" brought me to the time when I was jogging with Brad on Lake Shore Drive at night, and the waves from Lake Michigan crashed against the rocks on our left as we passed the old cemetery on our right.

"I hate you for killing me." The voice came from inside of the locked, iron gate.

"Who was that?" I asked the Lord.

"A demon, beloved; the demons lie when they accuse those I have called."

"You called me even then—even when I hated You?"

"Did you hate Me?" Jesus asked verbally. When Jesus asked me this question, His expression reminded me of my mother's face when she asked me a rhetorical question as a child, whenever I was hiding something. I thought about the answer for a while, knowing how I felt at the time, until the answer became clear.

"I hated the person I thought You were, because I thought God was angry at me." I replied. Jesus hugged me tightly and leaned His head gently onto mine.

"I was not angry at you, my beloved…I yearned for you to know Me and I mourned our separation. But I knew you would eventually receive Me. I knew that the hardness of your heart was because you yearned for the Father's love."

Then I recalled how my earthly dad had loved me. He served as my hero, but one year before my father died, he sat in his worn, brown leather chair and turned his head toward me. As I saw a tear settle in his left eye, he said,

"I never knew you."

"Yes, you did," I replied.

Deep inside, I knew that my dad's stoicism stemmed from a life of poverty and the deep trauma of witnessing the atrocities of World War II—plus his upbringing to "be a man and not show your emotions" from his Depression Era childhood, all of which settled deeply in his soul. He never said, "I love you" to me, but I knew that he did. His workaholic tendencies sprang from a young life where no one ate food without working to earn it. His upbringing and mindset deprived me of "father time" throughout my childhood, except for sports or the occasional trip or trite conversation during meals. Old age had finally tenderized his heart to muster the courage to apologize to me—an apology I appreciated but really did not require.

"Was I like my dad, who loved me but rarely showed it?" I asked. "Did I love You deep down?"

"No," Jesus answered. "I loved you first so that you might love."

"Thank You," I said. It was all I could say. I felt kindred to Jesus and the Holy Spirit, but the Father—He resided in a place I had not yet seen.

Jesus motioned to me with a downward wave of His hand, as an opaque window opened to reveal a cityscape below. Masses of cars crossed on opposite sides of two-lane streets, halting at red stop lights or speeding at yellow ones. People on sidewalks in jeans and gym shoes and some in suits and polished shoes walked solo or in pairs, and chatted without saying much.

It all felt wrong to me because people appeared destined for places, without going anywhere. I knew as I stood in Heaven that this scene was earth in real time and not just a life review. Jesus imparted the understanding to me as a sense of knowing. My spirit body could see telescopically as I hovered a few feet above a crowd of people who walked along a bustling city walkway. Some carried coffees and some chatted with others as they hurried to their destinations under the morning sun. A homeless gray-bearded man sat with a cardboard sign that read: "Vet in need of food money."

I also viewed shadows that hovered over several people and permeated their space to impart darkness. One woman wore a white polka-dotted, loosely-fitting dress that complemented her white hair. Her slow gait contrasted the fast pace of the others. Her wrinkled face, slightly hunched body and thick-rimmed glasses struck me. Hovering over her was an angel with wings that glowed white. The angel engulfed the woman with what impressed me as wonderful, glowing emissions of peace.

Before her stood a towering angel adorned in armor, like the warriors I had perceived while rising. I came to understand that this was the "second heaven." This angel waved his sword, which reflected the light of Jesus, as vaporous figures swerved to avoid the angel's sword, only to turn toward the many other figures who walked about. The vaporous figures enveloped most of the people and penetrated those whose faces appeared milky with crazy, diseased eyes, and who tottered and teetered aimlessly to somewhere, but really nowhere at all.

"What do you see, beloved?" Jesus asked.

"I see people going about their business in a hurry to get somewhere, but most of them—except for that one old woman, have no life in them." I paused, knowing that Jesus was leading me to an understanding, so I asked Him a question:

"What do You see, Lord?"

"I see their separation from Me, except for the woman with white hair, who is My child."

Then I noticed the faces of those who walked or stood along that busy throughway. Rarely did anyone smile. Those who did laugh or smile, only did so in a cursory sort of way. I beheld everyone with an understanding of their truest selves, not just their external appearances. I could understand how they felt. No one felt joyful, as I now felt in Heaven, not even the old woman, who felt only the partial joy I experienced in the fullness of Heaven.

"Inside, they are empty, Lord," I said.

"Yes, beloved, and so it is for everyone who does not know Me and those who ignore Me," Jesus said.

I looked at Jesus's downturned head. A moaning cry echoed throughout Heaven, but it did not come from Jesus. It blew throughout Heaven and emitted a sorrowful dirge that ushered in a somber mood. I knew the whirling wind that blew throughout Heaven was the Holy Spirit, as He blew comforting warmth. But in that cityscape, I sensed the cold desolation of lost souls, and it seemed that the Holy Spirit, the wind whom I knew as a familiar Person, could not reach these people. Therefore, no peace could enter them or that place.

My spiritual eyes beheld auras emitting from the minds of the people, creating an impenetrable force that walled them off from God's Spirit. Not even He could penetrate the aura that the people's ignorance and self-indulgences emitted—as powerful shields against the Holy Spirit. I knew then that all sorrow came from separation from God and that only the presence of God could usher forth true joy. Humility and truth-seeking served as the only antidotes capable of breaking down those shields.

Some of the people who walked along the street carried cancer and other diseases with them. I could sense the ailments within them that are caused by the world's separation from God and the compounding of generations of sins that corrupt and sully the world that people of flesh call "home."

My eyes now turned to one elderly woman who sat in a wheelchair and wheeled herself along the side of the street. Her raggedy clothes were dotted with holes. No aura existed over her personhood. Standing beside Jesus in Heaven, I could tell that she loved Jesus because He smiled down at her. Jesus's smile glistened like sparkles that reached over the old lady, and she looked up as if aware that Jesus was showering her with blessings. Even in her misery, she enjoyed closeness to Jesus.

Ah, the love of You, Lord, I thought. You desire closeness with everyone.

You listen well, said the Holy Spirit. Being in Heaven teaches everyone to fully listen for My truth.

In the next moment, I found myself witnessing my life review again. Now I saw myself accusing Christians of being hypocrites, yet in Heaven it felt like I was the biggest hypocrite of all. I saw myself at my fraternity before Mark, who I knew had lied about his grades and about his knowledge of different subjects. To me he seemed to be a classic example of a Christian hypocrite—someone who professed Christ while living a sinful life. But Jesus showed me that I had been a liar, professing myself as the judge of others when I was guilty as sin.

Because Jesus imparted a deeper understanding of all I beheld, I knew the life reviews showed that my rebellion against God had happened for a reason. I thought about my rebellion against God as a self-professing "devoted agnostic." But I wondered, *Why now? Why show me these vignettes that showcased my hardheartedness?*

I viewed the scenes in a space that, oddly enough, resembled a courtroom. There was a judge's desk, made of what appeared to be marble, and a vast, rocky white stand without blemish that seemed to reach for miles, with a gold, embossed book lying atop. Jesus knew what I was thinking before I could ask Him the question.

"Everything I am showing you could be used in My court to render a judgment as to whether you are worthy of entering Heaven, My beloved. I show you these things not to condemn you but to show that your life in the world has been defined by My grace, not according to My justice. You chose Me because you sought the truth, but I chose you long before, and I waited for you and longed for you. If I were to judge each trespass against Me by you, in no way could you merit My grace in Heaven. What you see is My Throne of Grace, and I have already written your name within the book that you see."

Indeed, a gold-laced, leather-bound book rested upon the Judge's bench. Jesus rested His hand upon the book and moved His hand along the red seal that rested atop the book. Even though the full measure of Christ's grace seemed unfathomable to me, I did understand His meaning. I was sealed by the blood of Jesus Christ.

I said, "So during the times when I thought You were not with me, You were with me, but I was not with You. And yet, I judged You and found You guilty of negligence against me. But in truth, You were always with me, so You *were* just, but I believed in a false justice—in the world's justice. But when it came time for You to judge me, I had done so many wrongs for which I did not repent, but Your grace…Oh my…Your grace, Lord, covered a *multitude* of my sins, because You judged my *heart* toward You and not just my head."

"You surrendered your heart to Me, beloved," Jesus said. And oh, how my understanding of God's grace caused me to rejoice in the awe of His love! God judged my heart, which yearned to know His Truth.

Jesus smiled at me and I knew that I was onto something.

11

LOST CHILDHOOD RESTORED

...for the kingdom of heaven belongs to such as these.
—MATTHEW 19:14 NIV

During the next scene in the "theater of life," I was a 23-year-old agnostic, crying out to God through my apartment window, saying, "I need to know You as more than just pages in a book." Only this time, I saw not only myself crying out to God through the bars of my window under the night sky, I also felt the innermost cry of my heart that desired a relationship with God.

"I tried to disprove Your existence," I said to Jesus, "but You knew my heart. Deep down, I felt abandoned by You and blamed You for everything—struggling to breathe, the bullying, feeling like a loser—all of it. But You really did know that I wanted You all along, didn't You?"

"Yes," He said. "I know all things."

During my next review, I was again locked inside the crushed car, with no memory of the crash that should have killed me, except for the woman who appeared at the window. I should not have known anything about that tragedy because I was unconscious. For the first time, I knew that I was seeing through the eyes of my soul, and that I was seeing an angel.

"You sent her, Lord, and You were telling me that I should have died, but that I wouldn't because You knew that my heart ultimately desired You. You saved me from death."

"My enemy intended to kill you, but I turned it for good," He said.

I remembered how the concussion had thrown me into a depression. It also forced me to dwell on God by stilling my mind. Oh my, God truly works in mysterious and wondrous ways!

Indeed, after suffering from a concussion for months, my mind surrendered to my heart. And God gave me a Christian friend who sincerely acted like a devout Christian, in order to disprove my theory that all Christians were hypocrites. Then God's Spirit gave me the desire to learn about the God of Jesus Christ; and miracles of miracles, I went to church and prayed to receive Jesus as my Lord and Savior.

"That was You, Lord—Your Spirit answered my prayer, saved my life, and then I finally surrendered to You."

I could see the celebration in Heaven that happened when I prayed to receive Jesus as my Lord and Savior. I saw winged angels blowing long, golden horns and shouting praises and lights beaming from Jesus in a glorious floral outburst of stars in the daylight. All varieties of colors spread forth in Heaven at the moment I received Jesus as my Lord and Savior. But the most prominent color was red—thousands of shades of red. It seemed as if all of Heaven celebrated my rebirth, with all of the varieties of God's grace, each of which represented the blood of Jesus that had been shed for me.

As I witnessed the celebration of my spiritual birthday, Jesus opened His arms and beamed with joy. I saw His wavy brown hair, His eyes glistening, the brilliant light shining from Him, and a river of liquid diamonds flowing from the hem of His white robe. This time I was not in a vignette. I was seeing crystalline water pouring forth from Jesus and the clear waters that flowed from Jesus throughout Heaven. After that, I found myself back in Heaven witnessing the full Glory of God's perfect creations.

For the first time, I turned to see Heaven in its fullness. Gentle lions lay with other smaller animals in fields of flowers and trees, in varieties and colors grander than anything I ever beheld in the world. People joined together in conversations and prayer. I saw an artist who painted a brilliant piece of art, worthy of the world's finest museums. She painted a surrealistic picture of Jesus surrounded by angels. In the picture, Jesus bent over to kiss the brunette-haired head of a woman, presumably the artist. In the background were clear waters running throughout deeply green hills—she had perfectly captured the imagery of Heaven. Perhaps through Christ's impartation, I knew that her artistry was enhanced in Heaven far beyond what her talent had been on earth.

Next, I beheld a man who was adorned in purple, with a golden sash, who was feeding others in a circle. Somehow, I knew that this man had been a beggar in the world. Now he fed the very ones who had fed him in the world. His regal stature now belied his status in the world before he died.

"Those who serve others in the world will be served even more here," Jesus said.

I turned to my right, still aware of Jesus's presence, but I didn't see Him. Looking over the river, I found Jesus holding a pearl-shaped bottle that held a liquid. He cocked His head with a quizzical tilt and a slightly bent smile. *That isn't like Him*, I thought. His comical gesture reflected a purpose, as if to signal that all things turn to joy in Heaven. As I stood across from Him on the other side of the crystal-clear river, Jesus lifted the bottle and turned it upside down, allowing its contents to pour out into the river.

Impulsively, I bent down at the water's edge. On bended knee, I cupped some water from the river and drank of its pleasant coolness. Joy instantly permeated my being. I jumped up and down and shouted praises to my Lord, in abandonment and glee. I felt lighthearted, as though I was listening to a funny joke and a moving symphony at the same time—giddy yet pensive, child-like but reverent. These contrasting feelings fit comfortably in my soul, like taking a nap and dreaming about something pleasant. It is almost impossible to explain, but I felt full of life. I looked over to Jesus for some response to my sense of wonderment, as He chuckled.

"Beloved, that bottle I held contained your tears. I have been collecting them all your life."

Oh my, the gravity of knowing that Jesus collected all of my sorrows throughout my life, struck me with a keen sobriety.

"Really? You collected my tears of sorrow?"

"Yes, beloved, not as a reminder but to fully exchange in Heaven, your sorrows for joy. You see, you grieved not because of your suffering. You suffered because of your separation from Me."

"You redeemed my tears for joy."

Jesus smiled. In the next moment, He appeared by my side. Now He slightly bent His knees and reached over to collect some of the living waters within His two palms, briefly exposing the scars at the base of His hands. Then He stood straight and reached His cupped hands over my head, baptizing me with the living waters by releasing them onto my scalp.

After this, a vision appeared before me of the Holy Spirit, in glistening sparkles that hovered above the waters and in front of me as a mist. I felt Him inside of me at the same time, as if God was revealing His omnipresence to me as both separate and internal. In that moment, I became fully aware of how the Holy Spirit indwelled me when I became born again—only then did I truly come alive. Before then, I was dead inside, lifeless and listless, in contrast to the fullness of joy I felt by ingesting the living waters of Jesus.

My spiritual eyes breathed in the fullness of Heaven as the very imprint of God. Every person I saw glistened with the same glow now bestowed upon me by Jesus and the Holy Spirit. I saw colors more vividly and sensed feelings more intensely. Everything in Heaven spoke of God's Glory, in both silent and spoken praises that evoked greater joy than words can express. I knew that this was the fullness of the Holy Spirit. I knew that this was life, not as an expression but as the imprint of life Himself, Jesus, God's presence—what I came to understand as the manifested righteousness of God.

"Beloved, My righteousness is without spot, and those bathed in My righteousness are cleansed like pure linens."

Jesus motioned to my right. Flowing down from a mountain was a waterfall that appeared to be made of white linens that rippled like waters, with the sound of hundreds of flapping flags that evoked the intoxicating aroma of a newborn. The flowing ripples met the base of the ground and appeared as satiny white waves. They were more elegant than the waves of the ocean, and they embraced my soul with their gentle nature.

Atop these waves frolicked thousands of children and new-borns, along with completely white angels whose gowns seemed to flow with the linens. Shouts of joy ushered from the mouths of the children and newborns. Giggles abounded from this place, as the angels bounced with the children the way an inflatable bounce house magnifies joy at a child's birthday party. At that moment, the Word of God was echoed in my thoughts, *"Fine linen, bright and clean was given her to wear"* (Revelation 19:8 NIV).

Yes, I remembered that fine linens represent the righteous acts of God's holy people.

"You see those who died as young children, and the unborn of the world," Jesus said.

His words struck me with the gravity of what brought these children to Heaven, especially knowing that many appeared before me who had been aborted in the world. But even that awareness did not sadden me, because God had redeemed their childhood in Heaven, restoring the absolute fun and feelings of blissful abandonment they had lost on earth. Even now, I tell mothers who aborted their babies and who felt guilty afterward that God restores their baby's joy in Heaven.

I also understood that the act of depriving a baby of its God-ordained destiny causes Jesus to weep. The "waterfall of linens" represents the tears of death that are turned to life. God's righteousness enjoined those tears to turn beauty from ashes, as the pristine, flowing linens of purity restored the innocence of childhood—replacing the pains of the children's final tragic memories of earth.

Indeed, God's righteousness brought life to every living thing in Heaven, and everything in Heaven was living—the flora, rocks, mountainsides, air, waters, and of course, God's most beloved, you and me. Nothing died—not ever. God perpetuates growth through the renewal of the Holy Spirit's impartation of life afresh. Like others in Heaven, I saw everything as though I was seeing it for the first time, even while repeatedly looking at the same sights.

Just as I began to soak in the wonders of Heaven, my translucent spirit body was transported through concentric circles, to another afterlife review in a separate space and time. This time I beheld my spirit in a hospital Intensive Care Unit. As Jesus informed me, my spirit came alive for the first time after I received Him as my Lord. So instead of seeing my fleshly body, I beheld my spirit body—the same body I was in as I experienced Heaven with Jesus. I'm not sure whether I was in Heaven at this point, or if Jesus had transported me to a different place to reveal my past, but Jesus never left my side while I relived any part of my life.

Now I witnessed before me the dying man in the ICU of the hospital in Freemont, Illinois. At the time, I was a new Christian who trained clinicians how to read their new vital signs monitors I installed for them. As one of the housekeepers had informed me, this man had attended church and was charitable in his life. Now his family stood at his bedside as the monitor confirmed his body was failing.

"What do you see?" Jesus asked.

"I remember thinking that this man was reaping his rewards for a good life."

"But, beloved, no man is good; only God is good," said Jesus.

"He served You, as I recall, my Lord."

"Yes, beloved, and yet his service to Me did not make him good. My righteousness in him justified him."

"And You made him good, Lord?

"I made his spirit holy in My sight. You saw the spirit of this man, beloved, and that seemed good to you, but I saw his righteousness through Me and Me alone. Apart from Me, he would be just like the other man you saw."

At that word, I now stood in the adjoining room, observing the man who caroused around the small town of Freemont. His face looked gaunt, like the boy I witnessed who was dying of cancer. But the boy had emanated joy. This man expressed a deep darkness that felt and even smelled like the air of a messy latrine. He felt lifeless, like most of the people I had observed walking within the cityscape. His eyes were pitch-black, and I realized that Jesus allowed me to see into his darkened soul through his dilated pupils. As I found myself in the scene of this life review, from whatever place I perceived these events in the heavens, I fully sensed the spiritual and physical expressions of all that I witnessed.

"What do you see?" Jesus asked.

"I see no life, Lord. He has no life, even though his heart still beats," I said.

"True, beloved, because those apart from Me are dead, even though they live. What else do you see?"

"I see a dark tunnel beneath him, Lord, and a deep pit and flames at the base of that pit. At the end of the tunnel lies the pit—deep beneath the earth, as if a boring machine tunneled to the molten core of the earth. And I see people in prison cells tearing at each other at the other end of the tunnel, screaming toward each other, and beasts like the ones I saw when I was being pulled by Your light, preying upon their bodies."

(I continued.) "They appear to be reaching out with their dull, flaky arms, like rubber bands, to grab onto the dying man. The flesh or outward appearances of those figures in the black pit, rot in perpetual decay. I see layers of skin peeling away and floating in the air and it smells like sulfur—and no light—absolute darkness. I feel nothing but hatred within those people and they have no hope. The ones beneath them are living in cages, like animals within burning flames. And those screams of terror…please, Lord, don't show me *anymore!*"

"You see hell. All who are not of Me reside in a place that is without life."

"Evil," I said.

"Evil, beloved, is not My design. That place was not made for those created in My image. Evil is like that waste you sense from this man. What is left apart from that which is good, is evil, wasted, and lost. Those who live apart from Me and who cease living in the world, wish for death—but they find no life and no death. They find only the suffering that comes from a life apart from Me, ruled by those who rejected Me, the fallen angels. Those without Me, beloved, have no life."

"And a life wasted turns to anger and hatred, Lord." It appeared I could read not only Jesus's thoughts but His intentions as well—something I later learned appears as revelations on earth.

"My Spirit has told you this, beloved."

After this, I passed through another spiral of circles before finding myself within another theater of my past. Now I was standing in a cornfield across from the house on Blood Point Road, as a crying sound like that of a lost child, blew through the wind. Behind me

I could see the gothic house with its vacant windows and a rod of lightning as it struck the house during a storm, and a wind that whirled through the house, tearing it to the ground like a swift wrecking ball.

"Oh yes, Lord—I was on fire for You and wanted to tell everyone about You, but I fell into temptation. I guess that I started taking You for granted. I did terrible things."

"You opened the doorway to Mine enemy, beloved, and you were entertained by the spirit of darkness."

"That child I heard in the cornfield—was the voice really a demon?"

"Yes, and each of the bizarre manifestations you saw. Did you expect anything else?"

"I was ignoring You," I said. "No, I knew better, but I assumed that You weren't watching me. I sinned against You without excuse, because I knew You as my Lord and Savior." Then I bowed my head—"So many offenses against You, Lord."

"My Spirit lived within you, My beloved, so of course, I always knew what you were doing. You grieved Me, beloved."

"Forgive me."

"I already did," He said.

"And why are You showing this to me, Lord?"

I suddenly remembered repenting of my indiscretions and offenses against God after returning to the house off Blood Point Road and seeing it leveled to the ground, but I felt something else. It was if I had caused Jesus to sacrifice Himself all over again for me—as if I was reopening the wounds of His persecution. Then I saw Jesus dying on the cross, with His blood dripping to the ground. I wept knowing that I was no better than the disciples who had rejected Jesus at His crucifixion.

"That's what sin does, doesn't it, Lord? Sin, for the believer, is a form of persecution against You, isn't it?" I asked. My spirit knew that sinning as a Christian crucifies Jesus all over again.

"Beloved, when one of My children sin against Me, he or she denies Me all over again."

"Denies You? Like the prodigal son?"

"Sin, beloved, is a rejection of Me. The unbeliever never knew Me, but My children know My voice, and when they sin, they refuse My voice. You thought that you were no better than My disciples on earth, but you were like Peter, whose foundation was established upon Me; and yet He chose the foundations of the world."

"And that opened me to hearing the voice of the demons? I rejected You all over again."

"Yes, beloved, you ignored Me. When I became your Lord, I breathed life into your spirit so that we could dwell with each other. When you sinned, you were like a runaway child, but when you repented, you came home to Me."

Strangely, I felt no condemnation from Jesus in seeing my sins. Rather, I felt even more thankful for His grace. He knew my heart and He knew that I wanted to return home, much like the prodigal son in the Bible. This was a huge lesson for me about God's grace. The believer in Christ may go astray, as I did all too often, but our heartstrings eventually call us back home. In truth, my soul never felt at peace while I was sinning.

When Jesus walked on the earth, He said, "No one will snatch them out of My hand," but we can run away from Him (John 10:28). I was saved and no one could take me away from God, but too often I had abandoned God.

A spirit born in Christ always desires to be home with Jesus and can never be fully at rest without repenting for having rebelled against God. I learned that the grace of Jesus is not a license to sin. It is a calling to return home. Once home, it is as if the sin never happened in the first place.

In Heaven, within my spirit body controlled by Christ, I desired no sin. I desired only to please God. My joy felt complete. But during the times I sinned as a Christian, I lost my joy and felt distant from God. Jesus is our Rock. He never moves away from us.

My heavenly imagination became reality, like a dream that turned into sights, smells, and sounds, as my spiritual eyes now investigated another realm. It is a place I can only describe as "the unknown" or the "unlived." Suddenly, a series of running vignettes flashed before my eyes. I saw myself running head-on into a car at high speed, and recalled the time in my life when I drove on a two-lane road late at night to work at a hospital. A car had pulled head-on into my lane at high speed. In the next instant, my car appeared to hop over the other car because I was seeing that car in my rearview mirror.

"That was You, wasn't it—You saved me from a head-on crash?" Jesus did not need to answer my question, because I already knew the answer.

Other flashes looked unfamiliar to me, such as a view of me receiving chemotherapy at a clinic. I saw a memorial service for me in a church, and a myriad of other experiences I had never experienced in the world, at least not yet. A whirlwind of blended tragedies streamed across my eyes, and all were accompanied by a sulfuric smell. In contrast, I now breathed in a fusion of pleasing fragrances in Heaven, which were a combination of crisp, clean air, soft floral bouquets and forestry aromas.

"You see the things that Mine enemy intended against you that did not happen, My beloved," Jesus said.

So, this is the power of God's love in my life, I thought. Jesus saved me from a multitude of trials that never happened because of His intercession.

Then another fragrance entered my senses, and I found myself standing on a golden path next to Jesus. I was staring into a gelatinous sphere that spread outward like an expanding jellyfish, exposing a clear opening that was filled in the center, with a pristine light that was whiter than white.

The smell of freshly baked chocolate chip cookies filled my space. Then a figure walked through the light and stepped forward, stopping about ten feet from me. Her hair glistened in browns. With gentle eyes, smooth skin, and an oh-so-familiar smile, she cupped her hands over her heart, as I perceived the essence of my grandmother. Only after my return from Heaven, would I look through an old photo album to see a younger version of my elderly grandmother, who had stood before me in Heaven. Her spiritual beauty sharply contrasted the stout grandmother I had always known in the world.

When I was a child, Grandma would bake chocolate chip cookies for me whenever I visited her modest home in Keokuk. Sometimes I would take them to the shoe shop, and by the end of my visit, all of them were devoured. That same fragrance permeated the space where I now viewed her essence. Her integrity, humor, loyalty, and love for me felt even more pronounced in that space. I realized that I had identified her in Heaven by her essence and intrinsic nature more than her physical appearance, because I had never seen my grandmother in her youth.

In Heaven, my grandmother's character spoke of who she was to me. Her features portrayed a faint familiarity, and her body appeared translucent, as did everyone in Heaven. But in Heaven, we knew each other foremost because the Holy Spirit imparted to me an understanding of her truest identity. Grandma mouthed the words, "I love you." Why we could not audibly speak to each other remains a mystery to this day, but I knew that I could only mouth back, "I love you."

Perhaps Jesus wanted me to wait before engaging in conversation with her, but I think it was because my full devotion and conversation needed to remain with Jesus. Even the gargantuan angel that journeyed with Jesus and me did not speak a word to me, nor me to Him. He had folded wings and an alluring, eight-foot or so high chiseled frame that was adorned in an ultra-white robe and a purple sash. His eyes looked more like fire and his hair flowed in golden strands.

His striking appearance commanded attention, as compared to Jesus's more modest features. Though Jesus was perpetually bathed in brilliant light, He appeared much like me or any other human. You may think I would be compelled to speak with the angel or my grandmother, but the presence of Jesus consumed my attention. No communication could ever compare to the absolute truth, love, and life that exuded from my Lord.

All this time, I somehow knew that a Storm loomed ahead. But for now, my spirit felt stilled by the calm of Heaven.

12

ANGELS ON ASSIGNMENT

*In my Father's house are many rooms. If it were
not so, would I have told you that I go to prepare
a place for you? And if I go and prepare a place
for you, I will come again and will take you to
myself, that where I am you may be also.*
—JOHN 14:2-3 ESV

My journey in Heaven was consumed with being in God's presence. It took only a nanosecond in Heaven to realize that my
home existed not in form but in the personhood of Jesus. Now I realize that God assigned a guardian angel to me for a lifetime on earth.
Indeed, thousands of angels of different varieties and forms circled
about Heaven. Their appearances varied by the color of their sashes or
by their faces. In the distance, I saw angels worshipping with choruses
of praises, whose features were more akin to humans. Each sang with
the force of ten human voices.

Some angels dove downward toward the world below. Jesus
explained them as warrior angels. They held silvery swords and were
adorned with tight-fitted silver suits that didn't reflect but absorbed
the light of Jesus. When they flew, the faces of the warrior angels
and the trails they made flashed like bolts of lightning. I knew from
the Holy Spirit's impartation that these were the warring angels

I beheld in the second heaven as I rose toward the third heaven, which is God's domain.

The Holy Spirit impressed upon me that these warrior angels respond instantly to commands from God's Throne—commands issued in response to prayers that work in combination with God's "appointments." The word given to me by the Holy Spirit that I understood was that all of this activity was part of God's design for each person's life.

Although the book of Enoch[1] mentions the archangels, I could not reference the angels by name, but Jesus elucidated their stature and heavenly assignments while I was in Heaven.

"I command each of Mine angels," Jesus explained. "They go forth to declare My Word. Some archangels battle for dominion of territories in the world. The guardian angels battle for each of My children. Some angels guard My Throne, in praise and worship to My Father, and some battle for the right to speak My truth to those who would listen."

I looked over God's Kingdom and saw people and angels coexisting and operating according to the Holy Spirit's inspiration. Some angels stood guard over a place off in the distance, which stood in the center of some villages I beheld around where we stood. These were the most spectacular-looking angels, whose brilliance nearly blinded me. Their faces and bodies glowed like cut diamonds and other gemstones. Their eyes looked upon Jesus even as they turned their heads like 360-degree camera lenses, although their eyes beamed forth light from the place behind them. In front of these angels appeared a series of circular gates, in spheres. They were somewhat like the spheres from which I saw my grandmother emerge. The awe of what I witnessed utterly bedazzled me, and Jesus sensed my desire for understanding.

"We will go there soon, beloved," Jesus said.

"Where?" I asked.

"To the place of creation, beloved," He said. "And there you will see Me with My Father."

"The Throne Room?" I asked, while implicitly understanding the answer.

"Yes, beloved, you will see that which is to come and you will see the fullness of Our Glory."

I implicitly knew that I could only see the Throne Room with my spiritual eyes, because no one could behold the full Glory of God in the flesh and live (Exodus 33:20).

Jesus swung His arm outward, and thousands of angels followed the emittance of His outspread light, like giant doves with human-like faces, that flew in perfect unison. I knew that the angels did not fly without purpose, because in Heaven nothing happens without intention. I also knew from the Holy Spirit that the angels were preparing something in response to Jesus's commands. Only later would I understand the monumental intention of Jesus's simple, commanded Word.

The absolute peace I felt in Heaven began to shift. I cannot explain the feeling, because my spirit mind flowed in attention to Jesus much like the angels; only my flight with Jesus took me to an endless city that had structures unlike any architectural designs I knew in the world.

"I have more to show you about your life, before we go into My Throne Room," said Jesus.

I hovered over gargantuan abodes made of crystalline stones that reflected swirls of incandescent colors. I saw people travel-ing in groups or families, as they walked through these places and into adjacent superstructures. Everyone knew one another and occasionally embraced in the tenderest of ways. Their faces beamed with a pleasant calm and peace as they journeyed with a dedicated reason for their activities. At the same time, everyone expressed a carefree attitude toward their destinations.

Some of the glorious structures appeared as behemoth homes that reflected the styles of the people entering them. Block-long and larger buildings had marble edifices and must have contained gifts, since people carried familiar objects out of them, such as books and materials of all kinds. Living trees, bushes, flowers, and flowing green grass lined each structure. There was no need for sidewalks since the soft, golden path on which I traveled with Jesus provided pathways everywhere within the pristine and sparkling city. It was a place dotted with expansive parks that were thousands of miles long and far grander than any I have seen in the world.

Millions of people traversed across this expansive space. Some walked and some glided like the birds that flew across the fair-weathered sky.

Some stood on the fertile ground in conversations with others, while some hovered above gentle-looking lions, bears, canines, and other animals of all species that appeared far softer than those on earth. The animals were more attuned to the needs of the human spirits, and I saw people cuddling with them. At times, animals such as horses bent downward to allow people to ride them. Not one appeared to need food. The animals' attentions focused solely on pleasing the people around them, and I watched as they obediently responded to their commands.

My eyes fixed upon a group of three people who were holding hands in a circle in the park. There were two men and a woman who had long brown hair that glistened from the light of Jesus. One of the men sported a goatee and another had kinky hair. Although their features differed, none of that mattered as they bowed in prayer for someone below. I knew they prayed for a person on earth, because their prayers appeared as tiny, sparkling stars that showered upon the world.

The most surprising appearance to me was Jesus, who stood in the midst of them at the same time He stood beside me. Then I realized that the Holy Spirit, the most ubiquitous or omnipresent of the Persons of God, could appear at any moment as Jesus. I perceived that the Holy Spirit enjoined the prayers of the threesome with the light of Jesus, and this caused the sparkling answers to their prayers, which carried the weight of God to earth. Before my eyes, I could see how prayer operates as a mixture of people's words and the effervescence of God.

"You see how I enjoin the prayers of My saints," Jesus said.

Then the Holy Spirit chimed in, with knowing, not words: And We always say "Yes" to the prayers of those who pray with Me, because when We pray together, the hearts of Our children only desire what We desire. But when they pray apart from Us, their prayers are like vapors—they evaporate with the winds of the world. But when I breathe life into their prayers, they shower the one prayed for with those sparkles that you see.

Like a spiritual shower, I thought.

"The light from Heaven speaks also to My angels," said Jesus.

With those words, I witnessed an angel diving toward the prayer recipient in the world. Then I realized that those sparkles were the angels that I had perceived from afar.

My warrior angels, the Holy Spirit replied.

"And the demons do not stand a chance against My appointed ones," Jesus said, with a voice lower than I had previously heard. Perhaps that was because of the gravity with which He battled in the spiritual realm—the same spiritual realm I witnessed before meeting Jesus. It struck me that Jesus did not relish defeating His enemies. He grieved for the fallen angels and for people who rejected Him, which necessitated God's judgment against the offenders.

Next, I witnessed a righteous anger that showed itself not as an expression on Jesus's calm face, rather, His anger revealed itself in a kind of blustering heat that made me wonder if the fires I saw in hell were remnants of God's righteous anger against those who had defied His righteousness—anger that had settled into their own self-righteousness, which left them with nothing but the stifling heat of their own rage. Suddenly, I realized that my theory was not a theory at all. It was the wisdom of understanding being imparted to me by the Holy Spirit.

I continued observing people in Heaven who were going about their activities with a joy that inspired me. Teachers were preaching in public squares. Builders effortlessly created masterpieces out of living stones that fit perfectly together, as people ran like the wind. No randomness defined their activities. Rather, their movements and words appeared orchestrated by the breath of the Holy Spirit, who spoke the same inspiration to them that He spoke to me. I felt as though I could write a masterpiece or teach with pure revelation.

All people in Heaven walked with a level of radiance about them, but some were brighter than others. The Holy Spirit explained to me that the closer one is to God on earth, the more of God's Glory will shine in and over them. The degree of their service unto God imparted a greater glow to them, making them more joyful. Their dedication to God on earth also enabled them to do even greater works in Heaven. So even though status did not define their position in Heaven, the degree of their closeness and service to God on earth imparted to them in Heaven a greater power and closeness to God.

The Holy Spirit directed me to one person who had continuously prayed for people on earth. She had also performed consistent acts of kindness toward others while teaching Bible classes. She gleamed more brightly than those around her. She taught others within a circle, and her command of God's Word and intellectual banter impressed upon me that she was a renowned scholar, although the Holy Spirit told me that in the world she had barely graduated from middle school.

She is highly talented and esteemed here because of her faithfulness on earth, the Holy Spirit whispered. She seemed to me as a dignitary in Heaven, because those around her honored her influence and position.

Everyone in Heaven busied themselves with meaningful activities and everything felt intentional, in accordance with God's intention. It all seemed like child's play, not work. I soon realized that the loss of innocence that occurs when children mature into adults, is returned in Heaven such that anything done is like play—with a renewed, inquisitive mind that can learn of God's wonder, in an eternal bliss. A profound lesson for me is that everything in Heaven serves a purpose. Everyone lives with the intention of fulfilling God's purpose for them, and everything is fantastically fun and deeply satisfying.

I also intuitively knew people at the core of their being—as friends, not strangers. It dawned on me that I perceived the essence of the people I viewed, not just their outward appearance. Their outward appearances seemed inconsequential as compared to their core nature. Each person reminded me of Jesus since I witnessed His reflection through them.

"You see them as they truly appear to Me," Jesus said, "and not as you saw them in the world."

"They appear so genuine," I said. "I can sense their purity and their personalities at the same time, Lord. I've never perceived people this way until now, here, but foremost at their core is a love for You and for one another as family. There are no boundaries, no superficiality, and no facades. It's pure communion with You and with one another. Oh my—this is truly Heaven!"

Jesus chuckled. "And do you love them, My beloved?"

"Yes! I love them like I've always wanted to love my dearest loved ones in the world, but I could never completely achieve that fullness of love. These are strangers to me, yet I feel like I've known them for a lifetime, Lord."

"You see Me in them," Jesus answered. "You love them with My love."

"But not as much as You love me," I said.

"No one can love My sons and daughters as I love them, but even a small fraction of My love would be exponentially greater than the greatest love anyone could feel for someone in the world. Here, you have the created fullness of My love for others. Only the Creator can love completely."

"And there are no carnal desires, Lord."

"Because you are not carnal, beloved. You are Spirit," Jesus said.

"Just as You are Spirit, Lord."

"Yes, beloved, you are Mine and I am yours," Jesus said.

"But we're not yet finished with your life," Jesus said. "I have more to show you."

I instantly found myself perched in my "theater of life." Now I was teaching a spiritual gifts church class at Crosswinds Church in Pleasanton, California, at the East Bay of San Francisco. My programmed way of teaching the class included Scriptures that I projected onto the screen as I tried to cover all of the gifts outlined in the Bible, including those I termed the "miraculous gifts" of healing, prophecy, miracles, tongues, and words of knowledge. But I had taught within a "seeker friendly" church, which rarely, if ever, practiced these gifts during the main services.

"I was so rigid," I said.

"You weren't listening to Me, were you?" Jesus said.

"No, I was trying to sound scholarly and it was hard, but I studied Your Word."

"This was good," Jesus answered, "but you would have been more effective had you sought My Glory," Jesus said. "When you operate in My Glory, beloved, you will not feel burdened. You will feel inspired."

I continued to look at this teacher (me) trying desperately not to make a mistake, knowing full well that the miraculous gifts we would discover within the student believers would probably wither away due to disuse.

"Was I teaching in vain, Lord?" I asked.

"No, beloved, My Word never goes void, but the teacher was My student, beloved."

"You were teaching me..." I didn't know what to ask next.

"I was preparing you to rely upon Me and Me alone."

I bowed my head and hugged Jesus while resting my head on His shoulder as He leaned into me. All this time I thought I was serving God, when the one who was being served the most, was me. Those first words He spoke to me settled into my soul: "Trust Me."

Was life's lesson that simple? Could the simplest answer to all of my trials be to trust God?

Jesus knew my thoughts.

"You can never catch up to My understanding, beloved," He said. "Nor can you please Me without surrendering yourself to Me."

"And my talk with the pastor about empowering the congregation, was that of You, Lord?"

"No one fit for the Kingdom can practice faith without works, beloved," Jesus said.

"So You require more of Your church?" I asked.

"My church is an extension of My body," Jesus said. "So if I am the head of My body, then how can the church live without the direction of My Spirit?"

"But the church as a whole had become too complacent, right?" I asked.

"If one within My church is not connected to My body," Jesus said, "then the church is not whole. Why do people in the world think of masses (of people) and not as one (body)?"

I knew the answer to that question. Jesus looked at me as if I was the only person in the world and the only one who mattered to Him. That is exactly how I understood that we are to see one another—as if the other person is the most important person in the world to God. They are to be seen as even more important than ourselves, just as Jesus considered His life on earth to be worthy of His sacrifice.

Then as Jesus motioned with His arm, several angels circled around me as if to create a movie screen for the next place I would find myself. Now I was sitting at the side of Annie's bed. I was rubbing her head and tearfully pleading with God to heal her of the spasms and night terrors.

"Heal her, Lord!"

At that time, my company's drug that was intended as a possible cure for Alzheimer's disease, had been pulled by the Food and Drug Administration and I was struggling to regain my financial footing after losing millions of dollars. During those desperate times, with all of our medical bills, I could not afford to pay the mortgage.

"Look, beloved," Jesus said. He motioned to a scene of me shouting for God to "show up" in my bedroom. I said,

"Show Yourself to me or else…"

My voice trailed off as I literally waited for God to appear.

"I'm so sorry that I doubted You, Lord," I said. I suddenly felt ashamed because I had contended with God. At the same time, I felt so thankful for Jesus's grace having put up with my severe lack of faith.

"I knew your heart and this grieved Me," Jesus said. His response surprised me. How could Jesus feel sorrow?

"Not sorrow, My beloved. I feel the pains of My beloved. They are always fresh to Me."

Oh my—did I die because of a rebellious demand to see God? Was death my punishment for challenging God?

"Does being with Me in this place seem like punishment?" Jesus spoke aloud.

My thought now seemed ridiculous, but I innately understood that defiance of God can lead to death. Yet death has no sting for believers, as recorded by the apostle Paul (1 Corinthians 15:55-56). As in everything in life, there is a purpose even behind our failures, which God turns for good—a phenomenon Paul also wrote in my favorite Bible verse: *And we know that in all things God works for the good of those who love him, who have been called according to his purpose"* (Romans 8:28 NIV).

"I don't want to ask You why, Lord, because I know never to challenge Your authority or to mistrust that You will turn it for good, Lord. Please forgive me?"

"That is what I wanted to hear," Jesus said. It was as if this entire experience had led up to my sincere request for forgiveness for having doubting Him during my severest trials.

Not wholly, the Holy Spirit spoke to my spirit. We wanted you to feel as We feel, and to desire that which We desire. I resided in you since you received Me as your Lord, and yet how many times did you acknowledge Me?

"So true," I responded. "I took You for granted. Everything You are showing me reminds me of Your love for me. You were with me always and I was with You only occasionally. I'm so sorry."

"Don't be sorry," Jesus replied. "Rejoice because now you are beginning to understand the depth of who I am to you."

I realized that Heaven lived inside of me, because the essence of Heaven is God. And once I surrendered my heart to Jesus, God deposited His Spirit within me. At the moment I died and met Jesus, I was the freest I had ever lived, because life at its fullest is entirely consumed with God; and life in the Spirit cannot occur until we are dead to our flesh.

Then I remembered what Paul wrote in the Book of Life. At that thought, my guardian angel presented me with the Book of Life, whose pages appeared as thinly-sliced gold. I dared not touch the Book, for a reason I did not comprehend, believing that only God could open the Book of Life.

"This Book was written at the beginning of your creation," Jesus said, "and here is what My beloved Paul wrote."

Jesus turned the page to Romans 8 and waved His finger as He declared the verses aloud:

> *And if the Spirit of him who raised Jesus from the dead is living in you, he who raised Christ from the dead will also give life to your mortal bodies because of his Spirit who lives in you. Therefore, brothers and sisters, we have an obligation—but it is not to the flesh, to live according to it. For if you live according to the flesh, you will die; but if by the Spirit you put to death the misdeeds of the body, you will live* (Romans 8:11-13 NIV).

Once again I caved in awe of God's words as spoken by Jesus, which cut to the core of my life. But what happened next brought me to tears. Jesus turned the pages to the latter part of the Book and pointed to some words. Those words were written as such:

רב ילש המישנה

My spirit knew that what I saw was written in a foreign language, Hebrew. Only one language existed in Heaven. I call it a language of love, but I also understood every tongue spoken, as the language of the Spirit and not of the flesh. In my spirit, I knew those Hebrew words, because the Holy Spirit spoke them to me in the language that was most familiar to me. I knew the words came from the ancient chosen language of God, but I dared not speak them.

"I know these words have meaning, especially for me," I said, through tears. "But I don't know why. They just settle in my soul as to who I am. Jesus, You called yourself I AM, and these words speak of who I am."

I have told you as much, said the Holy Spirit.

I knew that Jesus needed to declare the meaning of those words to me, because if I said them aloud, it would be an offense to God, so Jesus spoke forth these words:

"My breath in you."

As soon as He spoke, I began sobbing the way I did when I first met Jesus.

"This is who I am," I sobbed. "I am because of You and You breathed life into my spirit. You are my life!" I sobbed uncontrollably; my chest repeatedly heaving up and down. Then, just as He had done at our first meeting, Jesus lifted me up to look into His eyes.

"This is My name for you, My beloved, but you are not to speak of this name in the world. Only I can speak this name for you. It is your name and the name I have recorded in My Book. This is who you are to Me."

"Oh God," I declared, "I am…to You…as You are to me…for You are my all."

It was as recorded in Scripture, *"On that day you will realize that I am in my Father and you are in me, and I am in you"* (John 14:20 NIV). The sacred solemnity of that epiphany struck me like no other. He breathed life into me just as He breathes life into all of His children who surrender their heart to Jesus. Then He declared His name just as He did before His crucifixion:

"I AM."

At that, I saw a vision of people in the world who were cursing His name, but none of those curses could be heard in Heaven. Somehow, Jesus revealed the echo of those curses to me in the space of the second heaven. I could see the demons drinking in those curses, which affected them like an energy drink. They grinned with their fangs, shouted like laughing hyenas, and danced gleefully as the lost human souls in the world casually spoke God's name in vain or in anger. They did not realize they were crucifying Jesus with their words and declaring damnation against the One who loved them the most.

Jesus held His arms out to me, in this space halfway between the second and third heavens, to show me the scars at the base of His palms. Then He said, "This is why I wear My scars, beloved, because those who curse Me crucify Me until the end when hell will be sealed—until then, these scars shall remain."

Oh my God, I thought.

My attention returned to Heaven. I heard no more curses and the sickening sound of the demon cackling ceased. But then I heard the mourning dirge in Heaven as the cry of the Lord. It sounded like a soft, rolling thunder that was about to break. It was mixed with a tender, "Oh…" and followed by the blowing sound of wind, before it ended with an echo that resonated in all of Heaven. It was not a loud weeping. It was more like the soft sound of disappointment, only greater, as the sound of thousands of hopes and dreams fading into a space of nothingness.

Note

1. The book of Enoch is an ancient Hebrew apocalyptic text that is not considered part of Christian-inspired Scripture.

13

THE THRONE ROOM

At once I was in the Spirit, and there before me was
a throne in heaven with someone sitting on it.
—Revelation 4:2 NIV

Jesus waved His arm in the direction of a vast black hole in the place of the deep that was void of anything.

"These are the lost hopes and dreams of purposes unfulfilled," Jesus said.

I intuitively knew that once lost, these moments of opportunities for all people who reject the Holy Spirit's promptings—God's direction—during their lifetime in the world, would remain in that black hole.

Yes, the Holy Spirit whispered, *what you know is true.*

But the dirge, Lord, is that for the lost souls who have rejected You like I did for so long, or are they for the lost hopes and dreams?

Both, answered the Holy Spirit, *but the mourning sound is because I have grown weary from ages of crying for the lost. The mourning has faded into a soft lamentation for those who have no life in Me.*

"The ones in hell?" I asked.

No answer followed, but I knew the answer just the same. Hope remained for those who lived in the world. No hope existed for those sealed in death apart from Christ.

"I desire that none shall perish," Jesus said, "But I AM the only way here, none other."

With that, He turned His head downward. In His eye I saw a tear swell, before falling onto the golden path. I felt strangely compelled to stoop to the ground and cup the soil containing Jesus's tear. I did so and rubbed it between my palms, before touching it to my cheeks. I instantly felt the sorrow of my Lord to the depths of my soul. And I began to mourn in the same way I had heard the mourning cry of our Lord for the lost. It felt terrible beyond words.

"Feed My sheep," Jesus said to me.

Did not Jesus say that to Peter in John 21:17? Now He was telling me this, even though I was in Heaven and I had no influence in the world at that time—or so I thought until the Holy Spirit corrected me. Suddenly I felt I should pray. I thought of Renee, Annie, and Ryan, and how confident I felt in my Lord's ability to provide for them during the time I could not see them grow. Those thoughts did not sadden me, because I knew that God would give them all they needed. I was aware that my time in the world was the brief vapor that it seemed, and it gave them all God had required of me.

In life, I had prayed daily for my family and tried to model being a good father and husband. We had watched endless Christian videos together. I prayed for my children to receive Jesus as their Lord and Savior. We attended church and I taught them from the Bible. I prayed the so-called "Sinner's Prayer" with both of my parents, so I knew they were destined for Heaven. I loved Renee and tried to provide the security she needed, and we had prayed such rich prayers together. I could do the same in Heaven. I knew in the span of the fullness of eternity in Heaven that I would see all of them in a few moments of time, from my eternal perspective.

God would assuredly heal Annie, and my children would have families of their own. I fell short too many times; but in Heaven, none of those shortcomings mattered. God filled in the blanks—He would do the same in the future. He always did. I could still pray for them and others in Heaven, and I knew that. God could catch me up on their lives, as well as their victories. I was confident of that, and I asked Jesus to send them messages every now and then as "postcards from Heaven," as I later called them.

Fear was nonexistent in Heaven, because I finally and fully trusted Jesus. If only I had known these things in the world, how prosperous I could have been—but my fleshly brain would constantly remind me of my failures and my unworthiness.

"When you stop judging yourself, you will stop judging others," Jesus said.

After those words, I could hear birds singing as I remembered them on a typical spring morning. I felt the wind blanket me with warmth and appreciated the revelation that I had judged myself on earth. I thought about how that truth would have served me well in world. Indeed, I had judged myself as a failure so often that self-condemnation fed off a need to judge others, as a demented form of psychological deflection.

But as a spirit now not judging myself, why would Jesus tell me this now?

"I'm here though, Jesus, so I'm not judging anyone, least of all me."

"Not for long," Jesus said, as He hugged me tightly and kissed me on the cheek.

"Not for long?"

"I am going to return you, beloved."

"Oh Lord…" I hugged Him so tightly, never wanting to release. I thought that if I held onto Jesus, He could not let me go.

"I will never leave you," He whispered into my ear.

I knew that, but in the world it would be so hard to remember.

"I know how hard it is in the world, beloved," He said. "I lived there, but now you know, and what I am revealing to you will never leave you."

Suddenly a butterfly rested upon my shoulder. It was bright blue, red, and yellow—colors that reflected with an iridescent glow. It shed sparkly gold dust from the underside of wings that were dotted with purple eyespots and that gently flapped. I immediately felt calm and confident. I also knew that everything and everyone in Heaven performed intentionally, so I understood that God intended something from the butterfly's appearance.

"This butterfly represents My wisdom that will guide you in the world," Jesus said.

As soon as Jesus explained the meaning of the butterfly, I instantly knew that I needed to remain still so the butterfly would not fly away.

And so it is with wisdom, said the Holy Spirit, *be still and…*

"Know that I am God," said Jesus as He finished the Holy Spirit's sentence. I remembered the Bible verse: *"Be still, and know that I am God; I will be exalted among the nations, I will be exalted in the earth"* (Psalm 46:10 NIV).

Knowing that Jesus would return me to the world, I wanted to know the God-decreed plans for my return—a blueprint of sorts. As always, Jesus knew my thoughts and responded accordingly:

"Moment by moment I will direct your steps," said Jesus. "If I were to reveal your purpose in full, you would not remain dependent on Me."

Thus, I had learned the lesson of the butterfly—to get still, listen to the voice of wisdom (the Holy Spirit) telling me what to do, and to look for the opportunities to serve my Lord in the moments of life rather than worry about the grandiose scheme of achievement. Just after my revelation, the butterfly gently flapped its wings and flew into the blue sky, leaving its beauty imprinted within my soul.

But what about the latter part of Psalm 46:10? God is indeed exalted among the nations, but few people acknowledge Him as such.

"The nations, Lord—You were exalted in the world, but so many thought that You were not God," I said.

"I AM," He responded.

Later, I would correlate what Jesus had said with this verse: *Jesus answered them: 'I solely declare it: before Abraham came to be, I AM'* (see John 8:58). Indeed, that was the name God gave Himself when He first communicated with Moses (Exodus 3:14). Many people think of the Father as God and Jesus as the Son of God as an offshoot of the Father. And many are confused about the Holy Spirit; but in Heaven, the Holy Spirit was and is as real and relatable as Jesus. As for the Father, I had not yet met the Father, or so I thought.

"I will take you there." As usual, Jesus answered my thought. "But He has always been with Me and I with Him."

And I with both, said the Holy Spirit.

In the world, this often presents a point of confusion, but with my spirit mind, I fully realized what Paul referred to as the mind of Christ, or the Christ mindset. I understood that the three Persons of God were not persons at all. Rather, they were facets of one another, with each being one side of a three-sided personhood. If that still seems confusing, then just remember that there is only one God (Deuteronomy 6:4).

Although we are made in His image, we are not of the same makeup as God. Like God, we are comprised of three parts: a spirit person (controlled by God), a physical person, and a soulful person who represents the sentient or feeling part of ourselves.

"In the world, you saw things in part," said Jesus. "Now you see them in full. Now I will show you the Father."

With that, Jesus and I flew high above the ground, with Jesus's hand placed in the small of my back. I beheld what must have been billions of people, and a vastness greater than the sum of all galaxies. A "whoosh" sounded as we flew through orbs made of light. Angels flew through the second orb to what I presumed was the world below. A third orb beamed with the intensity of many suns, but it did not blind me because I could feel Jesus's presence shielding my eyes. He did this not with His hands but with His omnipotent Glory. Then I realized that the near-blinding light of God was indeed His utmost Glory. Bedazzled by it all, I didn't realize that we had settled upon a pavement of darkly glowing blue stones. Everything was blurred up to this point, except for where I now stood with Jesus.

I'm taking over from here, said the Holy Spirit.

I could still sense Jesus's presence, but not His figure.

Look up, said the Holy Spirit.

I witnessed a crystalline waterfall through which I could faintly see an altar and a towering, curved structure that was made of ruby red and opaque brownish stones. A crystal blue table stood at the center of an elevated stage of grey stone with flecks of mica interlaced with intense blue layers. A rainbow served as a halo behind this altar and extended to what existed below.

Living waters poured like a waterfall from the light that engulfed Jesus, but those waters did not soak anything they touched. They had another effect that I could not understand, but I sensed them as the source of life. Jesus reached His arms outward to form a cross with His body while He stood behind the stone altar. It was then that I noticed that waters flowed from His hands, which ushered forth the waterfall that I saw.

Those waters "gelled together" as an incline that curved back and spread out to form a glass-like seat that surrounded what appeared to be a mountain-sized melding of clear emerald gems, against an airy blue background. Walls of multicolored stones with the heartbeat of life reached thousands of feet into the air—as far as I could see.

To me, it seemed as if a portal or an open window existed at the base of the massive formation. Sitting atop this structure was a giant figure the size of a four-story building. His white hair flowed through the wind that was breathed from the Holy Spirit. I felt I was part of that wind since the Holy Spirit blew that wind through me and everyone within this sacred place. The brilliance shining upon this figure prevented me from seeing His features, if He had features. His white, flowing hair could have been the tendrils of the blinding white light that was brighter than the sun, but they appeared as strands of flowing clouds. His eyes blazed with flames that erupted like a volcano.

The figure blended in appearance with Jesus, though Jesus's eyes were constantly fixed on me. The larger and semi-distinct figure evoked an awe in me that bordered on fear as He declared words or sounds in a foreign tongue, with the utmost authority. In the strangest way, I considered Him to be *THE WORD*, the authoritative Word of all things. Until then, I had never in my life considered that the Word was a Person.

Within that instant, all of Heaven became beyond silent to an intense nothingness. A quiet that was thunderous. An absolute stillness of motion and sound settled after the Almighty's declaration—the calm before the Storm. And all of Heaven waited.

My feelings changed from comfort to pure and absolute awe. Somehow, I understood that nothing would ever be the same again.

14

GOD THE FATHER

Yet for us there is one God, the Father, from whom are all things and for whom we exist, and one Lord, Jesus Christ, through whom are all things and through whom we exist.
—1 CORINTHIANS 8:6 ESV

You see the Father, said the Holy Spirit. *Because you are spirit, you may behold Him for a reason yet to come. His is the Word, beloved, and before Jesus walked the earth, the three of Us abided as the Word. Your spirit understands what I am saying. None of your own words can explain this because the Word is We who existed at the beginning of all time; and the Word spoke life, and the Word spoke truth, and the Word spoke the way, and the order of these things was established first on earth as the Way and the Truth and the Life as born forth in the flesh on earth. But here, the Father remains as Word, such that no one can fathom His Glory, so that the Word of life is spoken as it was in the beginning.*

Although these words may sound confusing to those in the flesh, they made perfect sense to me in Heaven as I recalled the words in the Book of Life as first recorded by John: *"The Word became flesh and made his dwelling among us. We have seen his glory, the glory of the one and only Son, who came from the Father, full of grace and truth"* (John 1:14 NIV).

I could not see the outline of the Father's face because of the brilliance of the light upon Him, which illuminated everything around Him. I too glowed from the fullness of God's Glory. Then He spoke the Word in a thunderous, echoing roar:

"Behold, you see Me as I AM."

God spoke declarations in a foreign tongue that I could not understand, which ushered forth to the world below as light, through the portal at the base of God's Glory. Then Jesus, who was now only light, descended from the massive emerald tower and stretched His arm toward me, placing His right hand over my eyes.

As Jesus released His hands from my eyes, He spread His arms while bending His head downward to overlook the world below. Then He closed His eyes, turned toward the altar, and opened them again while lifting His head in the direction of the Father:

"I declare My Spirit over all flesh," He said.

My mind immediately recalled the verse that says that God would pour out His Spirit upon all people (Joel 2:28). In Heaven, through the inspiration of the Holy Spirit, I understood that the first outpouring happened to believers after Jesus ascended to Heaven and after spending forty days with His followers, while in His resurrected body. What I beheld now was the second descent of God's Spirit to the world within the last days—one that could not be denied by anyone on earth, except for the most hardened souls. A piercing light from Jesus now cut through the crystal floor beneath the throne, sending a laser beam downward that spread over all the earth.

"My Glory," Jesus said.

Something happened when Jesus gently pressed His hands over my eyes. I now saw the effects of the Spirit's outpouring over all people on the earth. A series of gelatinous dewdrops or droplets spread outward as they poured from Heaven. They seemed to clone themselves into long, connected chains that stretched around the entire globe below.

"Beloved, what do you see?" Jesus asked.

"The people look dazed but not confused. It's like they've been awakened from a pleasant dream," I said.

"What else do you see?" Jesus asked.

"Oh my," I said tearfully. "I see people rising from their hospital beds and even morgues! I see people walking out of their wheelchairs after Your followers, I presume, call out to them. I see those who cursed You crying praises out to You, Lord—masses of them around the globe—countless people praising You. I see sores disappearing. I hear praises wafting upward from the earth to Heaven, and I can hear them being echoed by Your angels here in Heaven. I see constructed idols all over the globe caving into ashes. I see buildings, temples, shrines crumbling. I see people all over lying prostrate. I see canes being thrown to the ground and laughter in the public places, even in cemeteries. I see joy…joy…and miracles of every kind. Oh Lord, Your Spirit covers all the earth!"

Jesus again cupped His hands over my eyes.

"Now what do you see?" He asked me.

"I see only You," I said.

"And so it is, beloved, those who see only Me shall be saved and healed," He said. Then He released His hands from my face.

"So, this is Your Glory come upon the earth," I said.

In my heart, I knew this as the final reign of the Holy Spirit on earth. And I knew the cleansing rain of God would turn into another Storm—one strikingly different from what I now beheld. The Glory I witnessed now showered the earth with transparent sparkles of fine dust that breathed a fire that did not burn. It purified what the Holy Spirit touched, as God breathed spiritual life into the people below.

Jesus cupped His hands over my eyes one final time and whispered:

"Look again," He said.

Jesus pointed to the world below. Instantly, I beheld new lives being birthed forth from mothers' wombs, diseased people awakening from their beds in full health, people rejoicing in God's Glory and speaking forth inspired truths, and humans of all colors and sizes being filled with the light of salvation. I saw revelations brought forth through various artistic works and teachings. Strongholds were broken over nations, towns, and cities as evidenced by a sense of freshness I sensed, like how it might feel to go from a mold-infected place to one where the air is purified. Peace was imparted to those who were anxious, and so much more. My spiritual senses were several times greater than the five senses on earth, giving me the ability to know reality from the perspective of Jesus. God spoke life over death and wholeness over brokenness. All of Heaven and earth rejoiced amidst the liberation and power of God.

The people I saw below even rejoiced amid sorrows, as oddly strange as that may seem. I kept hearing in my head these words: *Through the ashes new life is born.* That thought must have come from the Holy Spirit, because below I next witnessed a triangular shaped land littered in debris with what appeared to be the shape of a torch at its northern peak, and tens of thousands or so shouted in foreign-language-sounding words as they rose toward the Throne from that land and settled among the angels there. They shouted words such as:

"Praise our Messiah!"

"Hallelujah be the God of Abraham!"

"Yahweh be the Glory!"

Then I knew that God's glory had reached the outer edges of the globe. His fire had spread from Heaven to earth. To call it a revival would be a gross understatement. What I beheld could only be explained as a newness of life birthed from the Throne into a barren world. Heaven had temporarily come to earth not in form, but in effect.

Then Jesus ascended and joined His light with the light of Father, and they spoke in unison:

"Behold, it is good. So the last shall be first, and the first last."

With that, the massive angels around the Throne blasted their horns, which reverberated all throughout Heaven and earth. At this point, I knew what was going on, without the Holy Spirit needing to explain. It all seemed right and good and known. And I am literally shaking now as I attempt to type these words. I am sobbing and trembling as I remember the immense power of this place. God's glory filled Heaven and earth, if only for a moment in the span of eternity, so that all who earnestly sought the Truth would be given one final opportunity to acknowledge Jesus as their Lord.

A mass of people stood around the power seat of God, in the fullness of His Glory. They were adorned in white robes, with gold crowns upon their heads. The Holy Spirit, who dwelt with me in peace and understanding, blew His breath over everyone in this sacred place, causing the light to overflow. All I wanted to do was praise God as I shouted out with every superlative I could speak. I began shouting out not just in words but in a place of glorification from within my deepest center. I too expanded beyond my figure as an immersion in the light, to join the masses of angels and tribes around God's immaculate presence, to worship Him not just in words or body—I worshipped Him as did the others, with *who I am to God*.

My essence, my being, the core of my life, was born from God. Now, in this place beyond description, who "I am" reached out to Jesus. And He, the Father, and the Holy Spirit brought me unto themselves such that I felt entirely worthy—not because of who I am but because the God of I AM became my all. I had fully realized what Jesus called us to do: *"And you shall love the Lord God with all your heart and with all your soul and with all your mind and with all your strength"* (Mark 12:30 ESV).

In that moment of total immersion in God's holy presence, my adoration for God spilled out of me as supernally as the waters that flowed from Jesus, to cleanse and to birth "the new" in all things and to restore the broken.

A peace settled within me as I floated in a place of togetherness with God. For the first time, I fully understood what Jesus meant when He said that He is the vine and we are the branches (John 15:5). His life coursed through me and brought me not just to an awareness of who He is to me, but to the integral foundation of my life in His being. Oh, how I wanted to remain immersed in the fullness of God's Glory, in this place of power and life.

"He who is in Me has life," the Father spoke forth.

God could no longer be distinguished as the Father, the Son, or the Holy Spirit. They seemed as One to me in this place—fully enjoined and no longer distinguishable by their characteristics as Creator, Lord, or Comforter. And no longer did I need to understand how they spoke to me or why, because their oneness flowed through me as seamlessly as the waters that poured forth from the Throne and which filled me with life overflowing.

The Father is God, and Jesus is God, and the Holy Spirit is God. No one can come to this place where I found myself, unless the river of life flows through them. That happens only after one surrenders to Jesus as the Way, the Truth, and the Life, as described by Jesus in His Book of Life and as recorded in the book of John where Jesus declared: *"I am the way, the truth, and the life. No one can come to the Father except through me"* (John 14:6).

I heard those words from Jesus Himself in the Holiest of Holies, the sacred place of what has been described as God's Throne. They came directly from Jesus, whose presence echoed from the pages of His Word, as recorded by the ancients and blessed by God. I now know the Book of Life as the recorded book we know as the Bible. That's because the Book of Life rests atop the center of the altar of God and contains the recorded words of God as inspired through His authorized writers of the Bible.

"Beloved, we've kept a record of your life also," Jesus said.

"Where is it?" I asked. I wanted to see it.

Jesus then took my right hand and pressed it into His chest and said, "It is written within My heart."

The Holy Spirit now added, *And that large building you passed, that is the library of records, and your life is recorded within its walls.* As the Holy Spirit said this, I recalled the gargantuan, arch-shaped cloud formation in white stone. It had a water droplet-shaped entranceway that I now glanced down to look at while Jesus and I soared—enroute to the Throne Room.

I felt humbled that my life's record would exist for eternity within Heaven. As far as the Bible was concerned, I regretted that I had once doubted it. As a former agnostic, I had discounted the

Bible, tried to disprove it, and accused it of having flawed writings scribed by flawed human beings. But here, the Book of Life lay upon the altar of this sacred place. And what happened next would embed the truth of God's Word in me in a way I could never deny. Jesus lifted the Book of Life and presented it to me.

Why me? No…I thought. I am unworthy to hold the Book of Life.

"Here," Jesus spoke, "I give it to you."

"Oh God, only You, only You…" was all I could say.

"Beloved, My Word is inside you and all who call Me Lord."

I could not recall each sentence of God's Word, although some people have memorized the Bible. For example, many who are the persecuted church in the world are in places where they have no Bible. So, people memorize the entire Word of God in order to teach others for generations. But here, in this sacred place, I knew the answers even though the depth of what Jesus wanted me to do seemed to be the weightiest thing I have ever done in my life. I was to hold the Book of Life in Heaven?

Just as Jesus was beginning to rest the Book of Life upon my outstretched hands, I realized that the Holy Spirit's hands had materialized within my own hands, as one body. For the first time, with my spiritual eyes, I could see the Holy Spirit in me. He manifested as a glowing white form that melded with my hands and arms.

The next memory I have is the Book of Life resting in our hands—mine and the Holy Spirit's. Together, we looked upon the Word of God that is sealed with the blood of Christ. The Book was covered in a golden, leather-like material, with the embossed blood of Jesus. I knew it came directly from the cross of Jesus, where He hung during His crucifixion. I could not open the Book, but the Holy Spirit revealed each Word of the Book of Life to my mind. Those words flowed like a feast of delectable foods and sweet juices that fed my soul, imparting a richness of insight to me such that the words revealed the very mysteries of life.

You might ask—what were those mysteries? I do not recall them all because Jesus told me that when I returned to my body in the world, they would be kept within my spirit in a kind of "lock box," only to be released again when I returned. He would release only one mystery to me—a mystery that would soon be revealed through "The Storm" (His words).

After absorbing the mysteries of the Word of God through the Holy Spirit's revelations, we handed the Book of Life back to Jesus and He placed it back upon the altar.

"You know My Word?" Jesus asked.

"I know You," I answered.

"Ah," He said, "so now you know the answer, My beloved. My Word is written in the hearts of My children and no one can steal them away from Me."

"I did study the Bible," I said.

"Good," He said, "know that My Holy Spirit surpasses your understanding, beloved. For anyone who desires to know My truth, must listen to My Spirit. And when you listen with My Spirit, then My Word will be a part of you."

True; holding the Book of Life with the Holy Spirit revealed all of the mysteries therein. They felt as a part of me within my spiritual body, in a way that is almost impossible to describe. The Word of God was God, because the Word spoke life and Jesus is life and the Holy Spirit provided life to me. Apart from God's Spirit, the Word was interpreted through my own understanding. Having the Holy Spirit within us is the difference between divine impartation and mere human inspiration, and being full of the mind of Christ versus simple human mindfulness.

If that sounds too esoteric, I have good news for you—it will be clear to you in Heaven; and partly so in this world, if you know God's Word not just as pages in a book but as the manifestation of God's truth to your spirit. (Remember the voice of the butterfly—wisdom—inspiring you with what to think and do.)

Jesus gently and reverently placed the Book of Life back upon the altar. Then the Father spoke forth a declaration:

"All who hear these Words and abides by them shall live, and those who deny My Word and abide by their own self-righteousness shall know death."

Heaven trembled at the declaration of these words. I knew the tenderness of heart from which the Father spoke them, because I recalled the dirge of sorrow for the lost that I had heard in Heaven. I knew that God mourned for the lost, but wrath? True death to God is hard to fathom with the worldly mind, but my heavenly mind understood God's judgment was not a desire to destroy. I knew that God's judgment did not result from a loss of His temper or because He wished to mistreat those who rejected Him. Instead, His controlled judgment responded to a rejection of His holiness, with a release of what is divinely just.

There, in this sacred place of God's holiness, I witnessed a dynamic that burned into my soul. Those who surrounded the Throne, including varieties of humans and angels, carried unblemished white robes upon their personhood. The humans stood upon scarlet floors made of ruby-like stones, but the hem of their robes did not touch the scarlet floor. The flooring around the full Glory of God emitted flaming stones. The angels walked over sapphire-like stones, through flames that did not burn. Somehow, I understood that the flames would burn the humans, if not for the garments that covered them. As I pondered the matter, the Holy Spirit revealed what lay behind those brilliant white robes.

Do you see the blood of the Lamb? He whispered.

Yes, I said in my spirit.

"The fire…what is the fire?" I asked aloud.

"Me," said the Holy Spirit, in voice.

I knew that the fire was God's presence—the same fire that consumed the burning bush Moses encountered, as God. It was the same pillar of fire that led the Jewish people in the wilderness, as recorded in the book of Exodus and also the "tongues of fire" that represent the presence of God in the book of Acts. It's also that indwelling, burning passion that moves believers in the God of Jesus Christ to worship and act with power and revelation.

"So why do the humans not walk through the fire?" I asked.

"Because My fire is within them," the Holy Spirit answered in His whispery voice. "My fire burns away that which is impure, to cleanse unrighteousness with the Lamb's blood, but those who have not My fire are consumed by it."

Why fire, you may ask? In Heaven, I knew the answers even as the Holy Spirit spoke the answers into my heart, with both divine inspiration and understanding from the Word of God that had been burned into me. God's divine fire is the purest form of God's presence and was forged through the same elements that gave birth to all of God's creation.

The Holy Spirit inspired me with a vision of creation from the dawn of God-made life, when the fire of God formed substance out of the black hole I saw earlier, and where nothing had existed in the beginning—except God, who always existed. At the beginning of creation, the Holy Spirit breathed His fire, His presence, into the black hole, combusting life from nothingness. He created those things which I saw as paradise, in Heaven. They were spoken into being from the Throne of Creation, before which I found myself, so that everything was good and pure in God's sight. At the culmination of God's work, on the sixth day referenced in the book of Genesis, God fashioned His "masterpiece" that was made in His image—humankind. You know the rest of the story as recorded in God's Word (Genesis 1). The Holy Spirit inspired me with the reason why God created humankind, which He whispered to me:

We created you because We desired a family.

"And family was born through…Love, the Person," I said and paused, knowing the depth of God's love. "Those who receive Christ's blood born through fire have life, and those who reject love—the fire consumes…"

Oh my, oh my, oh my! Now I understood God's judgment. The fire—it burns whatsoever is not covered by the sacrificial blood of Jesus Christ. God's wrath is not a manifestation of hatred but of love. The spiritual cancer of sin destroys life but the fire of the Lamb gives life. God's fire burns away sin as a kind of "radiation therapy," to destroy what is impure so that life might thrive through the blood of the Lamb. And if one inhabits the blood of the Lamb, then the fire brings restoration, not death. But without the blood of the Lamb, that same fire burns everything in its path.

"I am your Redeemer," spoke God.

God's three voices spoke those words in unison, as the angels and the human tribes standing around the Throne burst forth with worshipful praises like ten thousand or so symphonic choirs.

All of Heaven rejoiced throughout the endless expanse of Heaven, and every living thing great and small shouted praises.

Then I saw a faded scene where a feast was set to display lavish dressings of foods and drinks.

This appeared to me as a vision of the future, not the "here and now" where I presently stood. After seeing this, my attention returned to the place of sacredness, with God in the Throne Room.

"I have set the table," Jesus said. "Soon, the feast will commence."

I knew that this vision represented a glimpse of the feast that is yet to come.

My attention turned to the rustling of fires and burbling waters. A quiet wind blew crackling fires across a vast sea of crystal-clear water that poured forth from the top of where the Father and Son stood. It was a tower with stadium-style rows of opal stands next to the clear crystal altar. The waters cascaded downward, as a waterfall into a rippling sea. I knew that the fires overtop the waters came from the Holy Spirit and that the living waters came from Jesus.

The Father spoke from within the vaporous clouds that mixed with light. His declarations streamed through what seemed to be thousands of large portals, to what existed below. His authoritative words, in a language unknown to me, manifested as shooting stars through a diffraction of the lighted clouds that appeared to spread out like spotlights over the darkness below. I watched what appeared to be an unending stream of thousands of lighted tunnels in the heavens, that were filled with vaporous waters and that reached into the world below. The light from the altar where the Father and Jesus stood as One, shined through the tunnels that connected Heaven to earth.

Next, Jesus commanded angels by calling their names. Immediately, the angels swooshed through the portals to the dim place below, and I assumed to the world as well. The angels must have known their assignments from the Holy Spirit, who spoke with the language of knowing.

Jesus and the Holy Spirit engaged legions of angels, who appeared as parachutists diving headfirst at the speed of light. Seraphim angels burned with the fire of the Holy Spirit as they flew with six wings that were larger than their bodies. They elicited shouts of praise above the Throne, with each one sounding as the voice of a hundred or so human voices.

Cherubim appeared freakishly different from all of the other angels. They had multiple heads which appeared as fearsome animals, the likes of which I had never witnessed. And their face was not unlike that of a human, except for its sharpened teeth. They guarded the portals. God sent some angels through the portals armed with ten-foot long (or so) spears that reflected the light. The grandest angels were what the Holy Spirit described as the archangels. They appeared regal, like the ones I saw fighting the demons when I rose through the second heaven. They were giants of at least eight to ten feet in height, with chiseled features and eyes of fire. They flew below at Christ's commands, as spoken through God's Spirit.

I understood from the Holy Spirit that these were the angels assigned to God's greatest creation—humans. As the Holy Spirit explained to me, we are created in God's image. When God looks upon us, He sees Himself in us; and above all of the voices that speak forth, God hears the voices of His children. He sees us through the eyes of a protective father (mixed with a mother's tenderness), and He always wants the best for His children.

An aroma of the sweetest perfume now entered my nostrils. It was unlike any perfume I had smelled in the world. It evoked a pleasantness of sweet-smelling bouquets that were mixed with a feeling of being home in the comfy senses of familiar surroundings. I will call it the pleasant evocations of home. This fragrance relaxed me to the point where I wanted to sleep, but I dared not miss what appeared before me. Something was about to change.

Home, the Holy Spirit whispered to me, you are home, here in this place, and what you are experiencing is the aroma of those who are saved from below and those who are coming home after finishing their assignment in the world.

I would later reference the Scripture that said the same as recorded by Paul: *"For we are to God the pleasing aroma of Christ among those who are being saved and those who are perishing"* (2 Corinthians 2:15 NIV).

Next, I heard the audible words of the Father speak directly to me as I inhaled deeply:

"Ah, beloved, you are the fragrance of triumph unto Me for all We have done for you, and for what you have done for Us from life to life. I bear witness of My Son's sacrifice for you and I give you the sweet aroma of life everlasting. Speak of what you see as a testimony to those who know Me not, so that they might testify of My sacrifice and be saved. Nothing gives Me more pleasure than the salvation of My lost children and the completion of the works of My saints."

I dropped again from the awe of hearing the Father speak from His heart. His love exuded through all of my senses—multiple senses beyond the limited senses we feel in the world in our physically bound bodies. The depth of God's love for His greatest creation was magnified through my full comprehension in Heaven—unhindered by my faulty, earthly brain, and free to experience all of the senses of my spirit body.

Here, I could take in the wonderful fragrances, feel more alive than I ever have in the world, feel as others feel, know beyond the bounds of flesh and blood, and rejoice at the feet of Almighty God who considered me His favored child—just as each of His children are equally favored and perfectly cherished by God.

Just as I basked in the fullness of God's Glory, I heard a rolling roar—and everything shifted.

15

THE STORM

From the sky huge hailstones, each weighing
about a hundred pounds, fell on people. And
they cursed God on account of the plague of
hail, because the plague was so terrible.
—REVELATION 16:21 NIV

All of Heaven went silent. A hush soon dissipated into an unsettling calm. I turned my head to see the Father's face blazing and spreading fires like the sun. His arms outspread with the brilliance of a starry galaxy glistening in light. The light engulfed my Lord so that only one figure appeared as a single stream. It was glorious and brilliant, as a conflagration of God's might to things below, and a tense calm to everything in Heaven and to those bathed in the shimmering light of Elohim, the Almighty.

Heaven quaked.

God's luminosity cut through the Throne Room, reflecting a prism of colors of every variety. Flashes of light thundered around God's presence. With each flash, I could see figures with halos of gold upon their heads—figures around Him who bowed in reverence. The icy surface around God erupted into fires of cobalt blue, through which figures that were adorned in satiny outfits reflected the colors of gem stones. Figures both strangely familiar and like nothing I could fathom, now hovered over the Almighty. They appeared not as humans but as creatures with fiery eyes that could see all around them. They shouted a depth of holiness unto the Lord that could be heard but not understood because of its greatness.

Their praises echoed through the roar of the Almighty in a chorus of venerations—"Holy is the Lamb. Worthy is the God of all creation. Glory and honor to the Lord of lords." On and on went the choruses that inspired me and everyone in the whole of Heaven. Next, I beheld a different figure, which roared. He appeared as a lion, but it was not so much the figure of a lion as it was the essence of the lion's strength that appeared to me as a lion—one unlike anything on earth. Jesus imparted to me an understanding of what I was beholding.

"You see not just that which is, My beloved. You see that which is to come and that which has been spoken of now," He said.

What I beheld defied any assimilation in the mind, but since I was entirely spirit, my spirit mind understood these appearances as the Righteous One. He was the Lion of Judah, the Protector, and He was the Eagle described in the book of Isaiah: *"But those who hope in the Lord will renew their strength. They will soar on wings like eagles; they will run and not grow weary; they will walk and not be faint"* (Isaiah 40:31 NIV).

He was the Lamb of God who hung upon that cross, and He was the Son of God who made humankind in His image. I saw all of these facets of God reveal themselves as creatures that honor God as a tribute to the One who created them—the Lion, the Eagle, the Lamb, and the Son. I saw each one bow before the Righteous Judge, who would execute His righteousness not in rage but in love.

I also heard the sorrowful mourning for the lost transition into a funeral dirge. It sounded like a mother's sigh birthed through empathy toward her lost child. Angels groaned with an operatic tone that ended with the wafting words, "No more…No more."

"These who are lost forever will never hear My voice again," came the words of Jesus, spoken through the undulating winds.

Suddenly, Jesus appeared at my side again as before, in human form and entirely relatable to me, unlike the visage of brilliant light He appeared as upon the altar. He wrapped His left arm around my left side now, as if bracing me from a fall. No longer did I sense the calming influence of the peace of Heaven. I found myself in a different place—one full of power and grace, righteousness and judgment, hope, and hope fulfilled.

I know these depictions may seem lofty and not entirely descript, but no description could adequately explain the shift I felt in this place. I found myself in a vacuum of time, both present and future. The only reason I can express this is because my spirit mind sensed the gravity of it all. God had spoken, and soon—I just knew that "as a thousand years is to a day," that what existed on earth would be never more.

"My Spirit tells you so," said Jesus.

Was God giving me a peek into the future?

"Yes," Jesus answered, "I show you that which is already established in Heaven and that which you will realize later, as a warning to My beloved. To them, it will be as if it were in the future."

Then I understood what the author of the book of Hebrews meant when explaining that the earthly Tabernacle was *"a copy and shadow of the heavenly things"* (Hebrews 8:5, 9:23 ESV). The heavenly Tabernacle was first formed by God, but the earthly Tabernacle, described by Moses and built under the direction of Solomon, was a copy of the one in Heaven. I witnessed that Tabernacle in Heaven. It is decorated with fruit-bearing trees, gold, and carvings of angels.

These same depictions also once adorned the earthly Temple that showcased the figures, to recall the grandeur of the Garden of Eden first created on earth by God.

All that I would witness in the heavenly Storm was not only destined for earth, but the Storm would bring closure to all who had ever lived upon the earth. Years later, I would search for the answers to confirm what I had beheld. I found these things in Scripture (Genesis 2:15; Numbers 3:7-8, 8:26, 18:5-6). All of these recordings echoed in my mind as I saw these things in Heaven, because in Heaven, the Word of God is always "top of mind."

Truly, the paradise of Eden mirrored the wonders I saw in Heaven. The sanctuary that exists in Heaven reflects the perfection that once existed on earth, when both coexisted in the first creation of this world. Sadly, sin eroded paradise and widened the separation of Heaven and earth and broke the covenantal relationship with Jesus. Now, as I beheld the perfection of Heaven, the Holy Spirit confirmed to me that I was about to see the unfolding of the new Earth and the new Heaven, which would once again reunite Heaven and earth.

Jesus and I soared to a several thousand-foot-high mountaintop. Though higher than any place I had ever been on earth, it felt warm at its pinnacle. I could see a Tabernacle begin to slide downward in what appeared to be a landslide not of mud, but of crystal waters. Then I noticed that the Tabernacle was a replica of the one that stood in the center of Heaven. The Tabernacle of Heaven still stood in Heaven below, so I asked Jesus about this strange appearance.

"Remember beloved, you see what is to come, and My Spirit tells you only what you need to know."

You see the Tabernacle of God (the New Jerusalem or Holy City), whispered the Holy Spirit, *and below is the new earth, which is to come.*

"I did dwell on earth," Jesus said, "and I will do so again."

I recalled "Jacob's Ladder," as explained in the book of Genesis, but I did not see angels ascending and descending a ladder, only the crystal waters from Heaven that turned vaporous as they drifted beneath the floor of Heaven to the place below (Genesis 28:12).

"Just as it was in the beginning of time, so it shall be in the end," Jesus said.

"I don't understand, Lord."

"In the beginning, Heaven and earth coexisted until sin separated us, but I will restore Heaven and Earth so that no one can destroy it," Jesus said.

"Jacob's Ladder," I said, knowing now from Jesus how Jacob's vision would come to pass.

"All that shall be established on earth will be blessed forever and ever," said Jesus, "but first must come the Storm."

The calm of Heaven dissipated into a rolling thunder. The angels and people around the altar of God stilled themselves. The angels around the Glory Place of God looked down as if they were expecting something. People beyond the Throne Room huddled together in prayerful chants.

"Let Your Glory reign," they sang.

"Let Heaven and earth rejoice," sounded many.

"Your will be established on earth," came voices from Heaven.

"Let not evil prevail upon Your people," called some chants.

"Let it begin," declared Jesus, in a thunderous voice. Then all who were in Heaven echoed those same words.

A sudden change brought heaviness to the air. Gradually the clouds from the Father ominously hovered above the Holy of Holies where God reigned in the Holy Place of God (the Throne Room), before spreading throughout Heaven. The dark clouds billowed like a wavy blanket that turned God's brilliant light to a shadier form. In those moments, Heaven turned the color of a cloudy fall day.

I show you beyond your eyes now, beloved, whispered the Holy Spirit. *You see through My eyes that which will precede the earth, because I have sanctified you.*

After the Holy Spirit spoke these words to me, the meaning of what I beheld became clear. I could now understand the mysterious effects of the Storm as they unfolded.

Next, rain dripped from the clouds, but they were not drops that dampened what they touched. Instead, I felt the drops much like I felt the living waters of Jesus when I first drank from the river that flowed from Him. The drops enlivened me and invigorated my soul—turning me to pray for those in the world, for the salvation of the lost, for miracles of healings to the sick, and for the full Glory of God to be poured forth upon the world.

"What do you see?" asked Jesus

"I see Your angels descending upon the world," I said.

"Yes, beloved," Jesus said, "the angels you see are for a time not yet appointed on earth."

I understood Jesus's words as clarified by the Holy Spirit to mean that what I viewed was for a future time in the world, not for the present. Perhaps a battle would ensue within the second heaven that would last for years. Perhaps God had somehow transported me into the future, to give me a vision. It all seemed real and it happened in Heaven in real time. I don't know how, but what I beheld in Heaven would be manifested on earth in the future. To say that it would be amazing would be the grossest understatement of all time.

Then God as Jesus released the angels as they responded to their assigned anointings for those upon the earth and according to the

Holy Spirit's leading. They swooped downward with the speed of vaporous rocket missiles. Because the angels were without sin, they could minister the purity of God's Word as spoken from the altar I previously explained—the altar upon which all creations and judgments would issue forth. That crystal altar now clearly appeared as a bright, velvety blue light, with colors and hues saturated in intensity.

"You see a host of My angels," said Jesus.

I immediately knew that these hosts functioned as an army of God's soldiers—"the armies of heaven" called out for spiritual warfare, as recorded in Psalm 89 and in 1 Samuel, chapters 1 and 17. As Jesus spoke to me, the verses of the corresponding biblical books were immediately illuminated for me.

The angels from the "Lord of hosts" spoken about in Isaiah 31 now descended into the heavenly bodies within the universe. I knew they had been called from the origins of space, from the Holy of Holies. I had seen them surrounding the Throne of God. Their assignments were to bring God's new life into the world.

"Do you see that angel?" Jesus asked, as He pointed to an angel that was bowing down before the altar of God.

"Yes, Lord," I answered, "he looks different, more like You."

"Beloved, he is written in My Word as 'the angel of the Lord,' and he was separate in purpose from the others because he went before Me as My messenger. He did represent My truth by My side, but when I became flesh, he did return to My altar."

I remembered the mystery of "the angel of the Lord," as referenced in the Old Testament. He exercised the prerogatives of God but he was not God. I think of this angel as a steward of the Lord, special and set-apart as explained in numerous passages within the books of Genesis and Exodus chapter 3, as well as several passages in the book of Judges and 2 Samuel. He wrestled with Jacob at the behest of Jesus. After the incarnation of Jesus on earth, this angel returned to Heaven and served God at the Throne all the days since, as *Malak YHWH*,[1] the angel of the Lord who now waits upon the Lord God, in anticipation of the new earth.

"Thou shalt worship no angel," Jesus said emphatically, in a guttural tone that went up in pitch on the first syllables and fell on the last syllables and with a rolling of His tongue that I imagine was an ancient voice. That He would use such an ancient dialect to declare that *no one should worship angels* may seem strange to some. But to me, it made perfect sense because although the angels are mighty in appearance, they were *the created*, not *the Creator*. No one should worship the created.

What better way to emphasize this point than to use an ancient, formal dialect that resonates with a truth that began from the time God created the angels? Were not the original sinners the fallen angels who defied God? Clearly, Jesus would ensure that no one in Heaven would ever rebel again. Only through creating humans anew through a perfect rebirth was He able to accomplish that perfection in Heaven.

In Genesis 18:3, we see that angels can appear in human form, just as the angel had appeared at the driver's side of my crashed vehicle. However, angels are created spirits as described in Hebrews 1:14. They are usually invisible to the naked eye; unless of course, you are in Heaven as I experienced after dying, or you are given a spiritual vision for a heavenly purpose. Now I heard the angels declaring the Word of God fluidly in the space of Heaven, as beings more knowledgeable of the Bible than any Bible scholar I knew in the world. This made perfect sense to me.

In Heaven, I had seen a kind of library where books were carried in and out by humans and angels. Although the angels existed prior to humankind, they appeared youthful, yet they carry the ancient past with them, making them more knowledgeable than humans. Still, we humans are positioned higher than the angels because of our union with Christ—we are made in His image.

That sense of knowing came upon me again, as evil lurked below in hell. I knew that satan could speak to God as he did in the case of Job, where God permitted him to be attacked by satan for a season. But all of that would soon end. Christ's justification would see to it.

Note

1. The Hebrew word malak means "messenger."

16

JUSTIFICATION

*I do not set aside the grace of God, for if righteousness
could be gained through the law, Christ died for nothing!*
—GALATIANS 2:21 NIV

My attention returned to the momentous disturbances all around me. I felt a cool downdraft as with the appearance of lightning before thunder. What I saw in the Storm continued to tense my body, as fiery angels that looked like projectiles sailed through the portals to what existed below. For the first time, my guardian angel spoke to me as I stood with Jesus. What happened next shocked me.

The angel bowed before me. Then he said:

"You will judge me one day, servant of the Lord Almighty, and I trust that my service to you will be acceptable to you on that day." With that, he arose, towering over me in height.

I was flabbergasted at first, but then the Holy Spirit gave me understanding.

Jesus was the last Adam and the second man, whispered the Holy Spirit, becoming the Head of the redeemed race, exalted above others.

With that inspiration, I knew that as the "redeemed race," we who follow Christ's sacrifice on the cross would be the ones who would see the second coming of Jesus.

"Behold," Jesus said, "I send Michael."

I saw the angel Michael, who carried a sword at least twelve feet long. Even so, it was dwarfed by Michael's gargantuan frame.

"He will slay the beast," Jesus said.

I had thought "slaying the dragon" (or beast) was a Medieval fantasy term found only in books and fairy tales, until I heard those words from Jesus. Jesus placed His hand over my eyes again, and I witnessed a scene so horrid, it chills me to this day. I saw a vision of Jesus standing in a lake of fire. A human-sized dragon or serpent stood before Him, amidst blood-curdling screams of terror and lamentations.

"It is done," Jesus spoke to the serpent.

Jesus then knelt and poured a cup of His blood that was co-mingled with the blood of the saints before the serpent, after which the serpent raged as fires burst out of him.

"Fool," the serpent said to Jesus, "they hung Your body on the cross and You do this?"

"You cannot have those who confess Me as their God," said Jesus.

"I hate the ones who You esteem as higher than us," the serpent said, "and then You would have us bow to them? NO!" The serpent's rage appeared to consume him with fire.

He appeared more like a dragon, half human-looking and half serpent, but his form seemed to vacillate between two figures. All at once he appeared as a vile-looking beast that had flared nostrils, a spiked forehead, narrow black eyes, and four flared wings atop a scaly body, with six claws on both of his hands and feet. Then he morphed smoothly into the most handsome-featured being imaginable, with piercing brown eyes and hair, and perfectly shaped ears and nose, with an alluring persona—one that nearly compelled adoration. I thought perhaps that his rage determined which figure appeared.

He looked at Jesus with more contempt than any being I had ever seen. Jesus looked into his eyes when satan appeared as the dragon. Oddly enough, I saw satan more as a man, although I absolutely knew that he was satan.

Jesus removed His hand from my eyes and the vision disappeared. Oh my—I had witnessed a vision of something I did not fully understand. Did Jesus place the sins of His children at the feet of satan? Was Jesus in hell? Was I seeing into the past? I asked the Holy Spirit to clarify my understanding.

Be not consumed with how Jesus redeemed the lost, the Holy Spirit whispered. Know this. What you saw was the place of the dead, but He who is Holy cannot be with the unsanctified, so what you saw was in two different places—the place of the living dead (those who were dead without the Spirit of God in them), and the place of the Ascension.

Then I remembered what Jesus said to the repentant criminal on the cross next to His, *"Today you will be with Me in Paradise"* (Luke 23:43 NKJV).

Jesus rose to Heaven from the cross and declared from His throne His authority over death. Jesus also declared to satan that His sacrifice was *"once for sins,"* as it says in God's Word, where He claims *"the righteous for the unrighteous"* (1 Peter 3:18 NIV).

I knew the plan of salvation and had been taught classes in church to help people understand how to become "saved," but in Heaven, salvation took on another dimension. Everyone in Heaven (including me) lived in perpetual thankfulness for God's gift of eternal life. And we fully understood that adoption was a transformative act of grace through Christ, because the spiritual infusion of the blood of Jesus Christ made us new.

The Holy Spirit reminded me of when Moses took the blood in the bowls and threw it upon the people as he said, *"This is the blood that seals the covenant which the Lord made with you when He gave all these commands"* (Exodus 24:8 GNT). Then the Holy Spirit reminded me of His Word, when Jesus said that He came not to abolish the Law but to fulfill it (Matthew 5:17).

"I said that unless one's righteousness *exceeds* that of the scribes and Pharisees—that person will never enter the Kingdom of Heaven," said Jesus.

Then I realized that the Holy Spirit acted to impart the "wisdom of the butterfly" so we who believe would know the mysteries of God's Word.

All who are in Christ are under the "Law of Christ," as is in the "Book of Life," whispered the Holy Spirit. No longer are those in the Age of Grace (post the resurrection of Jesus) justified by the works of the (Mosaic) Law, for no one is justified by the Law but through faith, and faith comes from...

"My Word," spoke the thunderous voice of the Father.

"Yes," I said, "we are justified by the blood of the Lamb of God (Jesus) and so were those before the resurrection!"

"My Spirit has told you so," said Jesus, "I came to fulfill the Law, and the belief in Me as the Messiah that Isaiah prophesized has always made the unrighteous pure. Who am I to you?"

As Jesus said this, I felt Christ's blood coursing through my spirit body. It felt warm, like a pleasant drink. It permeated my body and spread throughout it the way the iodine-contrast medium had flowed through my veins in the hospital radiology department before my death. However, this was entirely comforting to me and I instantly knew the answer to the question Jesus asked.

"You are my ALL, Jesus, and all of You is who I am."

"Behold," said Jesus, "what you understand now is an act of My love for the completion of My work. All who go through this (death and resurrection) will know that their justification is not of themselves but because of My grace. All who know Me are sealed by My blood and made inseparable to Me."

My attention was turned by Jesus to the future that I now beheld, as told to me by the Holy Spirit. Here, amid the beginning of the Storm, the sprinkling of raindrops evoked another feeling—power. The Holy Spirit's palpable power brought forth a warming wind that created undulating updrafts and downdrafts. The downdrafts pushed through the portals. Souls rose through other portals from the updrafts and were met by a welcoming group of people. Hundreds of thousands of redeemed souls appeared as vapors without form, but I knew that the vapors would inhabit their bodies on earth and that the vapors represented the power of the Holy Spirit in the Storm.

"You see the salvation of souls yet to be born anew, in the Heaven that is to come," Jesus said.

The new Heaven or the Rapture? Was I seeing into the future of the New Heaven that will be enjoined with a new Earth as Revelation 22 reveals? Or were these souls whisking into Heaven those who had never died? Instantly, I saw a vision of Heaven coming to earth, but that vision played out in my mind, not before my eyes, as when I was seeing Heaven with Jesus.

You see My outpouring upon the world, whispered the Holy Spirit. We are revealing what is happening now in Heaven but will be seen on earth long after your return.

"And those You will be taking during the Storm?" I asked. It seemed strange to me that I assumed the Rapture to be true since no one told me so, but again, in Heaven, understanding flowed from Jesus as common thought.

"I show you those undefiled by the wickedness that shall rule the earth and I gave you that vision of when I birth anew the earth, beloved, but you will see it soon," said Jesus.

So, it's true, I thought, the saints will be ushered into Heaven like Enoch, and within a second of time in Heaven, the Tribulation will end. Then after…what? Was I missing something?

"Beloved," Jesus said, "you see those who I conceived in Heaven."

I had written articles and presented teachings about salvation, and I know that my seeing the salvation of souls before they were born begs some questions. Did those souls live before their birth? Was I seeing into the future? Is there predestination in Heaven that determines who would be saved and who would not be?

While I saw these things in Heaven and clearly understood the answers, upon my return, my brain could not fully comprehend them. So, I will attempt to explain what God revealed to me both in Heaven and what I received after much prayer and revelation.

First, as confirmed in Jeremiah 1:5 and through my own experience, God knew all about us before we were born, although we never lived in the world until God birthed us there.

Second, I indeed witnessed the present in Heaven—one that had not yet been established in the future world. As I learned from Jesus, our future exists in God's past because it was first birthed in Heaven. It's just as the apostle Peter wrote, *"With the Lord a day is like a thousand years, and a thousand years are like a day"* (2 Peter 3:8 NIV). God was revealing to me there in Heaven and before my eyes, a span of a "thousand years," from the end of times to the creation of the new earth—and the very day the Storm in Heaven would be poured forth on earth. That Storm would commence with an outpouring of God's Holy Spirit in the world, and be followed by the removal of God's Holy Spirit from the world—and after that, a time of great anguish.

Third, while the Bible does reference predestination in several places, the focus of God's Word places Christ and salvation through repentance and faith in Christ at the core of God's creation of humankind. Think of it this way as I did in Heaven through the Holy Spirit's impartation: built inside of God's elect is the south pole of a type of spiritual magnet. The Holy Spirit represents the north pole of that magnet. God called everyone to be saved, but only those who draw closer to the pull of the Holy Spirit's magnetic force will connect to God and be saved.

"Those who draw near to Me will be made holy," said Jesus in that moment when I was in Heaven. "And I will draw near to those who draw near to Me."

Those words aligned with God's Word as I knew it in Heaven, and as I had studied it on earth after returning. When He spoke those words to me at the beginning of the Storm, I knew exactly what they meant. So many people strive for holiness as a discipline and fail. But those who draw near to God will be made holy through Him as a condition of the heart, which makes us want to please God in all things.

"So, holiness is not a state of mind. It's a positioning near You," I said.

At that moment, the wind blew forth water from the altar of the Lord. Flaming angels flew around the altar, their bodies partially cloaked in white linen that partly revealed translucent chests that reflected orange, blue, and greenish colors. Their exposed arms and legs were copper-colored. Their glowing faces and blazing eyes looked at God. What struck me the most about them was that each sang forth in a voice many times more robust than a single human voice. Their chorus erupted like hundreds of choirs, as they sang in unison: "Holy, Holy, Holy, is the Lord God Almighty. Precious is His Name. Blessed is the Lord…Holy, Holy, Holy…"—over and over again.

What had flowed from the altar looked like a flaming gas leak, only the liquid was pure and crystalline. It poured over me; and although I was immersed in its flaming waters, it did not make me wet or burn me. I somehow felt emboldened by the flames. I continued being bathed within the waters as someone recited:

"For with You is the fountain of life; in Your light we see light" (Psalm 36:9 NKJV).

I think it was my guardian angel beside me who spoke the Lord's Word. The Holy Spirit spoke next and said:

You are bathed in holiness, beloved, not because of what you do but because of who you are in Me.

Then Jesus stood nose to nose with me and said:

"You are Mine and I have made you holy, beloved. Do not think of holiness as anyone or anything other than My Spirit. Because of Me, you are made holy. You cannot obtain holiness without Me. The closer you are to Me, the more set apart you will be made."

Next, the Father descended from His Throne and appeared as an indescribable mass before me—greater than the sum of my understanding, and glorious to behold. He appeared to me as though I was looking into a thousand suns. Jesus and the Father and the Holy Spirit must have merged into this glorious apparition, or so I knew. The Father said in a thunderous declaration:

"The apostasy has begun."

With that, an inverse tornado sucked up the waters that had been flowing upon the earth through the portholes and back onto the altar, which overflowed to fill the surrounding pool of blue crystal that stretched for miles around the Throne. I kept thinking that it looked like an ice rink, but figures walked upon its surface as confidently as though they were walking on a track surface.

"What am I beholding, Lord?" I asked.

The Holy Spirit answered: My presence shall be removed from the earth before the final days, and then there will be no holiness upon the earth, because My holiness is within My children and about those who seek My truth.

"So your holiness comes from surrender to You? I asked. "And that thing that I saw was You lifting Your presence from the world before the last seven years of the world's history?"

"Those who reject Me have no life, and no life remains," said Jesus.

"Lord, You are so patient with us," I said. "The world cannot survive without Your love."

"You listen well," Jesus said.

"I guess not enough, since I doubted You before being rushed to the hospital," I said.

Then I remembered that I was no longer beholden to my physical body or brain. I was freed of all of my earthly concerns. So yes, my listening skills had immeasurably improved.

Jesus chuckled. "Look over there," He said, while pointing yonder.

Afar off, I saw Jesus praying with a group of three, even as He remained by my side. I realized that all this time, Jesus and the Holy Spirit operated as One, and never ceased being present in Heaven both in body and Spirit. As impossible as that may seem, in Heaven it all became crystal-clear. They functioned as the same because they are Spirit and the Father is Spirit.

Therefore, my spiritual eyes perceived them as one Person, all the time I sojourned in Heaven.

I suppose that one can only be freed of one's body, in order to experience the fullness of that realization in Heaven. My spiritual eyes could see spirits the same way my physical eyes could see bodies. But in my spirit body, the Father, Jesus, and Holy Spirit appeared as One, with each imparting unique facets of themselves. It was unlike any comparison I can make on earth.

"Let it begin," spoke a thunderous voice that I now realized was the Father's declaration. Or was it the voice of Jesus?

"I speak as One with the Father," Jesus said.

I understood that no separation exists between Them. Even though the Father appeared grand and majestic and Jesus appeared humanlike, They spoke with one declarative voice. But something felt different following this declaration from the Throne Room of God. I felt it, saw it, and absorbed it with a sense I had never felt on earth. It was an overriding sense of knowing, without the need to fully understand.

In this world, it is called inert knowledge, which is information that a person knows but does not fully understand. I could recognize some heavenly truths, without fully understanding what they meant. For example, I know that God exists distinctly as One being, but I do not understand how He could have been multiple places yet remain with me the entire time I spent in Heaven. God's omnipotence revealed Himself to me according to how I needed to know Him, while never leaving my side.

"Wisdom," Jesus said. "You knew wisdom as fleeting in the world, beloved. Here, wisdom abides in you as more than just telling right from wrong. You sense My thoughts."

Next, I spiritually sensed the wind descend from Heaven to earth as it spread its warmth. It was the calm before the greatest Storm in all of human history.

PART THREE

THE LAST DAYS ON EARTH

17

THE TRIBULATION

I watched as he opened the sixth seal. There was a
great earthquake. The sun turned black like sackcloth
made of goat hair, the whole moon turned blood red.
—REVELATION 6:12 NIV

Jesus spread out His arms to usher forth another phase of the Holy Spirit's winds. I felt a cool draft as God's Spirit pushed downward toward the world. It streamed below with the subtlety of the calm of a fall day before a storm. Then the wind brought forth a deep boom sound which echoed throughout Heaven and intermingled with a whirling, swishing sound.

Instead of seeing the clarity of the Throne before me, I now witnessed a host of angels swirling and spiraling in a circle as they formed the cone shape of a tornado. Somehow, I knew that the tornado was the Spirit of Jesus spiraling down from Heaven so the angels could literally traverse from Heaven to the new world below.

The brilliant light I saw emanating from the Throne faded in appearance, as the space in which I found myself turned gray, like the sky on a cloudy day but no clouds could be seen, only shadows over the space where the angels flew. Then the angels descended below in waves. I first thought it resembled a series of aviation brigades.

The first wave swooped down and was followed by another and another, and so on.

"Let it begin," declared God.

This time, His voice was not as thunderous as I had heard it before. Rather, it was a soft, sorrowful tone that was not a moan or wail. Understanding Jesus's thoughts, I knew that God declared a Word that He would rather not have declared, in the same way a relationship of a loved one must end because the other person hardened and refused their love. I might almost say that it seemed like the "goodbye" of unrequited love, but God's declaration brought with it an intensity of loss I could not possibly describe—deeply forever, never to be regained, forever lost. I also grieved, following the moments God declared what I later learned was the final judgment of divorce.

Preceding each swoop of the "angel brigades" was a sounding of angel trumpets around the Throne. They sounded like the "Taps" bugle call of a military funeral, only grander. The final brigade of angels swooped upon the earth after the seventh trumpet sounded out by the angels that encircled the Throne.

A cloud of black smoke now arose from the abyss below, from which a swarm of beastly angels emerged. The creatures resembled hornets buzzing from their nest, only they were dark angels with ghastly, charred forms. They gathered en masse while hissing and screaming phrases I dare not repeat because they were too unseemly and otherworldly. I later learned that one angel was "Abaddon," who flew above the pack of figures as he outstretched his long, sinewy arms, causing the others to do the same. Clouds of gray dust dispersed from their collective claws, to fall upon the earth. What followed next upon the earth could only be described as the rattling sounds of death.

After the final descent of the warrior angels from Heaven (where I witnessed this epic event), a lone trumpet sounded. The Holy Spirit told me that it came from the angel Michael, who had been assigned to Israel. I knew implicitly that Michael had been called to join Israel in battle. I could hear the Lord God declare these words:

"I have heard the cry of My beloved who first loved Me, and those who have been refined by the fires. They are the voices of My promised people."

Not until after my return from Heaven did I understand the prophetic fulfillment of this declaration. I later read the verse: *"And I will bring the third part through the fire, refine them as silver is refined, and test them as gold is tested. They will call on My name, and I will answer them; I will say, 'They are My people,' and they will say, 'The Lord is my God'"* (Zechariah 13:9 NASB).

Next, for the first time in Heaven, an angel directly approached me after Jesus waved him toward me. He did not possess wings on his back and his robe appeared scarlet red, unlike the other angels who were dressed in white. He carried a bowl made of marble, or a similar material.

Then I realized He was not an angel at all. This was Jesus, but an angel had handed Jesus the empty bowl, which is why I confused the two. Perhaps the angel had poured the bowl of what must have been blood over Jesus's gown by reaching over Jesus's head. Jesus then handed the bowl back to the angel, now standing to right of Jesus, and turned his head downward as he bowed before Jesus.

"Turn your head," Jesus said to me.

I turned my head away from Jesus and looked below, to see the most terrifying things upon the earth. For the first time, I lost my peace in Heaven as I viewed the scenes below. I saw human flesh peeling away to reveal skeletal muscles of hordes of people who were surrounded by smoldering pieces of buildings. I witnessed peoples' stomachs bloated from starvation. Those crying out to Jesus were being beheaded by beady-eyed marauders in tattered military outfits.

Fish, whales, and other sea creatures floated across deadened oceans. The demons, like those I saw as I rose to Heaven, now feasted upon the souls of those who walked about, like prey being devoured by packs of animals.

"Oh God, take my eyes away from this!" I shouted. "This can't be You. Oh Lord!" I cried. "How did this happen?"

"Beloved, fear not," Jesus said, "I came not to destroy but to save. All that is wicked shall be erased, to save the redeemed from their influence. Righteousness cannot abide with unrighteousness or all would be made unclean. Only perfection shall remain when I have redeemed the world. What you see is who they are without Me. It is written: "...Whatever is now covered up will be uncovered, and every secret will be made known" (Matthew 10:26 GNT).

After Jesus spoke that truth, I felt a peaceful assuredness that Jesus had done everything possible to save the lost. There existed no more grace upon the earth. Every chance to turn to Jesus had been offered to the lost by God. In the end, satan and his minions will ravage the world. The only remnant of good will be the tears shed by Christ.

I beheld the remnant of believers also, those who lived "as to the Lord" (Colossians 3:23 NKJV) but abided in the Spirit as it was in the Old Testament times, through a sense of knowing as confirmed through the prophets and the Word.

I have told you this much, whispered the Holy Spirit. These you see who show My Light shining upon them are equipped with a special anointing to endure the trials of the Great Tribulation, a gift.

"A gift?" I asked.

Then the Holy Spirit spoke audibly to me, as did Jesus.

"They have the gift of the martyrs whose blood was shed for Us, and great will be their reward. They treasure the Word and know the Word as only the persecuted know Our Word. They will be given beauty for ashes as spoken by Our beloved Isaiah who stands at the Throne."

My attention was drawn to a figure at the Throne whose long beard stood out the most to me. Jesus stood behind Isaiah and declared:

"This passage of scripture has come true today, as you heard it being read" (as Jesus said as recorded in Luke 4:21 GNT)—so the prophets of the Last Days will have seen the fulfillment of My coming and will be glorified and taken to Heaven, and the unrighteous will die for the completion of My Word."

Instantly I thought how right that Jesus would reveal His second coming behind the prophet who declared His first coming. Despite the horror of what I beheld, a peace endured. I felt not the judgment of God so much as the reaping of what the inhabitants of the world had sown. Jesus made it so simple to receive His grace, yet the world mostly believed in their own justification.

Know that what you behold is not the Word, whispered the Holy Spirit. What you behold testifies of the Word. Never share your witness as equal to the Word. Speak of what you see as confirmation of the Truth as evidenced by the Word.

Implicitly I knew that the Bible was the Word and the Word stood on its own, and that nothing I witnessed would add to or detract from its Truth. In Heaven the Word had become imprinted in my soul, internalized, even if upon my return, in the flesh, I would sometimes struggle to inculcate its Truth.

Instantly I felt the Holy Spirit blow His presence over me. The wind now formed a cushiony-thick blanket around me and I somehow slept while I was awake.

Beloved, whispered the Holy Spirit, you see as We see and you see that which has already been declared and you feel as We feel.

"Suffering is not of Me," said Jesus. "The ones you see were given all they needed to know Me, and they rejected Me, so I left them to their own and to those they worship."

Echoing within my spirit were these words:

> The great dragon was hurled down—that ancient serpent called the devil, or Satan, who leads the whole world astray. He was hurled to the earth, and his angels with him (Revelation 12:9 NIV).

"Your judgments," I said. "These are Your judgments—the bowls John wrote about in Revelation—Your judgments?"

"Judgments?" Jesus asked.

Why would Jesus ask me that question? Why would He pose that as a question and not an answer? I thought to ask the Holy Spirit for the answer, as my mind swirled with the terror of what I beheld. Then the Holy Spirit blew a soothing elixir into my right ear to calm my mind. I knew the answer. The judgment of God is executed through the loss of love. Without love, all hell breaks loose. God had removed His presence from the world, along with His protection. Nothing but the rendering of justice remained because there was no longer a Mediator for humankind.

"Those in hell do not blame You, do they? They know what is deserved and what is righteous. They understand justice in hell, just as we understand Your grace here," I said to Jesus. If you think it strange that I would say this, please know that all this time, wisdom spoke these insights to me.

Jesus nodded.

Years later, I would interview many people who died and went to hell, before returning. Each one said in one way or another, something along the lines of, "I deserved to be there and I accepted my fate." It amazes me that justice is known to everyone in hell who denied Christ.

This contrasts with those who know Jesus as their Lord, because they know true grace.

"You removed Your presence after showering them with Your Glory for a time," I said.

Then I beheld a glorious appearance like the northern lights, only their glowing rays were far more vivid, with shades of different colors. These rays comingled with one another like hundreds of different colored streams that crisscrossed each other before turning a blood orange color. Fire raged through these flowing lights so immensely brilliant that I could barely look at it with my spiritual eyes.

"Let it begin," roared a voice from the Throne.

Hovering over these lights was Jesus, who was bathed in white. His hand was lifted and upturned to reveal the scars in His palm. Then He turned His hand palm side down and a strong wind blew fire and light that began streaming toward the world below.

"As it was in the beginning, so it shall be in the end," declared Jesus.

The Holy Spirit explained to me that just before the judgments, Jesus had released God's Glory upon the earth so that God could once more save all who would be saved. In a vision, He showed me people below who were dancing and laying hands on the sick and shouting praises, as well as people lying prostrate in reverence to God.

In my spirit, I remained curious as to why the order of events that I witnessed did not seem to be in the order I expected them to occur in the world. I wondered, *Why would God reverse the order of the end-time events? Or was my understanding skewed given that in Heaven there is no time and God's declarations could only be translated through inspiration, rather than just understanding.* I had just witnessed the judgments being released upon the earth because of the absence of grace. Now I beheld God's Glory released on earth. Was the Glory of God not released before the Judgment?

How do you see things in the mirror? asked the Holy Spirit.

"In reverse," I answered.

"Ah, beloved," Jesus said, "you see things as they are now in Heaven, but on earth you will see them in reverse."

Then I remembered: *"For now we see in a mirror dimly, but then face to face; now I know in part, but then I will know fully, just as I also have been fully known"* (1 Corinthians 13:12 NASB). That still did not answer the question for me, but my spirit knew the answer.

When I returned to this world after being resuscitated, the answer eluded me, as strange as that may seem. It suggests to me that God confounded me of certain things that would appear on earth, things I had first witnessed in Heaven. However, after much prayer while writing this account, the Holy Spirit spoke to me again so that I could explain the answer to you. He said:

What you saw in Heaven was the order of judgment. Judgment must be rendered before mercy, or else mercy would be given for nothing. The world has always been under judgment, but the Messiah's mercy and grace delivered the righteous from judgment so that no one who is covered by the righteousness of Christ need suffer the penalty of sin. In Heaven, you saw Our Glory, which affected the righteous and the unrighteous, but it followed the righteous judgment of Him who is Holy. This is grace—to forgive that which has already been judged as guilty.

Ah…my spirit comprehended what the Holy Spirit told me, just as it had been in Heaven. In Heaven, I witnessed the judgment that would be rendered on earth. The Glory of God followed, but on earth, those would be reversed. God's mercy would once again prevail on earth. His Spirit would be manifested on earth as one final opportunity for humankind. I knew that the greatest revival in the history of humankind would either precede the Tribulation, or be in the midst of it; but, God's judgment had already been established as well as His mercy.

What we will behold on earth is a reflection of what has already been established in Heaven. In His mercy, God would release His Glory on earth one last time before it would be evacuated from the world. Once removed, God's protection over humankind would no longer be evident on earth. Never in the history of humankind had God's presence been absent from the world—until the Tribulation.

"Tell them to focus on Me, not the world," said Jesus. "The spirit understands what the mind cannot fathom."

After understanding this epiphany, my mind thought back to Heaven. As humans the tendency is to focus on the end times as some form of entertainment, but each person lives in their own end time. Heaven shifted my attention toward an immersion in God's presence as the only thing that mattered. I was there again, in Heaven, and the Holy Spirit spoke to me as my body and brain lie lifeless on a hospital bed.

For a season We brought Our Glory to earth, the Holy Spirit whispered.

I knew that when the Holy Spirit spoke in the past tense, He referenced what had already been established in Heaven but not on earth, so I fully expected the Glory to be forthcoming. As strange as that may seem, try to conceptualize something you might build in the world, for example, a mobile home. Once built, you transport the home to your destination.

Heaven is what I call "the manufacturing plant." This world is "where Heaven's creation is placed." Everything in Heaven is everlasting; but in the world, sin corrupts God's creations, like rust and mold that eat away new structures. This explains how God's paradise on earth became sullied, and how the first humans, who were created to live forever with God in paradise, suffered the debilitating effects of sin—and which all of humanity has subsequently suffered, across centuries of existence.

In Heaven, Jesus now appeared to me, dressed in a gown that was whiter than snow. The skies around Heaven cleared as brilliant sparkles of colors now gleaned throughout Heaven. I looked toward the altar of God as it stood against the backdrop of gloriously shining stones. Suddenly, the Godhead appeared before my eyes. The Father, Jesus, and the Holy Spirit stood faintly defined, not as towering figures but as the image of humans, only far grander.

Their features blended together as they were cloaked in light. They smiled down at me with a love so profound and consuming, that I felt the same as when I had caved to my knees in awe and gratitude during my first meeting with Jesus. I worshipped them with every fiber of my being. I dared not speak, because to do so would be trivial as compared to the reverence I now felt. Once I regained my composure to reason again, I began to speak as one drunk with wisdom, understanding, and absolute thanksgiving.

"Your love is perfect," I said. "I know love only because You first loved me."

I later learned that I had paraphrased 1 John 4:18-19. In Heaven I was reminded of God's Word, so I knew the answer to all of my questions, since knowing God's Word allows me to fully know God. I answered my own question about God's judgment:

"Your judgment in someone's life stems from the absence of Your love in them," I said.

With that, God implanted a vision in my mind of a blazing fire bursting down upon a person. Above that person was a shield that deflected the burning flames. I knew that all of this time and before God would remove His presence at the time of the Tribulation, His love protected the world from judgment. But the rejection of God's love by people of the world causes the "shield of love" to be removed. Therefore, the flames of judgment devoured them. They turned against each another in hatred, for lack of any semblance of true love.

Justice is rendered to those who deny the truth because they have surrendered to the lie and there is no absolution without truth. I secretly knew that lies are always exposed by the truth, and that the consequence of lying always follows after those lies are exposed. That is judgment. That is the consequence of sin—not being covered by the shed blood of Jesus the Messiah. Without Jesus's forgiveness, judgment must be executed to restore what is right. After coming to this realization, I felt profound gratitude toward Jesus, God, *Elyon* (Hebrew for "God Most High"). He did not have to sacrifice Himself for me or for you—if not for love.

Then I remembered the flames around the Throne that did not burn those who walked through them. That's because they walked with the power of God's love, so God's judgment was not deadly to them. I knew those flames brought life, not destruction. The burning flames of God's love are intense, like the sun as it spouts forth flames, but these flames soothed those covered by the blood of Jesus. Those bathed in righteousness rejoiced as though they were plugged into a power source. They were reinvigorated, enlivened, and enlightened spiritually and intellectually by the God of Jesus Christ.

Those who are not cloaked in His righteous blood burned in the world as evidenced by their boils and discolored skin. The flames consumed them from among the smoldering wastelands of the world. And the things that were *not* of God, such as hate, vengeance, unforgiveness, and envy, ate through them like cancers.

"Well done," the voice of the Threesome now spoke to me in unison. "You see not through your eyes, but of Mine. Speak not of what you see until I have appointed you to speak. For now, this is for you to grow in what you have learned, but I will give you that which you need to fulfill the purpose I have ordained for you."

"When My Word speaks truth to those made in My image," they continued, "then they speak in love and truth and wisdom. Apart from My Word, there is no truth. My Word is who I AM, for as it was, My Word became flesh, and My Word is love, and no one knows love who knows not Me. Without love, there is hate and without truth, there are lies, and without life, there is death and without the way, there is confusion."

"Yes!" I cried. "Just as You spoke through John, You are the Way and the Truth and the Life, and no one comes to You except they come through Jesus" (John 14:6).

At that, all of Heaven began rejoicing. I think it was because whenever an epiphany of understanding happens within a person in the world (or for me as one who would be returned to the world), it births a newness of revelation. There is rejoicing that begins at the Throne Room and that ushers forth throughout all of Heaven.

Now, if I were to attempt to describe the rejoicing in Heaven that was enjoined by the seemingly billions who inhabited that place, words would ridiculously pale in comparison to what my spirit saw, heard, and felt. You see, in Heaven, we not only hear God's Word but we also live it. His Word imbues us with joy and unfettered thanksgiving. In Heaven, we realized the fullness of God's revelation. And the repentance or revelation of one person in the world, compels all of Heaven to rejoice.

But the Storm—I remembered the solemnity of the Storm and the birthing of new souls from the outpouring of the Holy Spirit, and the judgments pouring forth in the absence of love. In the distance, I could see what appeared to be lightning pouring forth from the Throne, in flashes that crackled in a space of blackness. I could visibly see the wind push against the space of nothing, in a place far away. Beyond the void, only the lightning could be seen. It appeared as the most striking contrast—light against the darkness.

An anvil-shaped cloud hovered over the darkness but began dissipating as the sparkling rain from overhead twinkled like stars disappearing into blackness. The scene was unlike anything in the world. I felt in my spirit that it was devoid of existence, yet once seemed to have had form. The once towering mass that rained upon the darkness finally turned into a wispy vapor and faded away.

"Let it begin," a voice roared from God's triune figure from within the Throne Room.

I noticed that the altar had faded from my sight. In its place appeared a winding pathway down a long slope. Toward the tip of this trail was a series of stairs that formed step by step. The pathway did not penetrate the space of Heaven but seemed to descend toward the world.

My eyes turned to Jesus, who emerged from the triune God and began to step downward. As He walked, a host of cherubim angels followed alongside Him. One held a white horse beside Jesus, who mounted the muscular animal that was decked in a golden saddle, with three golden, twisted cords and scarlet tassels on each side. He carried a crossbow trimmed in gold and red, and wore a king's crown dotted with several jewels. His flowing white hair and beard matched the brilliant white of His robe.

Then trumpets sounded and Jesus descended upon His horse from Heaven to the sky below. I could see Jesus and the angels emerge from clouds juxtaposed against a blue sky. Jesus appeared regal upon His horse, surrounded by tens of thousands of angels driving chariots. People below looked up. Some bowed before Jesus. Others screamed in bitter, scathing cries, while some yelled words such as:

"Not yet!" "Go away!" "Don't look at us!"

God revealed the world below to me through a kind of telescopic lens. What I saw began with a view of the round earth, which quickly descended from concentric circles onto a view of masses congregating at a large stadium. The people within the stadium who were not cloaked in the righteous blood of Jesus burned from the light of Heaven. They screamed all kinds of foul language. I never witnessed such hatred toward God in all my life. Their loathing of Jesus was proven by their mocking taunts.

I saw demons surrounding them. Some had faces with protruding eyes and slithering figures that had clawed feet but no tails. One turned his reptilian face to the side and an attractive face appeared. The demon donned black or dark brown hair, bright brown eyes, a perfectly-shaped nose, full lips, and high cheeks. As it took a step, its body no longer slithered but appeared like a well-toned male model dressed in casual designer clothing. Now his bright figure looked up at Jesus and shouted these words:

"You denied me Heaven and now You deny me earth! Cursed be Your creation made of flesh and give me them at least!"

The ones below who bowed before Jesus and His armies were bathed in God's light. They mostly teared up with joy while lying prostrate, even while attempting to raise their arms in praise. The serpent's spit landed on those who cursed Jesus, but the ears of those bowing before Jesus seemed to hear nothing but the shouts of praise from the angels who surrounded the glorious figure of Jesus. Our Lord now looked majestic with His long, flowing white hair. He was like the figure I had seen upon the Throne as the Father, only He was at least ten times in size as He was before and wondrous beyond words.

All of Heaven and earth shook as Jesus declared these words:

"It is finished."

With that, the serpent and those who cursed God were sucked into the black hole. At the base of the black hole, flames appeared that burned but did not kill. They tormented those who were consumed within the flames. Those flames were diametrically opposed to the soothing flames I had beheld around God's Throne.

I knew as did all in Heaven that the flames of hell burn forever and consume those who are there, but not with death because death would be welcome. Those flames consume all those who curse God in a continual remembrance of their evil deeds. The Holy Spirit explained that all those who are in the fire feel justified in themselves and are without remorse. They loathe God with their insults and repeat the words of the demons around them who feast upon them as prey.

Fear not, the Holy Spirit whispered to me, for those who call upon the Name of Yahweh will be refined with fire that gives life. But those who deny His resurrection were already made dead through the fires of truth because of their rejection of the truth.

Those fires burned the earth. Jesus summoned those bowing before Him to rise above the fires, so they arose in a space between Heaven and earth. After that, the growing pathway I witnessed earlier now stretched downward from Heaven. As it did, a new Earth began to take form. This took place in the same order that God called forth life on the first earth, as recorded in the book of Genesis. Its birthing emerged from blackness as a four-dimensional rendering of an artist's painting of paradise emerges from a black canvas.

Such began the end of Christ's Second Coming. He looked at me. I teared. In that moment all that remained left me with one lingering thought, *Why did I ever worry about the future?* God never left the Throne, just as He never leaves us.

18

THE NEW EARTH

Then I saw "a new heaven and a new earth," for the
first heaven and the first earth had passed away, and
there was no longer any sea. I saw the Holy City, the
new Jerusalem, coming down out of heaven from God,
prepared as a bride beautifully dressed for her husband.
And I heard a loud voice from the throne saying, "Look!
God's dwelling place is now among the people, and
he will dwell with them. They will be his people, and
God himself will be with them and be their God."
—REVELATION 21:1-3 NIV

Light spread forth from the Throne. A breathtaking, cloudless sky formed. Seas stretched beneath the sky and parted to form lands sprouting forth with all kinds of wonderfully colored flora. Trees were adorned with fruits, greener-than-green grass, and bushes that burst forth with flowers. The light came not from the galaxy of the universe—it shined directly from God above.

Planets seemed to move in alignment, as giant particles of dust blew from Heaven. The new Earth was larger in size than several planets put together. Fish of all kinds swam and birds flew and each could traverse from their own environments to others. Heaven was enjoining a new Earth.

Look, the Holy Spirit whispered, as He turned my attention toward Heaven.

Through the darkness and off in the distance, a glorious waterfall emerged that gushed forth with living waters in Heaven and skipped over Heaven down into the world below. Something new now emerged from the living waters.

This thought immediately came to my mind: God is creating a masterpiece from His blank canvas.

In an instant, I moved downward within the wind and settled on the ground.

I have brought you to that which is made new, the Holy Spirit whispered.

I found myself standing in a field of cushiony grass that ran for miles farther than my eyes could see. Within the field stood countless numbers of people walking along golden paths who could not speak to me and I could not speak to them. Instead, the Holy Spirit spoke for them.

They are those who did not die, the Holy Spirit whispered.

Oh, I thought (or knew) these include Enoch and Elijah who did not die and the ones taken into Heaven through what we have termed the Rapture.

I knew that they must have been taken before the angels descended upon the world, or before the shield of righteousness had been lifted. That's because they had already appeared in Heaven, before the final outpouring of the judgment. But these people appeared to be waiting, like those enjoying their time outside of a concert before entering through the gates—only I sensed that the gates of Heaven were opening to a far grander show.

"Turn around," said Jesus, who stood by my side.

When I turned, I beheld the gates of Heaven behind the place where I stood. There were twelve of them and they were adorned with gems that dotted gold and silver facades, and all of them opened outward. Jesus led me and others who were behind me, through the gates and into a lush paradise that was filled with every natural luxury one could imagine. There were warm pools and animals of every kind that frolicked about in harmony with one another. I saw rolling hills, mountains, and vast waters full of fish that one could see with the naked eye. Angels bantered with humans, and songs of joy were sung by many. I could go on and on describing what one would normally ascribe to paradise—only this was far better.

Jesus walked from my side and began climbing a small hill. He stood upon the hill as all looked up, in anticipation of what He would say.

"My beloved bride, welcome to Our Marriage Feast."

Thousands or millions of tables lay before us. Merriment filled the air as angels sang songs of joy. Set before our eyes were mountains of luscious foods of every variety to satisfy anyone's hunger or thirst. I couldn't even see the tabletop because of the abundance of foods and drinks, except for the spaces where one could place their food upon crystal plates or drink from silver mugs. Then it dawned on me that I was hungry for the first time in Heaven—but was I truly in Heaven? Thousands, if not millions mingled, while others sat upon regal-looking throne chairs with red and gold cushions.

"Blessed are those who now attend the Marriage Supper of the Lamb," shouted an angel who stood to the left of Jesus, who was now seated at the head of one of the tables. He was adorned in light and color. There were supernaturally elegant, asymmetric arrangements atop the yellow-laced table. "Let the feast of a year begin."

Welcome to the new Earth, beloved, whispered the Holy Spirit, for now, Heaven has enjoined earth, making all things new.

"Am I dreaming this, Lord?"

No, whispered the Holy Spirit, you are in that which is established in Heaven but is yet to come on earth. Do not share what you have seen until the appointed hour, when I rain forth the blood and fires from the Tabernacle.

How will I know? I whispered in my mind.

When the heavens Storm, beloved, answered the Holy Spirit.

"When the heavens Storm?" I said aloud.

Look to the place above the earth, the Holy Spirit answered. Know the signs. The Word speaks of that which is to come and the heavens declare God's Glory.

"Do you see My Tabernacle, beloved?" Jesus asked, while I journeyed with Him on the new Earth.

Indeed, the Temple I observed only faintly in Heaven now appeared in plain sight and not more than a hundred feet from where I stood amidst the paradise of this new Earth. It had multi-levels of stone, wood, and gems, and an open gateway made of golden gates that led to a long courtyard with floors of red, white, and blue marble that were lined with palm trees. Figures were carved within its wood-paneled walls. As I walked within its gaping corridors, the smell of cherry and oak woods filled my senses. Within the inner chamber, I observed towering crystal walls. Gone was the altar I had seen in Heaven. The presence of God was realized by the sheer Glory that filled the Temple and the new Earth.

But where is the Father? I thought.

Sanctification has come upon this place, the Holy Spirit whispered. Do you not see Him as you see Jesus and as you know Me?

True, I thought. I did sense the Father's presence as real to me as knowing the voice of the Holy Spirit and the appearance of Jesus.

The ordinances of Heaven had been sealed in the center of the Temple square, with a book that lay atop a marble table. Four angels stood at each of the four sides of the table, to guard the Book of Life. I did not observe any humans in the Temple. Perhaps it was because they feasted outside. But the angels walked around its floors above and below as if standing watch. What were they guarding against? No demons existed, and all had been sanctified on this new Earth, so nothing would interfere with the sacredness of the Temple.

"Ah, beloved," said Jesus, who now stood beside me, "the earthly Temple was where My revelation would be received, but here, nothing is hidden from My saints. Are you not still the Temple of My Spirit? So why do you question the Father's presence in you and in this Temple? Surely, you should know that My will has been fully established on this Earth. You desire to see the Father, so look no further. I, the One who is with you now, am He" (John 4:26).

Oh my, I thought. The Father stood with me, not in the grandiose appearance I had beheld in Heaven. Rather, He appeared in the flesh within a body as tangible as mine. I cannot fully describe His face or figure because His visage almost defied explanation. It would be like defining the embodiment of perfection, encircled within the brilliant Glory of God that masked His appearance as larger than life itself. His skin still looked the same brown as when Jesus appeared to me in Heaven, but His fuzzy hair was pure white, and his previously aquamarine eyes flamed with the intensity of the sun and the softness of a soothingly warm afternoon. As I glanced at His feet, I saw that the fires of Heaven had burnished them with a chestnut color that still glowed. God had brought His glory from Heaven to earth in form and impartation because His Light illuminated all the new Earth.

At one point, I questioned whether He was the Father, thinking maybe He was Jesus. This figure appeared regal yet warm—indescribable beyond words. All I could think about while in His presence was: *So this is the Father I always yearned to know, personal and mighty, tender and strong.* He loved me so infinitely, beyond comprehension.

Then clearly, Jesus, the One who was familiar to me, stood by my side and hugged me tightly. He seemed to have walked through the Father in some kind of symbiotic formation that to this day I cannot adequately describe. No creation in all of time can even approximate their harmonious nature.

I asked, "But why is the Temple here and the Glory so strong here, Lord? And what are the angels doing?"

"Beloved," Jesus answered, "I had sealed the written Word. Now I seal the words spoken to My beloved. All that you hear now comes directly from Me. And this Temple is not guarded by My angels. It is revered by them because it contains My letters to those I most esteem in My Kingdom."

Then it struck me. The angels respected each of us who received Christ as our Lord and Savior. The angels could only *reject* God, but humans who are made in God's image were made to *accept* God. I now remembered God's Word: *"For if their rejection brought reconciliation to the world, what will their acceptance be but life from the dead?"* (Romans 11:15).

"We, not the angels, were Your ambassadors in the world," I said, remembering the Scriptures: *"There is no greater honor"* (2 Corinthians 5:20; John 15:13 NIV).

"And so," Jesus said, "in this Temple I honor you and all My saints, for in this place I established My righteousness, and in your heart you accepted My righteousness. You are made righteous through Me."

I heard a heavenly version of Psalm 24:3-5 being sung by the angels in the Temple:

Who may go up on the mountain of the Lord?

Who may stand in his holy Temple?
Only those with clean hands and pure hearts,
who have not worshipped idols,
who have not made promises in the name of a false god.
They will receive a blessing from the Lord;
the God who saves them will declare them right.

"Praise be the Lord God of High," an angel shouted.

And then all the voices in the Temple enjoined the angel's words. Again, I realized that the Temple did not only represent God's presence, but God's presence also made the Temple holy, and the Glory of God made each of His beloved children holy. Here, freed of our earthly bodies, we realize the fullness of God's holiness, to experience holiness on the new Earth, as it is in Heaven.

"That was the prayer You gave Your disciples, Lord—'thy will be done on earth as it is in Heaven,' and this place is the fulfillment of that prayer," I said (Matthew 6:9-13).

Jesus smiled—oh, that wonderful smile, so kind and knowing and affirming. I so missed that smile after my return, and I so very much miss that smile upon writing this account. But do you know the good news? Just as I thought of Jesus's smile and how much I missed it, He gave me a vision of His smile, even as I sit in the office and write this. Now, that's Love.

Thank You for that, my Lord, I said, and smiled in return.

While in the Temple, I said to Jesus: "You said that I am returning, but my physical brain on earth couldn't possibly tell what I have seen in this place or in the place before…"

Jesus immediately took my hand and walked me outside of the Temple. Then within the garden outside of the Temple, Jesus placed His right hand over my eyes as the Holy Spirit blew into my chest. When Jesus removed His hand from my eyes, I found myself hovering over one of the portals I had previously seen. Next I saw Jesus's visage before me. His eyelids drooped. His eyes were downcast and His slanted eyebrows arrested my feelings of joy.

He stepped back and reached His arms toward me, and I moved forward to grasp His hands, but then I felt as if I should not touch His hands. Instead, I looked down at His hands and again saw the scars at the base of His palms.

"Fear not, My child, for in due season I will reveal My timing for you. This was our time and I will direct your steps. Remember the butterfly."

Jesus waved His right hand in the air and formed a circle with His arm. A multitude of butterflies flittered above my head, and each adorned a different variety of colors. One settled on my right shoulder. I stood perfectly still and breathed in the sweet aroma of gardenias' closing my eyes, instead of darkness I saw the Light of Jesus in blended shades of whites and blues.

"What do you see?" Jesus asked.

"I see You, I suppose. I don't see Your form; I just see Your Light."

"You see My Light amid darkness, beloved. Know this, no darkness shall prevail against you because I am with you always."

I opened my eyes to see the butterfly that rested on my shoulder. It gently waved its wings before my eyes. It stayed there for the longest time until I reached my hand toward the butterfly, and it rested on my forehand, and then it turned to sparkles of dust that seemed to enter through my skin, sending a warmth from my hand to my chest, to my head, and finally to my feet.

Indeed, wisdom would give me the assurance of what is right, and the right thing to do.

"Beloved, Truth shall be your guide. My Righteousness shall be your protector. My Word shall give you comfort. Faith in Me shall guard your understanding. And victory shall be gained through My Spirit. Fear not."

I started tearing up and my chest heaved as I cleared the tears from my eyes.

"Oh God…promise me I will come back here, please."

He nodded. "Most assuredly, I will say on that day, 'Well done My good and faithful servant.' I will never leave you."

"Don't…let…me…go," I sobbed.

"Never," He responded.

Then He stepped forward and hugged me so tightly and so gently at the same time, as only Jesus could do. Finally, He released me and stepped back. I heard the angels singing around me as a choir sang a song unfamiliar, yet altogether enchanting:

> *Abide with me; fast falls the eventide;*
> *The darkness deepens; Lord, with me abide;*
> *When other helpers fail and comforts flee,*
> *Help of the helpless, oh, abide with me.*[1]

At first I thought the lyrics strange for angels to sing, but they were beautiful, comforting, and glorious en masse. What I heard was sorrowful and longing in their rephrase, so beautifully sung with purpose, as a prayerful request to my spirit.

Remember beloved, the Holy Spirit whispered, *I go with you wherever you go, and I am He, the One who always comforts you. Trust Me.*

I could hear the voice of Jesus through the Holy Spirit—He made a Sssssssshhhhhhhh sound, like the sound of static that was both audible and a feeling, but without words. At that moment, I felt myself glide down a tunnel that felt as if I was on a slide. The farther away from Heaven I went, the more frightened I became because I knew my destination. Never had I felt such separation before. My true home was behind me.

Note

1. The song "Abide with Me" was written in 1847 by Henry Francis Lyte; Timelesstruths.org; accessed May 17, 2023.

19

THE RETURN

*Above all, you must understand that in the last days
scoffers will come, scoffing and following their own
evil desires. They will say, "Where is this 'coming' he
promised? Ever since our ancestors died, everything
goes on as it has since the beginning of creation."*
—2 PETER 3:3-4 NIV

No longer could I hear the Sssssssshhhhhhhh of rustling waters. Jesus spoke only as the Holy Spirit, in that sense of knowing that resonated within my heart. As the slide slowed me back into my body, I began to sense pain, foul smells, and a feeling as if I had awakened into a recurring nightmare. Now, a new heaviness and pain in my chest contrasted so miserably to the way my body had felt in the presence of Jesus.

"Mr. Kay, can you hear me?" said a woman's voice.

As my eyes opened, I heard a couple who were singing a prayerful song, in perfect harmony:

Abide with me; fast falls the eventide;
The darkness deepens; Lord, with me abide;
When other helpers fail and comforts flee,
Help of the helpless, oh, abide with me.
Swift to its close ebbs out life's little day;
Earth's joys grow dim, its glories pass away;

Change and decay in all around I see—
O Thou who changest not, abide with me.
I fear no foe, with Thee at hand to bless;
Ills have no weight, and tears no bitterness;
Where is death's sting? Where, grave, thy victory?
I triumph still, if Thou abide with me.
Hold Thou Thy cross before my closing eyes;
Shine through the gloom and point me to the skies;
Heav'n's morning breaks, and earth's vain shadows flee;
In life, in death, O Lord, abide with me.
Abide with me, abide with me.

You may know this song by the title, "Abide with Me." Only years later would the Holy Spirit remind of this song in full. What immediately struck me as I lay in that hospital bed with tubes and wires strapped to me like a limp puppet, was that the couple were singing the exact song that had echoed in the chambers of Heaven just before my resuscitation.

For thirty minutes and forty-nine seconds, my body lay dead, according to the monitor. Nobody understands how long I may have been unconscious, but already the red blood cells had been sinking and pooling in various parts of my body, causing the stiffness of early rigor mortis.

My foggy brain could not grasp the irony of hearing the angels in Heaven singing the exact same song as the couple who stood by my bedside. Later, I would come to understand that the prayerful song of that couple was ushered unto God's Throne Room as the couple prayed for my return. And that same song was enjoined in Heaven as an answer to prayer.

For weeks, I couldn't walk without assistance. My lungs, heart, and vascular system had been damaged and a small bleed in my brain persisted for days. Slowly, I would follow a physical therapy routine as I pondered the idea that *dead people usually never return.*

But after my return and during the period when my speech slurred and I couldn't move well, the contrast between the space of Heaven and the disturbing space in which I now found myself on earth, left me confused. I asked myself, "Why? Just why?"

I could still smell the faint but sweet fragrances of Heaven, which sharply contrasted the hospital disinfectants in my room. If the heavens speak of God's Glory, then surely this place spoke of humanity's lowliness. But at least I knew that I could no longer doubt the sovereignty of God or His kindness or unyielding love. I could not walk to the bathroom but I could soar in remembrance of how Jesus and I had glided over hilltops and valleys as easily as the water that flowed through them.

I remembered the butterfly. Moment by moment I would walk in my purpose. For now, that meant a smile to others through the pain of recovery while attempting to walk again. When my wife first met me after my mind-blowing experience, I said this to her with understated enthusiasm:

"I met Jesus."

I could say no more without tears flooding down my cheeks. Besides, in no way could I adequately explain what had happened. What followed would be a change in my attitude and empathy toward others. I could feel what other people felt, like never before.

Having trained people in the corporate world for much of my career, twice I had taken a "versatility" assessment to determine my level of empathy for others. That took place before I visited Heaven with Jesus. My scores had ranked toward the bottom of the mean or average, which determined that I lacked empathy during my BH (Before Heaven) life. Months after my recovery, I took the same validated assessment multiple times. I now scored at the top of the spectrum, meaning that my post-Heaven empathy had exponentially increased—along with my faith.

God had implanted within me the imprint of His love for others. I now saw people in a way similar to how I beheld them through my spirit in Heaven. Now I could see their essence, not just their outward expressions. However, this did not make me an "enlightened" person. My flawed brain still filtered life through my programmed tissue more than my Christ-controlled spirit.

But always—always, the lingering effect remained of having once been freed to think spiritually through the mind of Christ. The apostle Paul wrote things that often reminded me of who I am and who each of God's children truly are. We are orphaned spirits in a physical world.

Recovery took weeks in the hospital. One day my new boss with Johnson & Johnson called me, completely unaware of my debilitating condition. She said:

"Can you fly to New York City next week for a surgical conference? We'd like to introduce you to everyone. They're excited to meet you." She spoke in an enthusiastic British accent, in contrast to my weakened voice.

I politely declined, given my condition. But more than a month later, I started to travel. Renee accompanied me on some of the trips, in the event of a relapse. My first solo trip happened in Seattle, Washington, as I limped and stopped every few steps to drop my luggage and suck in air. When the representative for that area led me into the operating room of the hospital to observe a cardiovascular case, I thought of asking for a chair. I worried that there was no way I could stand for four hours. Instead, I took breaks in the hallway, looking out the window toward the cloudy blue sky as I thought, *Lord, this is so hard and I need Your strength so desperately*.

Looking back, I wonder how I endured the strenuous, long-hours traveling across the nation and internationally. The answer should have been obvious. God was strong in my weakness. I threw up numerous times on a flight to Dallas, Texas, where I was to attend a minimally-invasive training of cardiovascular surgeons. Imagine me rushing out of my airline seat as my stomach insisted I be first in line, lest I share last night's barbeque dinner with those patiently waiting in line for the lavatory. This happened at least a dozen times. So after a very long day of training surgeons and proctoring (helping with) scheduled cardiovascular cases in Dallas, my nausea eased into extreme fatigue.

I still had to catch a flight to Sacramento, California, to help with a 6 a.m. heart case. The surgeon was practicing our company's procedure on a patient for the very first time. Thank God, the case proceeded successfully before I had to hop another flight to another surgical training in Los Angeles. This time, I temporarily lost my vision during a migraine headache. Thank God again, that we did not lose one single patient, despite a number of complex cases including patients whose life expectancy included the probability of death.

I prayed over every case. The surreal moments seeing a patient's exposed heart caused me to marvel at God's most wonderful creation. Heaven never left me, and even the smallest details now seemed so profound.

This went on for several years, while in the back of my mind I knew that the damaged valves throughout my circulatory system might result in cardiac arrest—death. But that possibility did not really phase me because I knew my ultimate destination. Still, my doctors told me that I should quit my job or I might die (again).

I called that a "win-win" situation, although my family might not agree.

Each night while I was out of town, I scribed my experiences and corroborated them with Scripture. I searched the Bible looking for any contradictions but found none. At no time did I ever intend to share my experience publicly. My experience in Heaven was mine alone—or so I thought. Besides, who would believe such an astounding experience that I could not fully explain through my physical brain—even if my spirit mind in Heaven knew the meaning behind every detail?

Yet, those recollections of Heaven remained vivid within my memory to the remarkable effect that I could recall the minutia of Heaven even years later. Compare that to how I could forget my earthly experiences that happened just days before. A key lesson for me is that the spirit mind assimilates the ethereal. But filtered through the brain, fleshly experiences get lost within the mind's tissues between the synapses, stored memories, and interpretations.

However, the spirit logs everything that is of Christ and remembers heavenly experiences forever. The memories and numerous sensations I experienced in Heaven somehow translated into my body as the knowledge that Heaven is more real than this world.

Returning to my flesh and re-experiencing all the defiled aspects of this world allowed the realization that I was now extraordinarily different. Heaven felt like home. This world felt like I had returned to a musty, rat-infested house. Still, I felt a compassion for God's children and a new appreciation of every living thing that had not existed in me before Heaven. The cliché to "stop and smell the roses" bore fruit in me as I soaked in the sights, smells, and sentience of all of God's creations.

In my spirit, I felt the abuse that triggered abusers, which made me less judgmental. I sensed people's overwhelming need for God, including my own, which caused me to pray unceasingly. And I found myself in constant conversations with the Holy Spirit—even over the most trivial of matters.

What should I do today? I would ask the Holy Spirit in thought.

Do you see that person over there, beloved? The Holy Spirit would whisper to my soul.

Yeah, I do, and I'm supposed to pray for that person, aren't I? I asked.

Yes, he doesn't know Me, whispered the Holy Spirit. Silently pray that he might turn his attention toward Me.

After praying, I could sense a shift within the person. Not physically—I sensed it in my spirit. On more than one occasion, the person's countenance would even show something like a smile or an inquisitive look. Some people would look at me as if they intuitively knew I had somehow instigated a change. Each time this happened, I recalled the shift in Heaven I had felt whenever people prayed.

Prayers sent up from earth to Heaven could be seen when I was in Heaven. They caused a supernatural move of God that rolled out of the Throne of God like waves of pronouncements that flowed in supernatural colors. On earth, prayers now felt to me like a bolt of *aufklärung,* which is a German term that explains inspiration that is felt within. An example is how we respond to the inspiring music of Mozart, the poetry of Robert Browning, or the *le soufflé createur* (French for creative inspiration) of Monet's artistry when it rouses the soul.

We can become so accustomed to the camera's eye in this world that we miss the subtleties of what lies beyond the lens of our own point of view. We see the seen but not the unseen, yet both are equally real. I suppose sin and suffering can do that to a person, but Heaven changes our perspective.

I would have to deal with the aftermath of my health crisis, such as the way my blood pooled within my circulatory system, the valves that were damaged by blood clots or the effects of having sepsis that had damaged my organs.[1] But none of these ailments rivaled the pain of living in a world that is largely alienated from God.

Upon my return to this world, I initially felt that I was living more in Heaven than I was on earth. I felt like an alien in this world and avoided as many worldly experiences as possible. I considered them to be trite interferences to my intimate time with God.

At the same time, I felt love for others more profoundly than ever. Gradually, and sadly, the freshness of God's intimacy in Heaven faded into the coarse nature of this world. Once again, I felt the world's toxic infection settle into my soul. I was becoming more flesh and blood again and less spiritually inclined. I kept trying to hold on to the effects of Heaven but felt them slipping away. The vivid memories served less to assuage me than they were reminders of what I had lost.

However, what still lingered in my mind was a part of my experience that defied explanation. I knew that my heavenly experiences with Jesus as we traveled in paradise clearly ministered to me, but that Storm meant something entirely different. The Storm signaled something prophetic that would be established on the earth during the end times.

I also remembered what the Holy Spirit had said to me. He told me that a signal would be given to me that would trigger when I could share the meaning of the Storm. Even so, I did not intend on sharing any of my experiences in Heaven, except with a handful of people who were closest to me.

Most of all, I yearned to experience Jesus again, the way I had in Heaven. And just like the gracious God I witnessed in Heaven, Jesus would reveal Himself to me on earth, one more time.

Note

1. I suffered sepsis from Methicillin-resistant Staphylococcus aureus or (MRSA), a potentially fatal bacterium.

20

MY REUNION WITH JESUS IN TAHOE

Then Jesus said, "Did I not tell you that if you
believe, you will see the glory of God?"
—JOHN 11:40 NIV

I prayed for some explanation from the Holy Spirit as to the meaning behind the Storm, but He always remained peculiarly silent on the subject. One event would change that. I joined an expedition to Lake Tahoe with some men from church for a retreat. Our family owned a cabin about a mile down the street from the lake, where I and three others would stay. My friend George owned a gargantuan house that would house everyone else and that overlooked the lake and the surrounding snowcapped mountains.

We gathered one evening to pray beside the seven-foot-tall stone fireplace that burned with an unusual intensity. That night, the cold January wind rattled the many frost-covered windows. At first we prayed openly for whatever the Holy Spirit placed upon our hearts. Then the prayers with the Lord turned silent.

All this time, I prayed in the spirit in an unknown language called "tongues," as in the Bible. Tongues are supernatural prayer languages that are given as gifts to believers, and languages that are only understood between our spirit and the Holy Spirit. No one, including demons and God's angels can understand what I spoke in prayer, including me. Only God heard and knew my prayers. The apostle Paul wrote about this spiritual gift and said that he desired for everyone to speak in tongues, but that he preferred believers to have the gift of prophecy (1 Corinthians 14:5).

After a period of prayer, I drifted into a place beyond my reasoning mind, to a place not described by physical attributes. I found myself consumed with absolute peace, comfort, and love. My eyes closed. I sensed the presence of God within a faint orb of reddish-orange light and nothing else.

Great to be with You again, my Lord, I thought.

Within a space of time that seemed to last only a minute, I soaked in the deep, internal space of stillness—awake, peaceful, peaked stillness—that coursed through me. Later, I supposed that this might have felt similar to how a baby feels in the womb. There was a consummate quietness and a deep, complete awareness of God's presence. I was in a place that appeared like the beautiful, dancing waves of the northern lights.

Once again, I felt full of life—God's light of life spoken about in the book of John (John 1:4-9). My awareness of God during these moments was non-conceptual, without definition yet completely known within my spirit. For a brief moment, I was completely walled off from any sound in the room and separate from any mind clutter.

I was home again with God, isolated from the world. God gifted me during this time with an awareness of His embrace. I can only surmise that during this moment between us that God embraced my spirit wholly and apart from anything in or of this world.

I awoke rather suddenly. As my eyes opened, I felt as if my soul had been shocked by electricity of a thousand volts. None of this energy felt physical but my soul was on fire! I slowly stood up and staggered like a drunken man without inhibitions except for a consuming desire to speak forth words that came out of my mouth with uncharacteristic loudness and conviction.

Never in my life did I feel so bold, so invigorated, or so unhinged, in contrast to my rather tailored, conservative, and introverted nature. I looked at the fire in the massive fireplace, partly with my physical eyes and partly with my spiritual eyes. Next, through my spiritual eyes, I saw the flames reach across the room and wash over everyone without burning anyone. At this point, I felt I was in the spirit more than the physical world. I turned to a thirtyish man and pointed at him.

"The Lord God Almighty has delivered you from the abuse inflicted on you as a child and you are freed in the name of Jesus Christ!"

The man fell to his knees and began sobbing as other men around him placed their hands on him in an effort to comfort him. Then I turned to another man and pointed to him.

"Yeshua says to you, do not wait any longer for the calling to be released in you—no longer are you a part-time servant. Go and prophesy and teach full-time."

The man slowly caved to the ground and lay there, completely still. Then I turned to another man and pointed to him.

"The Lord God has told you to stop, and you know of what I am speaking—no longer do that which He has told you *not* to do!"

The man stood there as his jaw dropped as far as humanly possible. His eyes opened so wide that even his pupils seemed to bulge.

These declarations continued for several minutes as my reserved nature had been totally obliterated. Never in a zillion years would I normally have spoken like a wild man—speaking prophetically and with healing to these men, many of whom were complete strangers to me.

Later I would learn that the young man had indeed been abused as a child. Since that night, he felt free to live with confidence and without harmful thoughts. The other man confessed to an affair. Another man over whom I had spoken, started a deliverance ministry and taught in churches. Some of the prophecies were later revealed to me as true. Because several of the men were strangers, some left the retreat without confirming what was spoken and I never heard from them again. Healings of different varieties did occur, both mental and physical. But what happened next had never happened before, and has never happened since.

After speaking declaratively—no doubt surprising all of the men in the room—one of the men who knew me said, "Who are you?" My body went limp as I staggered and swayed around the room. My speech became slurred and I rambled on with words while laughing at the silliest things.

"Hey Dan—God loves you so, so much!" I said, in my drunken state.

"Hey brother—keep the faith!" I said to another man in the room.

The owner of the house told me that I lay on the floor for over *forty minutes*. During that time, I was prostrate on the floor as the other men bantered around the room. Some verbally prayed for others while I remained oblivious to it all. To me, it seemed as if I was communing with God for only a minute.

The drunken stupor continued for several minutes until the three men staying at our house in Tahoe needed to carry me out to my car. "Big Dan," as we affectionately called our tall brother, drove the three-mile distance to our cabin on the icy roads, as I sang whatever worshipful lyrics I could remember from popular Christian songs—surely as off-key as it was heartfelt.

After walking me up the stairs of the house, the three men carried me into the lower bedroom and placed me on the bed. They asked if I would be okay, to which I replied with laughter.

"Of course, I'm with Jesus!"

Then they walked upstairs to the bedrooms on the second floor. Fully cogent and pleasantly imbided in the Spirit without any alcohol in my body, I looked on either side of my bed only to see seven-foot-tall angels standing guard on either side of the headboard.

Okay, I thought, *I've entered the "Twilight Zone."*

As a scientifically minded person not prone to fanciful thinking, my first thought was that I was dreaming, but nothing appeared dreamlike. This was clearly a holy apparition.

"Whoa…you dudes look awesome!" I said.

The angels stood straight and stared ahead while appearing like opaque ice sculptures. The left hand of one angel and the right hand of the other grasped silver rods with spear tips that reached slightly above their heads. They looked straight toward the opposite wall. Upon their heads were helmets that fit snuggly over the top and sides of their heads. They donned armor like what I beheld when I saw the angels battling the demons as I rose toward Heaven. They looked regal and had humanlike features, with long noses, square jaws, and stern eyes. I wanted their attention but they would have none of it. The angel on my left spoke slowly and with a deep voice:

"Speak not to us when the Lord is in your midst."

I knew then that I was on sacred ground, in a place apart from the world. I was somewhere between the realms of Heaven and earth but the room looked the same. Nothing appeared different to me except for the two towering angels on either side of me.

I didn't see Jesus but I felt Him. We spoke congenially, as best friends at a reunion. In my spirit, I felt that the Holy Spirit, my constant Companion, somehow deferred to Jesus. I know that may sound strange, since the two operate as One. But I walked with Jesus again, although the surroundings appeared far different from those in Heaven. Instead of seeing glorious stones shining like pure crystals, I looked at the room's weathered carpet and off-white-colored walls.

Instead of meadows covered with flocks and valleys mantled with grain, the faded trees outside the window bore no leaves. Instead of the cleansing waters that streamed from Jesus and revitalized everything and everyone who drank from them, I turned on the faucet and tin-tasting water poured out. Instead of being bathed in the otherworldly glow of God's light, the light bulbs from above barely broke the darkness. I could not smell the fragrances of spices, fruits, and floral perfumes as I had in Heaven. Instead, I smelled the musty odor in the room. All of that was okay though, as I communed with Jesus again. Nothing else mattered.

"It's so good to be with You this way again," I said.

"Beloved, I never left you," Jesus answered.

I spoke verbally, but not Jesus. After dancing in the room, I lay back on the bed and closed my eyes. Then I heard the soft, entrancing sound of the voice of love, my Savior, my Lord, dear Jesus:

"Why did you miss Me?" Jesus asked in my spirit.

Just for a moment I thought that I had actually heard His voice. I felt that the answer would have been obvious to Him but then I recalled that Jesus never asks a question to learn the answer. Instead, He asks the question to bring the answer to us.

"It's not the same, Lord," I replied. "It was so easy in Heaven."

"So, stop thinking with your mind and think with your spirit," He said.

Bing...Jesus always strikes at the core of everything, I thought.

"Because the core of who you are is Mine," Jesus said after hearing my thoughts.

"I don't like being in this world anymore," I said.

"Then don't think of yourself as being in the world," Jesus said.

Our conversation seemed glib but there was a depth to the merry nature of our talk.

"Remember how much fun it was to be with family in Heaven, Lord? It had a different feel to it."

"I know," said Jesus. "Heaven does that to people, so dwell on the things of Heaven, My beloved."

It dawned on me that Jesus was teaching me as we exchanged pleasantries—even as I brushed my teeth. Jesus knew my struggles readjusting to the world, and this brief manifestation was His healing gift to me.

"This toothpaste tastes foul," I said.

"I didn't invent it," Jesus said, followed by my chuckle.

Again, our conversation was like two friends chumming together. Now that I have processed our conversation, I think that the reason we spoke so casually and entreatingly as compared to the holiness spoken in Heaven, was due to my spiritual inebriation. The lack of depth of everything on earth is incomparable to Heaven. Because I was not completely in the spirit at this point, my mind brought me to trivial matters. My thoughts were not fully controlled by my spirit the way they were in Heaven.

I was thinking about the lonely times I felt separated from God, and I wondered why He chose this time and place for what was perhaps a once-in-a-lifetime visitation on earth.

"Why?" I asked.

"Ask not why, beloved, but ask what you will do with this time."

"Hmm?"

"Why do you hear Me now, this way, but not always?" He asked.

I asked the Holy Spirit to reveal the answer to me since I had no clue as to what Jesus wanted me to say. Then I realized that I was in a type of "transfiguration moment." In the New Testament, the transfiguration of Jesus was an event where Jesus is transfigured and becomes radiant in Glory upon a mountain. Jesus took three of His disciples (Peter, James, and John) up on a mountain, where Moses and Elijah appeared and Jesus was transfigured. His face and clothing became dazzlingly bright. It was a period in history when Heaven came to earth in a small space and where Jesus could speak to His children (Moses and Elijah) who had already passed into Heaven.

In my case, I believe that because I had been to Heaven before, somehow the Glory of Heaven enabled me to have a similar kind of conversation. Please know that I am no Moses or Elijah. I am probably unworthy even to wash their feet! But as Jesus said to me, Heaven changes a person. Perhaps Heaven consecrates a space for those who carry His Glory from Heaven to this world—not because we are special, but because even a remnant of Heaven enables a person to live more confidently in Christ. This is especially true for those of us who have tasted of death before Heaven. So-called "seers," or others who claim to have visions of Heaven, have not been fully freed of their body and brain.

I thought about the question Jesus asked me. I answered Him in a rather flippant manner: "Because I'm drunk with your Spirit?"

Jesus chuckled. "Ah—you let go." Jesus said.

"Yes…yes, it's that easy—letting go?" I asked.

A warmth came into my cheeks and I just knew that Jesus was spiritually cupping my cheeks as He had done in Heaven. I gave thanks to the Holy Spirit in advance of knowing the answer to my question. Then I knew the answer, without Jesus needing to say anything.

"It's that easy and that hard." I answered my own question. "It is easy through faith but hard through doubt, and this world breeds doubt in place of trusting You, Lord. Those first two words You spoke to me—'Trust Me...'"

"Now you know why I said those words to you. They are the most difficult and the easiest words to abide by in the world," Jesus said. "Think not with your understanding, beloved, but trust in Me."

I immediately thought of the Scripture: *"Trust in the Lord with all your heart and lean not on your own understanding; in all your ways submit to him, and he will make your paths straight"* (Proverbs 3:5-6 NIV).

"You had to make me spiritually drunk to know that?" Again, I knew the answer before Jesus could reply, because wisdom spoke the truth. I suddenly remembered the butterfly.

Just to clarify, being drunk in the Spirit releases freedom, whereas being drunk with alcohol or drugs enslaves a person. The Holy Spirit brings wisdom and the freedom to commune with God, but worldly drunkenness brings a temporary fix that calls for another fix and another and so forth. Drunkenness in the Spirit of God brings life. Drunkenness in the world brings death.

I was drunk in the Spirit because I surrendered my thinking to God and fully trusted in Him for that moment in time. God honored that trust by imparting His presence to me once again—bringing Heaven to earth, if only for a fleeting moment in eternity.

Then I remembered the Storm, when Heaven would come to earth forever. I saw it, but why did I see it in Heaven? I asked Jesus that question within my thoughts.

"In due season," Jesus said. "I will give you a sign and when I do, what you saw shall be upon the world."

That was fine with me because I trust Him.

Jesus and I spoke throughout the night—often about the silliest things. We laughed about bugs being beautiful and ugly at the same time; about the foolishness of people inventing "religious" beliefs out of thin air; and how for ages, humankind has tried to disprove God. I had done this in my early years as an agnostic, to no avail. We even laughed about the taste of broccoli. I asked Him:

"Why couldn't You make it taste like chocolate, Lord?"

Every silly question required no answer, but Jesus often chuckled with me. The answer always ended with the same knowing:

"Trust Me."

Before our conversation ended in the early part of the morning, Jesus said:

"Tell them not to ignore Me. I am in their midst. Too often they care more about the things of the world than they do for that which is of Me."

Then Jesus and the angels disappeared.

At the time, I had no forum through which to communicate Jesus's message. The pastor of my church of about sixty people only asked me once to do something—usher Sunday service. Later, Jesus would give me a voice to speak with others. No doubt He knew that His message for others would not go void, since He knew you would be reading or listening to this story.

In the morning, I went downstairs feeling refreshed and invigorated, despite a lack of sleep, and yet I felt as though I had slept a full eight hours.

"You seemed really drunk last night, but I know there wasn't any alcohol," said Big Dan, as he chuckled. He continued, "The things you said—it wasn't like you."

"We heard you talking downstairs," said Mark.

I now vividly remember all my conversations with my friend Mark Crouse, unlike the other conversations I had with the men at the retreat. Only later would I know why. Mark died of pancreatic cancer years later. I think that Mark's presence in Heaven today somehow illuminated our earthly conversations. Heaven does that to people. Those who have returned (like me) sense that Heaven is more real than this world. For those who are in Heaven now, the memory of their life on earth is softened in the light of how they now exist in Heaven. Heaven washes us anew, allowing us to see people in a way similar to how Jesus sees them. That explains why the memory is often kinder—it culls out the bad and remembers God as God remembers us.

But would anyone believe this? I thought. My answer at the time was "no." I was content with keeping my treasure to myself. For fourteen years, I shared nothing about my experiences in Heaven with anyone but a handful of people.

The morning after my reunion with Jesus in Lake Tahoe, the four of us munched cereal in our cabin. I could drive my car at this point, but Mark volunteered to drive just to ensure we didn't drive over a snowy embankment. A pleasant hangover settled over my being like a faint anesthetic, although I was fully cognizant and alert. I found myself in the most relaxed state I could ever remember in my earthly life. Its bliss allowed me to enjoy the wondrous variety of falling snowflakes that melted on the windshield, and the pleasant swoosh-swoosh-swoosh sounds of the windshield wipers.

Rolling down the car window, I could clearly see the white-blanketed mountains hugging the deep blue Lake Tahoe. The air felt warm as the sun kissed the lake's rippling surface. The sight meshed with the pristine smell of air that had been cleansed by the snowstorm the night before. I listened carefully to the chorus of chirping birds as they welcomed the sun's warmth to expose areas where they might feed. Everything felt deeper, richer, more real, and more precious. I had tasted of Heaven again.

I quietly praised the Lord for giving me this much-needed respite in the wake of my sad return to this world, after the Glory of Heaven. I suppose Jesus knew that I needed that special time with Him, in a place somewhere between Heaven and earth. The visit healed my soul and returned the joy of Heaven to my heart.

After entering my friend George's house, I briefly took note of the stares from the other men who were in the living room to my left, before rushing downstairs to call Renee.

"I met Jesus again, honey," I told her.

The afterglow must have passed to her from me, because she sighed before saying, "Oh my, you needed that. Tell me about it."

I told her of the casual conversations with Jesus and the angels on either side of the bed that stood guard. I also shared about the time before with the men when I acted like a madman, declaring words over them and how I felt a little embarrassed now as I remembered my excessive boldness—even though I knew in my soul that my actions were just.

"God gave you those words," Renee said, knowing that I needed some comfort before facing the men again.

"I need to come home," I said to Renee. "I just need to come home."

"I agree," she said. "Come home. We miss you and I want to hear all about it in person."

I gave my car keys to Mark so he could drive my car and the other two men back to San Diego, while I caught a cab to the airport in Reno, Nevada. I just could not sleep another night in that bedroom at our cabin, knowing the profundity of what happened there the night before and throughout the early morning. I just needed that memory to linger for a little while longer—just a bit longer, before the world invaded me again.

As a renewed vigor overcame me, I began to think about the Storm I beheld in Heaven and what it meant for the world today. I needed answers.

21

THE REVEAL

The mystery was made known to me by revelation.
—EPHESIANS 3:3 ESV

Normalcy soon took the place of the supernatural as I eased into the routine of life. Renee, Ryan, Annie, and I continued attending the church in Encinitas, California (north of San Diego) that had prayed for me during my hospital stay. The pastor asked me to walk to the front as a living testimony of the power of prayer. As I stood before the congregation of about two hundred people, I began to collapse from the fatigue caused by a pooling of blood within the damaged right leg where the blood clots had begun. But none of that really mattered, considering my encounters both in Heaven and in that bedroom in Lake Tahoe.

My pastor and mentor in the San Francisco Bay Area, Rich Marshall, asked to meet me during one of his speaking engagements in San Diego. During dinner, he invited me to be interviewed on his *God@Work* television program on GodTV in Orlando, Florida, because I had authored several self-help books and occasionally authored articles for business publications.

I had authored the book, *The Power to Thrive.* It was based on my thirty-year study to determine the skills for thriving in life. Rich asked me to share about how to bring one's ministry into one's career and life. Rich authored a book by the same title, about how God uses "priests" and "kings"—meaning pastoral staff and lay Christians (or simply Christians) operating in their gifts at the workplace. Rich also happened to be one of a handful of people who knew about my experiences in Heaven. Just before airing the episode, Rich asked me if he could ask me about my afterlife encounter on the show. I thought, *Well, Lord, if this is what You want, then I can't say no.*

Sure enough, after discussing the extensive research about thriving that I wrote about in my new book, he asked the question. I started to cry while briefly sharing my account. After the interview, Rich jokingly said, "Don't worry, Randy, you just spoke to about three hundred million people." That was it—the proverbial "cat" was out of the bag.

On the return flight to San Diego, I began sipping on my apple-cranberry juice when I suddenly heard that now-familiar voice from the Holy Spirit. He spoke in the same silent whisper that I had experienced in Heaven—the self-evident awareness of God's declaration, in a supernatural voice that cannot be denied as a pronouncement of His truth and direction.

I want you to record our special time together, He said to my spirit.

I began writing a manuscript in a notebook that was about turning suffering to joy through Christ. I was using what I learned about thriving in life and briefly mentioned my time in Heaven. A book was eventually published, titled *Dying to Meet Jesus.* Some of the comments that came from people who read the book went something like this:

"I wanted to hear more about your encounter in Heaven."

So, I authored *Revelations from Heaven*, which summarizes thirty-one revelations I had gleaned from Heaven and mentions numerous experiences I had while journeying with Jesus.

The popularity of *Revelations from Heaven* brought me before several Christian audiences. I talked about the book as I flew to television stations and spoke at various venues around the nation. I am what can be called a "reluctant messenger," since I never desired for my intimacy with God in Heaven to be made public. As my personality leans toward being introverted and private, for the longest time speaking publicly about something this immensely private proved profoundly difficult for me. Going public defied both my nature and my desires.

My friend and publisher, Shaun Tabatt, started marketing *Dying to Meet* Jesus at Chosen Publishing before moving to Destiny Image Publishers. After that, he asked to publish *Revelations from Heaven* at his new publishing house. He also asked me if I would like to do a joint podcast that we would eventually title *Two Christian Dudes*. Our first interviews were about near-death experiences (NDEs), to coincide with the launch of *Revelations from Heaven*. Our plan was to record several NDE interviews before transitioning to episodes about spiritual warfare.

Shaun continued recording shows for his popular podcast, *The Shaun Tabatt Show*. At the same time, we recorded *Two Christian Dudes*. Meanwhile, I received several messages from people who claimed to have experienced an NDE. Separately, Shaun interviewed a variety of authors and experts about spiritual warfare on his show.

I prayed for God to release His direction for Renee and me. About ten years prior, a prophet had placed his hands over Renee's and my clasped hands to impart a special ministry calling. He said:

"When you pray together, God will speak to you directly from His Throne and you will see miracles, power, and direction for your lives."

He also said that we would serve as messengers to help usher forth Heaven to earth. At the time, we didn't understand what this would mean. But from that day forward, when we joined our hands in prayer within our bedroom or family room, the Father, Jesus, and the Holy Spirit began speaking direction and prophecies to us. Renee would speak in tongues (the language of the Holy Spirit) and I would interpret her words into English (1 Corinthians 14:1-40). God told us about a destruction that would occur in the "center" of the East Coast—before the 9/11 terrorist attack on the World Trade Center buildings—so that we could pray for America.

Jesus told us about the seasons of our lives, including the "desert" (financially dry) times and the harvesting (ministry) times. Each prophetic utterance happened as God directed our steps by either telling us to stop or by telling us how to go forward. God told us that we would reach the ends of the earth with His truth, which seemed impossible at the time. Then Jesus declared this mission for me. He said:

"I want you to take back the narrative about Heaven and hell. Those who have abandoned Me are spreading lies about what I created. I want you to tell those who will listen about My truth."

I knew what God meant but I did not have a clue how this would happen. Universalists, "reincarnationists," and other religions that believe in false gods were dominating the airwaves with afterlife accounts that glorified a place apart from God's loftiest invention, Heaven. God wanted to reclaim the truth about Heaven and hell. After all, God created Heaven, not the false gods who tend to take people on a roller coaster of experiences—for which there is no way to verify them prospectively in an objective manner and/or they run contrary to how the Bible explains the afterlife.

After Shaun and I completed a series of interviews about the afterlife, I continued recording NDE interviews on a platform eventually called *Revelations from Heaven,* on the "Randy Kay" *YouTube* channel. Thousands of people reached out to me. Multitudes battled illnesses and other sufferings. Most needed prayer, often after a crisis. The most desperate asked me for a reason to live.

After the Covid-19 crisis hit, the floodgates opened, with people from around the globe needing prayer and counseling. Their only answer stemmed from this critical fact that I perceived in Heaven: God loved them as though each one is the most important person in His sight. Love as a Person, not just an emotion, consumed people with the truest understanding of God.

I realized at this point that these growing outreaches came from the "alienated church"—those who either did not attend a church or were not being closely pastored within their church. I came to realize that the church in the Western world was not fundamentally built to pastor large numbers of people, especially within the so-called megachurches.

While many churches developed a "small group ministry" to foster closer relationships, the essential need for interdependence within the body of Christ had largely failed. A Pew Research Center poll projected that the number of Christians of all ages was shrinking from 64 percent to little more than half (54 percent) and would be just above one-third (35 percent) of Americans by the year 2070.

The average church could not fulfill the bursting needs that only the God of Heaven can satisfy. I began building a ministry team of people with my wife Renee that we eventually called (rather unimaginatively) Randy Kay Ministries, in order to reach the millions who now poured into our various channels. We became a "virtual church" to thousands, if not millions, while triaging the most desperate individuals in need of personal follow-up. We hosted livestreams to pray for people, with numerous topics that ranged from Bible teachings to prophetic messages, including visions and dreams that God began downloading to me.

I received dreams of revivalist winds sweeping God's Glory throughout the world. On several occasions, visions arose of God opening a series of doors and calling my fellow afterlife survivors and me to help lead others through them. During several of my dreams, I beheld a mysterious series of doors that led to rooms. The first door opened to a view of the second heaven, where angels and demons battled. I walked through the warring angels unharmed and opened another door on the other side.

The second door opened to people praising God and being healed of the worst kinds of ailments. Then I walked through a third door, which led to a darkened, empty room. Walking through that empty room, I came to the fourth door, where I heard piercing screams. I did not want to enter through the fourth door for fear of what I might see, but God insisted. So I ran as fast as I could through the screaming bodies that were clawing at their skin and shouting all kinds of profanities. I could not wait to open the fifth door. When it opened, I walked into the same paradise I had witnessed in Heaven.

God's Holy Spirit revealed to me that my five journeys represented the coming periods of the end times. The first door revealed the spiritual warfare that has intensified during our present day. The second door led to a worldwide outpouring of God's Glory, greater than any in all of history—and by the way, that revival has already begun. The third door opened to darkness, when God lifted His presence from the earth, leaving no hope and no light, when the absence of believers caused no light to remain. The fourth door revealed the afflictions after God's protective covering was removed from the world, allowing demons to devour humans as prey. The final, fifth door followed Christ's return when God formed the new Earth as I had viewed in Heaven.

These dreams not only mirrored what I saw in Heaven, but they followed the biblical eschatology I had studied after returning to the world. But the signs of the times still perplexed me. Jesus and the Holy Spirit told me in Heaven that I would see signs. Jesus even told me to "look up," to know the times. Although I would never know the exact time or day, I believed that God would reveal the season of His return.

A burning in my soul told me that it would come quickly.

22

THE LAST DAYS

But understand this, that in the last days
there will come times of difficulty.
—2 TIMOTHY 3:1 ESV

Having now interviewed hundreds of afterlife survivors, most of whom are my friends, I learned that the story of God's love triumphs over understanding when presented within the celestial infiniteness of His abode; or even the contrasting lack thereof, for those who experienced hell without knowing Jesus as their Lord and Savior. Oddly, excitingly, the stories of people like me who experienced Heaven or hell in the afterlife have proven to have ushered forth one of the largest evangelical and faith-building impacts in the world.

We vetted hundreds of stories submitted to us through our RandyKay.org site and accepted only a fraction of accounts that passed our qualifications by asking these questions:

1. Was the account Christ-honoring?
2. Could the account be verified either through hospital records or witnesses?
3. Did any of the testimonials conflict with the Word of God?
4. Did the pre-interview of finalists confirm in the Spirit that those accounts were true?

5.   Did the afterlife account pass the "gut check"
     since I could assess experiences in the light of
     my own Heaven encounter, a kind of "heavenly"
     discernment?

We introduced a series of teaching videos, along with my interviews on our show and on subsequent shows, about miraculous
encounters that Renee hosted. Messages poured in of people getting saved through Jesus Christ and healed through His power.
Many of those healings were the result of prophesying during one
of our channel's programs.

I appeared on the Sid Roth show *It's Supernatural* and became
close with many of the *It's Supernatural* (Messianic Vision Inc.)
ministry team, as well as becoming friends with the icon himself,
Sid Roth. He is a man I will forever consider to be a giant in the
Judeo-Christian faith. And I believe he is one of those who will be
honored with a seat around the Throne of God. The ministry team
at Messianic Vision who produce the It's Supernatural Network
(ISN) and Middle East Television (METV) programs are minis-
tering first to the Jew, then to the rest of the world. This fits perfectly
with my understanding of how God would bring forth the end-
times fulfillment.

Messianic Vision Inc. owns the broadcasting rights to every
home in Israel and provides bomb shelters to this war-torn nation.
They help thousands of Jews come to know Jesus (Yeshua) as their
Messiah. I also had the pleasure of meeting several of their dynamic
ministry leaders who are part of the revivalist ministry I know will
help usher in the "Greatest Holy Spirit Revival Outpouring" in the
history of the world. God's Glory will be manifested on earth as it is
in Heaven, to reflect His splendor and holiness.

Why do I know that this world will experience this revival within a generation living in this world today? And that the subsequent Tribulation period explained in the book of Revelation will arrive and that the Rapture of Jesus the Messiah's beloved children will happen? I believe it because I saw it in Heaven!

During the years of preparation toward my full-time ministry and after thirty years in the clinical and business worlds and also having taught part-time in churches, God told us (in advance) about the seasons of Renee's and my lives. First, He said that we would be in the "barren season," which lasted seven years. We would start minimally successful businesses at a small fraction of my corporate salaries.

Then God told us that we would be in the "planting season," which lasted four years, as we volunteered on ministry boards and assisted with Christian charities, without the finances to do so. Next, God told us that we would be in the "harvesting season." This is when people would start coming into our lives who wanted to join our activities, over a three-year period.

Finally, God told us that we would walk in the "bountiful season," not just of finances but of partaking of the fruits of our labors. That season began with my appearance on GodTV to talk about the marketplace ministry. There, I inadvertently mentioned my afterlife experience to a large audience. Later, I learned that God almost always follows a pattern when directing peoples' lives. I tell you this because like me, you have seasons of life that follow the same pattern:

1.   **The Barren Season**
2.   **The Planting Season**
3.   **The Harvesting Season**
4.   **The Bountiful Season**

As I learned, our bountiful season may or may not be prosperous in worldly terms, but it will most certainly be prosperous in our Kingdom work. My Kingdom work continued as I described earlier. But it began with death—the *Barren Season*. Death precedes life in the natural, and oftentimes in the supernatural as well. Ninety-four (94) Bible verses reference "dying to self." Jesus said, *"Truly, truly, I say to you, unless a grain of wheat falls into the earth and dies, it remains alone, but if it dies, it bears much fruit"* (John 12:24 ESV).

Whether death in the flesh that leads to Heaven, or death in a worldly dream that leads to a Kingdom purpose, or even death to self (the ego) that leads to being heavenly minded, at times we must all endure the Barren Season. But we must also keep learning and planting opportunities that might bear fruit. Then when an idea, work, or ministry bears fruit, we must harvest it by sharing it with others. The final season is when people find value in our idea, product, or service.

Fruit-bearing is the most evident marker of God's move in our lives. Jesus even noted this when He said that *"He cuts off every branch in me that bears not fruit"* (John 15:2 NIV). We bear fruit when people desire what we have to offer and when that desire provides sustenance for our life and for the continuance of God's calling. We bear fruit when the fruit of our labor proves spiritually and sustainably profitable.

This might seem off-topic when talking about Heaven and the end times, but I did not understand the seasons of God's work. At least, not until I looked back and realized that all this time God devised a plan of action that follows the same pattern. Today, I make a paltry sum as compared to my executive days within the secular world, but my Kingdom riches are overflowing. Death precedes life until Heaven makes death no more. Then those Kingdom riches turn into a closeness to God that—believe you me—is the greatest wealth of all.

I first realized the pattern of God's plan for me when my fear came full circle. God gave me a dream of myself dying, years before my physical death, and that may have foretold my eventual death. In that dream, I lay in the casket like Uncle Carlyle. Everyone sat there looking at my waxy profile. Surrounding me were those sickening-sweet flowers. I lay in the same funeral home where I saw Uncle Carlyle's wake as a child, Graves Funeral Home in Keokuk, Iowa.

Later, I would realize that it was not my profile that I beheld. It was the profile of my father. He died in the trauma unit of a hospital in San Diego, California, from a fall while visiting my family. While speaking words of encouragement and verses into my earthly father's ears as he heaved his final breaths, a pleasant aroma filled the space. I turned around to ask if anyone could smell the heavenly smells, but the four people in the room said "no." It then struck me that I was smelling the same pleasant fragrance of the saints who were perishing that I had smelled in Heaven (and as recorded in 2 Corinthians 2:15-16).

The next day, his body was flown to Keokuk. I sat in the front row next to my mother and sister. At the funeral home, I found myself looking at his waxy profile from the same spot I had observed Uncle Carlyle forty-six years earlier. It was only the second time I had seen a dead body in a coffin. Instead of evoking terror as happened when I was in this same place as a child, I felt perfect peace.

Death had lost its sting. Finally, I could speak of Heaven without even a passing thought of death.

To this day, I believe that the fear of death—even if a fear of losing a loved one—must be overcome before the fruits of eternal life can be born forth. No longer did I mourn the death of anyone, especially that of my revered father who I led to Jesus years before. Certainly, I did not fear my own death because of my experience in Heaven. I was ready to begin my ministry.

As my father's closed casket found its final resting place in the reserved plot at Keokuk's National Cemetery, I stood for a few minutes to see the coffin placed into a vault and then into the pit below. A storm started settling east to west over the Mississippi River, but it was not just any storm. Dark gray clouds billowed over the sky, like rolling waves which settled above my head. Then the rain poured. I froze while the water drenched my black suit as I stared at the grave.

I could feel in my spirit, soul, and body that the storm meant something. As the lightning crackled in the distance, I remembered similar sounds in Heaven as the rain eased over those portals to earth, as they awaited God's final words:

"It is finished."

A shift had taken place in my soul. This was different. This time was unique. Now a sense of urgency was imposing itself upon me. God spoke another season into our lives as Renee and I prayed together. He said:

"Now is the Season of the Storm."

| 23 |

THE JOSHUA GENERATION

Even so, when you see these things happening,
you know that the kingdom of God is near. Truly
I tell you, this generation will certainly not pass
away until all these things have happened.
—LUKE 21:31-32 NIV

One sacred rule within Renee's and my prayer time as a couple with the Lord is this: we cannot ask God questions once He speaks. We would simply listen to God. Each occasion we pray in the spirit is a time for our spirits to intercede on our behalf and for God's Spirit to speak in response, through my interpretation of Renee's tongues. After prayer, we confer as to what God meant and confirm our agreement with one another; and we always stand by God's words. Renee records the Spirit of God's words to ensure that we remember them.

I was left with a lingering question as to what God meant when He told Renee and me that this is the "Season of the Storm." Then I remembered the four seasons through which each of us must travel that I mentioned earlier. Here is how I interpreted the four seasons that have occurred *within this world* as they lead up to the Storm:

1. **The Barren Season:** This began after the first humans rebelled against God, bringing the devastating effects of sin.

2. **The Planting Season:** This was the season after Noah's voyage, when a new generation would honor God.

3. **The Harvesting Season:** This began when the Jews entered the Promised Land of Israel under the leadership of Joshua, establishing the presence of God within the Temple in Israel.

4. **The Bountiful Season:** This would be during the "Grace Period" that followed Jesus's ministry on earth—His crucifixion, resurrection, and post-ascension after He sent the Holy Spirit to indwell all believers in Jesus as their Messiah.

I still wondered which season would include the Storm, so I prayed for the answer. I had witnessed the Storm in Heaven. God told me while I was in His presence that at His appointed time, I would share what I had seen concerning the Storm, but I first needed to understand it.

One day while walking along the ocean, I listened to the soothing crash of the waves on my left, which danced beneath a pink and orange sunset. All at once, a spiritual lightning rod struck my heart with an inspiration that must have come from the Lord, because it resonated with the same sense of knowing I had heard in Heaven from the Holy Spirit as He whispered into my soul:

As it was in the time of Noah, so it is now, but I shall not destroy the earth to rebuild it. I shall pour out My Spirit and this generation shall not pass until the hour of completion, as it was in the Joshua generation.

Although this may sound somewhat cryptic, when interpreted through wisdom—remember the butterfly—those words became spectacularly clear to me. The Holy Spirit told me that the "Joshua Generation" lived today, in our world. I intuitively knew what God meant by the Joshua generation. In the time of Moses, exiled Jews wandered in the wilderness for forty years because they lacked faith. They worshipped false gods, just as many people today worship false gods and religions. Moses was told by God that he would not be permitted to enter the Promised Land and why:

> *This is because...you broke faith with me in the presence of the Israelites at the waters of Meribah Kadesh in the Desert of Zin and because you did not uphold my holiness among the Israelites. Therefore, you will see the land only from a distance; you will not enter the land I am giving to the people of Israel* (Deuteronomy 32:51-52 NIV).

Instead of Moses reaching the Promised Land, an entire generation passed. The next generation led by Joshua carried the Ark of the Covenant into the Promised Land and possessed the land. Thus, the presence of God went with Joshua and his followers to Israel, a land often referred to as a "land flowing with milk and honey," for its abundant fertility. Joshua and his generation of followers ushered forth God's Glory into the land of Israel.

To understand today, we must begin at a time when the biblical King David first declared: *"Pray for the peace of Jerusalem"* (Psalm 122:6 NIV). During his reign, Jerusalem became the location for God's Glory on earth, inside the Holy of Holies of the Tabernacle where the Ark rested. (Later, David's successor, his son King Solomon, built the First Temple to house the Ark.[1]) Not until the Israelites reunified Jerusalem after the Six-Day War of 1967 was the covenant promise of God to the Jews finally fulfilled, and the exiled Jewish people returned to the Promised Land.

Nearly a generation has passed since Jerusalem was reunited with Israel. Could it be that just as with the Joshua generation of long ago, that the generation of Christ followers who live today will witness God's Glory being restored upon the earth? If so, will that Glory take the form of the most powerful revival ever witnessed in history—just as I had witnessed it in Heaven?

I knew that God's Word tells us to *"test the spirits"* (1 John 4:1). Well, I was invited to a group dinner before the day of my interview with Sid Roth, which I attended. Seated to my right was Bishop Bill Hamon, a man who is known as the "Father of Modern-Day Prophecy." This nearly ninety-year-old man has accurately prophesied to more than 75,000 people, so I took the opportunity to test the word I had received about the Joshua generation.

"Bishop, I have received a word that I believe came from the Lord," I said to him. "He told me that we are living in the Joshua generation and that this generation will see the fullness of God's Glory on earth."

He looked me squarely in the eyes and said, "I agree. We are living in the Joshua generation. I don't know if I'll live to see it, but I believe that you're correct."

I subsequently asked others about my word from God, including seasoned believers, and none disagreed. What I saw in Heaven was about to pour forth on earth. Surely the Storm is coming and will have arrived after these phases in modern history:

1. **The Barren Season:** The time when the Jews were exiled from the Promised Land (around 589-587 BC).

2. **The Planting Season:** This is the time when Jesus ministered on earth (about AD 27-34).

3. **The Harvesting Season:** This is when the spread of faith in Jesus as the Messiah began to turn Christendom into the largest faith in all of history (John 4:35).

4. **The Bountiful Season:** This is when the Holy
    Spirit will pour out His presence over all the
    earth—and it has already begun.

The Promised Land today is not simply a territory as it was in
the ancient days of Joshua, when he and his tribe conquered the
Land of Canaan. When the Jews possessed Israel, their most trea-
sured place was not the dirt beneath their feet. It was the location
where they would build the Tabernacle to house the presence of
God, and eventually the Temple. The Ark of the Covenant that they
had carried with them was the place of God's presence—where the
Lord was present among His people. To the believers in Yahweh,
God's presence meant more than just a nation. And redemption for
the ancient Jews, just as it is for us today, can only be found through
the abiding presence of God's Spirit.

I believe that understanding the final plan of God's redemption
can be found squarely within the Bible. After my trip to Heaven,
I compared my personal revelation with Scripture, which further
served to validate what I had seen. From Heaven, I had witnessed
God's presence coming to the earth and I was shown that all of
Heaven represents God's presence.

Jesus declared a prayer to bring forth God's heavenly purpose
on earth. He said, *"Your kingdom come. Your will be done, on earth as it
is in heaven"* (Matthew 6:10 NKJV). In order for this to occur, God
will create the new Earth that I had witnessed in Heaven. But before
Jesus takes His "Church" (body of believers) to Heaven prior to exe-
cuting justice on the earth during the Tribulation period, another
event will occur, which I also saw in Heaven. The presence of God
will be poured out over this existing world. I had seen God's final
plan to save every individual person who would be open to knowing the truth about Jesus the Messiah and who would receive Him
before it is too late.

The good news is that God's Glory is arriving right now. What is the Glory of God? The Glory of God is the Holy Spirit's presence, God's presence. Revival is to be revived by the Holy Spirit, which means to be filled to overflowing with God's presence and to experience the outflow of God's power.

Beloved of the Lord Yahweh, soon to come will be the largest revival in history—a world revival! God's Glory will burst forth from Heaven and countless people will be saved. Millions of believers will be anointed with miracles and with gifts including prophecy, evangelism, teaching, deliverance, and healing.

Move over world, because Heaven is about to invade the earth!

Note

1. The First Temple period was roughly 516 BC to AD 70.

24

THE RETURN OF JERUSALEM

*Pray for the peace of Jerusalem: "May
those who love you be secure."*
—PSALM 122:6 NIV

Heaven's invasion that I sensed in my spirit lingered within my soul for years after my heavenly encounter with Jesus. I knew now that I had been released to share my afterlife account, with one exception—the last days that I saw birthed in Heaven from God's Throne. Earlier I mentioned the confirmation of the Joshua generation that I received when the Holy Spirit began speaking to me about the end-times revival. God's presence, His Glory, will be poured forth over the earth. But a second revelation came to mind.

The Holy Spirit began unraveling the mysteries of the ancient times in light of the future end of this world as we know it. It began with the numbers "seven" and "forty." These numbers play a significant role in marking the advent of the last days that I beheld in Heaven.

It probably took about seven years for Joshua and his tribe to conquer Canaan. As communicated in Israelite culture and literature, the number seven (7) conveys a sense of "fullness" or "completeness." Indeed, the number seven is the most important symbolic number in the Hebrew Bible. We know from the book of Genesis that God rested on the seventh day *Sabbath* (Genesis 2:2). This seventh day rest was also commanded in the Law of Moses (Exodus 16:29-30). Also recorded in the Bible is the culmination of the end times, which happens after the seven-year Tribulation.

The number forty (40) also represents a significant identifier within the Bible. In Scripture, the number forty signifies new life, new growth, and transformation. It took forty years of wandering in the wilderness to bring the Jews to God's offer of a Promised Land for Abraham and his descendants (Genesis 17:1-16). One hundred and forty-six (146) times, the Bible references the number forty, symbolizing a period of testing, trial, or probation.

Jesus fasted for "forty days and forty nights" in the Judean desert before His temptation, as recorded in the Bible in multiple places (Matthew 4:2; Mark 1:13; Luke 4:2). The rain of the Great Flood also lasted forty days and nights. Jesus spent forty days with His followers after His resurrection. God even designed human pregnancy to last for forty weeks.

In and of themselves, the numbers seven (7) and forty (40) mean little, but the God of order appropriates a plan with meaningful perfection. In the book of Revelation, the apostle John notes seven churches, seven angels, seven seals, seven trumpets, and seven stars. People tend to place too much significance on numerology—the study of the spiritual meaning of numbers. In my case, I think these numbers point to what the Holy Spirit told me in Heaven, when He told me to know the "signs."

In my spirit, I sensed that forty years would mark a significant event for Israel. The Word of God speaks prophetically in numbers and also of God's Glory in the heavens. God never speaks without purpose. And since His Word is eternal, it applies "on earth as it is in Heaven." In the Bible, God refers to Israel as He does to no other land on earth. God raised Israel to be a light to the Gentiles;

and indeed, the Jewish disciples spread the Gospel of Jesus as the Messiah to the world.

In Heaven, I knew that the Jews and Israel received God's everlasting attention. And I witnessed the archangel Michael swoop down from Heaven upon Israel, to arm the Israelites as prophesized:

> *...For in Mount Zion and in Jerusalem there shall be deliverance.... The Lord also will roar from Zion, and utter His voice from Jerusalem; the heavens and earth will shake; but the Lord will be a shelter for His people, and the strength of the children of Israel* (Joel 2:32, 3:16 NKJV).

So, my attention became keenly attuned to the events of Israel as a prophetic sign of what I had seen in Heaven and an indicator of when God's Glory would be poured forth upon the earth. After the Covid-19 pandemic hit, an interesting article was brought to my attention. I believe it was significant for my understanding of "Heaven's Storm."

In 2021, seven years after the Holy Spirit prompted me to go public with my Heaven experience, Israel celebrated forty years since Israel declared Golan Heights sovereignty. Israel conquered the Golan Heights from Syria in the Six-Day War of 1967, and claimed sovereignty in 1981. The return of the Golan Heights finalized Israel's return to its original territory from the time of Joshua, thereby fulfilling God's covenant with the Jews to give them the Land of Canaan and finally return the Jews' Promised Land.

Referred to as "Bashan" in the Bible, the Golan Heights area was considered part of the Land of Israel and was assigned to the tribe of Menashe (Deuteronomy 4:43; Joshua 13:29-31, 21:27). Names of Jewish tribes in Britain and Europe, who mainly moved to North America, are those clans from Manasseh (Menashe), the first son of Joseph (Genesis 41:50-52).

The Golan Heights includes Mount Hermon, also called the Mount of Transfiguration. This is one of the mountains which represented the northwestern limit of the Israelite conquest under Moses and Joshua. Some people believe that the mountain where God gave Moses the Ten Commandments is the modern-day Mount Hermon mentioned in the Hebrew Scriptures. The significance of Golan rejoining Israel after forty years did not escape me since the event marked the reunification of the Promised Land taken by Joshua and his army.

Just as God had told me in Heaven, it seemed to me that the signs of our times were fashioning a timeline to prepare Christ's body of believers for the Groom (Jesus the Messiah) to return for His bride (His beloved body). God was revealing to me the signs for His return through the fulfillment of His promises to the descendants of Abraham.

Why is all of this important in the scheme of things? Remember how Jesus told me to look for signs? God chose not to reveal the time of the last days to me, but He would reveal the *season*.

Under the Mosaic Covenant—the covenant God made with Israel—the Israelites were instructed on how to commemorate seasons and feast days. Earth's cycles and seasons are important to God and He established them during the first "week" of creation seen in Genesis. The feast days and seasons of the Mosaic Covenant not only prophesied the coming Messiah, but they served as shadow pictures for the patterns and events first established in Heaven and that play out in real time on the earth below (Genesis 1:14).

The prophet Daniel talked about signs: *"How great are his signs, how mighty his wonders! His kingdom is an eternal kingdom; his dominion endures from generation to generation"* (Daniel 4:3 NIV). Another Scripture from the book of Daniel has this to say about signs: *"He rescues and he saves; he performs signs and wonders in the heavens and on the earth. He has rescued Daniel from the power of the lions"* (Daniel 6:27 NIV).

In Scripture, Jesus condemned those who were looking for signs—but with their flesh, not signs given by the Holy Spirit to believers (Matthew 16:3). Jesus blessed Simon Peter as "Simon son of Jonah," since he divinely discerned Jesus as the Messiah. We may recall another Jonah, a prophet God spoke to who was asked to warn the people of Nineveh to repent. Jonah ignored God and had to repent to be saved—a prophetic picture for us. I could not help but believe that the United States of America (USA) is like the people of Nineveh today, a place and people corrupted by iniquity who are called to humble themselves and repent of their sin, from the leaders on down. If, like Nineveh, the people of the USA repent, God's blessings will follow, and this nation's place in the last days will be likened to that of Israel's.

Such were the epiphanies consuming my attention. God's revelations began to pour through me like the rivers flowing through Heaven. Scripture reveals the fact that God gives revelations (Matthew 16:17). Jesus reinforced our need to seek *His* signs and wonders, for they reveal *His Glory* as seen in Jesus's earthly ministry works, in believers who follow Him, and in the heavenly signs as His Spirit reveals them.

The ministry works of Jesus and His disciples marked the beginning of the "planting season" that I mentioned earlier. Jesus's works first appeared on earth as signs. We might note the rapid transition within the following passages. First, Jesus instructs His disciples about His ministry. Then He ascends into Heaven where He works with His followers (once filled with the Holy Spirit) to confirm His Word on earth by the same works He did and greater works in all who believe in Jesus (John 14:12; Acts 1:2, 2:3).

> *"And these signs will accompany those who believe: In my name they will drive out demons; they will speak in new tongues;…they will place their hands on sick people, and they will get well." After the Lord Jesus had spoken to them, he was taken up into heaven and he sat at the right hand of God. Then the disciples went out and preached everywhere, and the Lord worked with them and confirmed his word by the signs that accompanied it* (Mark 16:17-20 NIV).

When I visited Heaven, God informed me that the signs on earth would mean something to me. Meanings are personal, whereas facts are just facts until they convey a personal meaning. God always knows how to strike a personal chord in our lives. He revealed to me in Heaven that what is first established in Heaven—and what I witnessed—is then released upon the earth. I saw the Storm and I saw it come to earth. As in Scripture, God used numbers and events to speak a sense of "knowing" to me on earth as He said so in Heaven. His command for me to watch for "signs" when I returned to earth is to me a reiteration of the signs seen in Scripture, including Luke's gospel, where we are warned about the heavenly signs of the last days (Luke 21:25-28).

To understand the reason for the spiritual Storm in Heaven, we must also understand the purpose of the Tribulation that will occur on earth as it relates to the biblical representation of numbers. In Scripture, numbers usually have more significance than just as quantitative indicators. Again, seven represents perfection and fullness of completion. It is also the number of the Holy Spirit and the number of God's Covenant.

Eight (8) is another number that is significant. In Hebrew, eight is *sh'moneh* and means, "to make fat," abundant, be made new. Eight represents the number of salvation, resurrection, and (to an expanded degree) the Second Coming of Jesus Christ. Together, the numbers seven and eight represent an eschatological meaning of spiritual completion. Seven covenants were revealed in the Old Testament.

The eighth covenant (with Christ) in the New Testament was shadowed under the Mosaic covenant (the covenant God made with Israel) in the "Eighth Great Day" feast. Under the old covenant, the eighth day was a day when all of Israel's newborn infant males were to be circumcised (Exodus 4:25; Leviticus 12:3). The eighth day was also the last day of the eighth-day feast, called the Last Great Day and *the closing assembly* of the *Feast of Tabernacles*, the last day of feasts for the year, and a holy "day" of rest (Leviticus 23:36).

The Last Great Day represents the last day before the White Throne Judgment and the reward of eternal life for believers. In Jesus's day, people wanted to know if, when the Messiah came, He would perform more *signs* than "this man"—Jesus (John 7:31). A few verses later, it says: *"On the last and greatest day of the festival, Jesus stood and said in a loud voice, 'Let anyone who is thirsty come to me and drink'"* (John 7:37 NIV). Jesus was talking about His death, resurrection, ascension, and the Holy Spirit outpouring that would come to all those who believe in Him (John 7:39).

In the book of Revelation, the apostle John records seven visions. The seventh notation is repeated using the Greek word *kai eidon* (meaning "and I saw") for the *eighth* time (Revelation 20:11-12). Under the new covenant, Jesus taught that circumcision is *of the heart* and hinted of a great day when Jews and Gentiles alike would live together as one new man with all under the new covenant—Jesus as Messiah, Savior, Lord, and King (Acts 10:28; Romans 1:6, 2:29, 3:22; Ephesians 2:11-22). Today, the Judeo-Christian faith serves as the foundational belief upon which the Jews and Christians would fellowship together on earth and in Heaven. I witnessed from Heaven the Jewish believers in Jesus as their Messiah being raptured into Heaven and placed around the Throne during the last days.

The numbers seven and eight signified an important last days event to me when I researched contemporary history related to the Jewish people, as it related to my own experience. In world politics, as Egypt and Israel signed the Camp David Accords peace treaty in 1978, it was the same year I cried out the window of my apartment as an agnostic who was earnestly asking God to reveal Himself. My cry was followed by God's release of the Holy Spirit from Heaven to me, as His reply. So I should not have been surprised when in Heaven I saw seven angels releasing their shields (or "seven bowls" of wrath as the apostle John called them) upon the earth. Heaven had been personally related to me from the times I became born again, and it became my only reality when I entered Heaven as a spirit. Thereafter, I discovered the unraveling of what I beheld in Heaven through the events of modern history related to the Jewish nation, which is the eschatological marker of the last days. Paul tells us that in the last days people will believe they have finally attained peace, but destruction will come instead. Indeed, today we stand at the precipice of what I beheld in Heaven:

> Now, brothers and sisters, about times and dates we do not need to write to you, for you know very well that the day of the Lord will come like a thief in the night. While people are saying, "Peace and safety," destruction will come on them suddenly, as labor pains on a pregnant woman, and they will not escape (1 Thessalonians 5:1-3 NIV).

Recent peace discussions have centered on Palestinian demands that the Israeli borders be returned to the pre-1967 demarcation line when Jordan controlled the West Bank, thereby denying the original land promised by God to Moses. The Storm is underway. When I read a Pew Research Center article published on December 8, 2022, I was surprised to read that four in ten US adults believe that humanity is "living in the end times." In prayer, I asked the Lord to bring light to my understanding of the season. The numbers seven, eight, and forty clearly resonated in my spirit—confirming to me that the last days are upon us.

According to the prophet Daniel, there is a seventieth "seven" (seven years) that were yet to come. Daniel's entire prophecy of the "seventy sevens" speaks of the nation of Israel. It is a time period when God focuses His attention especially upon Israel as a fulfillment of the covenant He made with the Jewish people. God's covenant with Israel is based upon God's promises that He made to Abraham. God's covenant with Abraham established the basis for the birth of a nation that would be known as Israel. The reference to Abraham appears several times in the Exodus narrative (Exodus 3:15-17, 6:3-8).

The "seventieth seven," or the Tribulation, must be a time when God deals specifically with Israel during the Tribulation period, which is presumably after the Rapture of believers (1 Thessalonians 4:15-17). The "blindness" of Israel noted by the apostle Paul will be removed during the Tribulation. This will occur as the fullness of the Gentiles is complete and the Jews are awakened to their Messiah, Yahweh, during the last days (Romans 11:25). Therefore, the purpose of the Tribulation will be to reestablish justice for the world and a covenantal relationship with Israel. Those who are born anew through Jesus are already covered under the new covenant in Jesus

Christ: *"This cup* [of redemption through Christ] *that is poured out for you is the new covenant in my* [Jesus's] *blood"* (Luke 22:20 ESV).

This was the spiritual Storm that I beheld in Heaven and that is soon to be released on earth. The first sign of this impending heavenly Storm was the regathering of the Jews, which triggered the season of the last days, with the establishment of the Promised Land given to the Jews, according to God's covenant with them. Most importantly was the annexation of Jerusalem, which was completed by the occupation of the Golan Heights. This completed the ancient geography of the Promised Land that was originally conquered by Joshua and his army.

Why was the annexation of the Golan Heights to Israel in 1981 an important marker to foretell the last days? There, several ancient cultures entertained idols. But later on, the prophet Elijah and the righteous kings Hezekiah and Josiah tore down these types of "high places of [false] worship" as they confronted idol worship of Canaanite gods. In the Golan Heights, Jesus pointed out that no evil, no idol, and no false god would stand against the greatness of His body—the Church.

A divine conversation took place in the Golan Heights when Jesus asked His disciples: *"Who do men say that I am?"* (Mark 8:27 NKJV). He purposely took them to this setting, where lewd acts of pagan sacrifice had occurred, in order to reveal Himself as the Son of the Living God. Peter was the first one to proclaim Jesus as the Messiah, and to which Jesus replied, *"...flesh and blood has not revealed this to you...and on this rock I will build My church"* (Matthew 16:17-18 NKJV).

When the *"city of refuge"* named in Joshua 21:27 rejoined the nation of Israel, it marked the completion of Israel. Even as various presidents of the United States and Israel negotiated the rights of the Golan Heights between Palestine and Israel, God had already established this territory as a demarcation between good and evil. Today, it remains a contentious point between nations and religions. But its position in history signifies that the restoration in 1967 of the Messiah's divine establishment in Israel as an important sign for the land God gave to Abraham—and where Jesus would soon return.

I believe other indicators of the outpouring of God's Glory upon the earth and the ensuing Rapture and Tribulation relate to my heavenly experience, as well as the numerous testimonies of others who have died and experienced Heaven and hell.

As I related earlier, one night while praying with my wife Renee, the Holy Spirit silently spoke to us about our need to "take back the narrative" of near-death experience (NDE) stories from the "universalists" (New Age) narrative that dominated this space. After all, God created Heaven, so He should get the credit for it—not some mystical religion. And for such a time as this, God chose to open a floodgate of stories through our various programs, during which I publicly interview afterlife survivors.

Sometimes I would associate my interviews with afterlife survivors as "transfiguration experiences." What this means is that each afterlife survivor experienced a change of form or appearance, as most of us received new bodies in Heaven, having witnessed the glorified Person of Jesus.

A biblical transfiguration experience occurred as Jesus walked the earth, when He took three of His disciples (Peter, James, and John) up a mountain. There, as Jesus was transfigured, Moses and Elijah appeared with Him. Noting the figures, Peter asked if he could build three *tabernacles* for them—indicating the important Third Temple period (Matthew 17:3-4).

This certainly points to the rebuilding of the earthly Temple in the last days, but if we look closely, the tabernacle that Peter is speaking of here is the Greek word *skēnē*, which is a *tent or tabernacle made of green boughs or skins*. Scripture refers to people as "trees" (Mark 8:24).

The Israelite's tabernacle in the wilderness was a tent of meeting. That tabernacle was a pattern after which the Jerusalem Temples were built. The tabernacle, the tent of meeting was moved from place to place until it found rest in Jerusalem during David's reign. However, a *third tabernacle* is revealed in the New Testament. The Tabernacle of Heaven is not the one built by human hands, but by God, for believers are the Tabernacle of God on earth (Matthew 17:4; Acts 7:48; 2 Corinthians 5:1).

During the transfiguration, due to the Glory, Jesus's face and clothing became dazzlingly bright, as recorded in the gospels of Matthew, Mark, and Luke. We saw the shadow image of this same Glory upon Moses's face when he returned from the mountain with the Ten Commandments (Exodus 34:33-35). Moses covered his face with a veil before the Israelites, because sin does not allow us to see the Glory. But believers are not like Moses, whose veil kept the Israelites from *"seeing the end of what was passing away"* (2 Corinthians 3:13 NIV). That veil was torn down forever in the Temple of Jesus's day when He died on the cross for sinners. That same veil that kept people from seeing the end result of their sins in Moses's day still covers the hearts of all who do not call Jesus their Messiah today (2 Corinthians 3:15).

I believe that Jesus is bringing Heaven to earth through these "transfiguration" (afterlife) experiences. God's revelation of Heaven through an unprecedented number of believers in Christ who all died and witnessed Heaven and returned, is a critical sign of the times that foretells the coming Storm. It's the same Storm I saw in Heaven and that began in Heaven and will soon begin on earth with the outpouring of God's Glory.

I beheld that same Glory hovering over the ones I witnessed in Heaven as a "glow" about them. Later God would clarify to me that the increased glow of some people over others testified of the greater Glory that will abide within those who grew closer to God in this world. So, the degree of devotion and closeness you realize to God now, in this life, will directly correspond to the degree of God's Glory that you experience in Heaven. Just as Moses descended with a glow about him after being in the presence of God atop the "mountain of God," you too will one day carry that Glory in Heaven, and it will never leave you.

You are closer to Heaven than you think.

25

THE STORM IS HAPPENING NOW

When you pass through the waters, I will be with you;
and when you pass through the rivers, they will not
sweep over you. When you walk through the fire, you
will not be burned; the flames will not set you ablaze.
—ISAIAH 43:2 NIV

Heaven tells us everything we need to know about our world and God's plans. Remember how in Heaven I saw that the fires from the Throne Room did not burn God's children? God promised that He would protect His beloved, but that does not mean that the Storm will not affect us. This world can be very oppressive.

Our world tends to confuse matters, while Heaven makes them clear. What could be understood so easily in Heaven did not translate so readily on earth. With my spiritual eyes, I could see the rolling out of God's end of times in Heaven; but within my body and brain on earth, I could not easily deduce when all of what I witnessed would manifest on earth. That is because for now, as the apostle Paul wrote, in this world, *"we see in a mirror dimly,"* but in Heaven we see all things clearly. In Heaven, it seemed as though God was manifesting His final outpouring of His Spirit and His judgments in real time. Only later would I understand that what I beheld in Heaven would be realized on earth at a much later time.

Wanting answers, I turned to my fellow afterlife survivors, with whom I interacted over the past several years. Of the hundreds of afterlife survivors I have interviewed, a narrative began to emerge to help me piece together some answers. This was confirmed by my own experiences, which I offer here, to more clearly detail the story of the future of humankind in this world. One of these pieces included the reasons why God is causing so many afterlife accounts to surface today. In fact, one of the most common questions I am asked is:

"Why do you think so many of these afterlife or near-death accounts are being shared today?"

Please know that most of us afterlife survivors did not want to share our stories, at least not initially. But we felt *compelled* to tell our account—even feeling a direct pull from God to do so. To say that we are looking for publicity or notoriety is frankly absurd (to most of us). The type of "notoriety" I received after sharing my story did not reflect any type of recognition I desired in my career or life.

Never did I desire to face the questions, doubts, and sometimes ridicule that comes from skeptics, even though I used to be one myself, before my own afterlife experience. Neither did I want to divulge the intimacies that I cherished the most from my journeys with Jesus. "Do not waste precious things on people who will not appreciate them" comes from a saying of Jesus from the gospels, *"Do not…cast your pearls before swine"* (Matthew 7:6 NKJV).

To answer the question as to why so many afterlife accounts are surfacing now I believe goes beyond simple explanations, such as greater access to social media, better life-saving medical interventions, or people feeling safer to share their stories given those who have gone before them. The afterlife stories that are coming to the forefront in greater numbers serve to prophetically call people to Jesus, in anticipation of His soon return. Those who have died and experienced Heaven (or hell) can leave little doubt that Heaven and hell are real and that the God of Jesus is real. The accounts lead many to believe in Jesus as their Lord and Savior. After all, God desires in these last days that *all* people will come to *know* Him—not just know about Him.

Perhaps the most telling sign of these last days is the expanded unveiling of God's heart to the lost. He loves us far too much to continually expose us to the ever-degrading aspects of this fallen world. Jesus is returning to save the remainder of the lost and retrieve His beloved bride before the end of all time—a timeframe that appears to be upon us today.

As I recall the Storm, I am reminded how the good that happens in this world often mirrors what takes place in Heaven. Throughout the Bible, Jesus used several worldly analogies to explain heavenly truths, since nature mirrors the paradise that I beheld in Heaven, in appearance and truth. Even earthly storms follow the patterns I witnessed. The clouds come, then the rain, then the clearing of the air, then the water comes for all living plants, animals, and people. Sometimes the Storm brings destruction.

In a similar but spiritual way, the Storm in Heaven initially hovered over the earth. The rain of God's presence fell upon the earth, causing revival and giving new life to those who previously had no life in Christ. Next, I saw Jesus mount His white horse, along with His entourage, and summon His beloved children (saints) to Heaven—without them dying, just as God had done with the ancient prophet Elijah who was taken to Heaven while he yet lived. This "taking up" translates as the Rapture.

The Storm I saw in Heaven then brought destruction, as God lifted His presence from the earth and the seven "bowls" were spilled. But the bowls looked more to me like bowed shields that rendered the justice God had withheld from the earth while His presence had yet remained in the world.

The way I saw the events in Heaven, all of the injustices manufactured by humans during all of earth's existence had amassed for centuries. God's grace withheld from me the cause of our inhumanity toward one another, but from Heaven I beheld the resulting atrocities through the heavenly portals. I did not want to see them because a mere glimpse revealed the horrors of diseases and destruction that were compounded by centuries of human atrocities. But there they appeared horrible to the extreme. Only martyrs slain by demonically possessed reprobates can relate. Each time God lifted His shield of protection, another effect of sin was loosed, as if a levee had broken open to release a flood of swirling cesspools. I did not go into vivid detail of what Jesus showed me in Heaven because He protected my sensitivities from witnessing the fullness of the destructions on earth.

When John wrote about the "seven seals" of judgments in the book of Revelation, I suspect he:

A) was seeing something he did not understand, or

B) he wanted to disguise his terminology, to avoid the Romans from disposing of it, or

C) he witnessed the shields from below, thinking that they were bowls.

I tend to lean toward answer "C" because I witnessed God releasing His judgments from above, while John presumably witnessed them from below. This distinction is important to make in order to understand how and why God will soon release His judgments. But you do not have to take my word for it. Look at what Peter scribed around AD 64-65:

> *If this is so, then the Lord knows how to rescue the godly from trials and to hold the unrighteous for punishment on the day of judgment. This is especially true of those who follow the corrupt desire of the flesh and despise authority. Bold and arrogant, they are not afraid to heap abuse on celestial beings; yet even angels, although they are stronger and more powerful, do not heap abuse on such beings when bringing judgment on them from the Lord. But these people blaspheme in matters they do not understand. They are like unreasoning animals, creatures of instinct, born only to be caught and destroyed, and like animals they too will perish* (2 Peter 2:9-12 NIV).

In the second heaven, I witnessed the angels carrying long, triple-edged, silver swords that glistened as they dripped with the blood of the Lamb, Jesus. The angels declared words steeped in divine blood that shielded them from demons. The archangel Michael and his angels fought against the dragon and his fallen angels, with those same blood-stained swords (Revelation 12:7-9). Eventually I witnessed in Heaven God's release of Michael to watch over Israel, because God made a promise to the Jews in the time of Abraham, and God never breaks His promises.

Was the Day of Judgment part of what I witnessed in Heaven? I fully believe so. When God declared "it is finished" in Heaven from His Throne, He was releasing His Word—the Word that had already been recorded for the end of the ages. The angels then let down the sword of the Word and released the fallen angels to pour out their vengeance upon humankind, whom the fallen ones despised.

God did not create evil. Rather, He allowed it for *the absence of good* because of those who still reject God's Way. In Heaven, I witnessed fallen angels below that intended harm, as well as the instances when God had stopped them. But when God's protection is lifted from the world, He will command His angels to "drop their swords" and permit satan and his demons to have their way. This means that for once in all of world history—during the Tribulation period—Heaven's angels will no longer defend humankind.

What is the Tribulation? According to biblical prophecy, the Tribulation is a seven-year period that will impose havoc upon the world. During this period, evil will spread throughout the world, but without restraint. What is the Rapture? It is most clearly presented in 1 Thessalonians 4:13-18, which encourages living Christians who at the Rapture will be *"caught up"* and reunited with those who have died in Christ before them. In verse 17, the English phrase "caught up" is translated from the Greek word *harpazō,* which means "to seize upon with force," or "to snatch up."

A few verses later, Paul says this about believers, *"For God did not appoint us to suffer wrath but to receive salvation through our Lord Jesus Christ"* (1 Thessalonians 5:9 NIV). The book of Revelation implies but does not explicitly confirm that Christians will escape the seven-year nightmare of the Tribulation:

Since you have kept my command to endure patiently, I will also keep you from the hour of trial that is going to come on the whole world to test the inhabitants of the earth (Revelation 3:10 NIV).

Still, there will be a great harvest of souls for Christ during the Tribulation, meaning that many who are currently lost will be converted, fulfilling the prophecy of Matthew 24:14. I witnessed these events in Heaven through some form, although I did not understand the timing or the day of their occurrence, only the season. I also witnessed a vision of either a millennial earth or a new Earth that replaces the millennial Heaven and earth, as scribed by John (Revelation 21:1). In reference to the new Earth, "the heavens" does not include the third heaven, where God dwells. The word translated as "heaven" likely refers to the first heaven, meaning earth's atmosphere and/or space.

Know also that the word *new* in Greek is *kainon*, meaning, "new in quality," or "fresh" (Revelation 21:1). Since this verse notes that "the sea was no more," and the millennial earth contains large bodies of water, I can only assume that John is referencing the eternal Earth (Isaiah 11:9; Ezekiel 47:8-10; Zechariah 9:10, 14:8).

When people speak of "the millennium," they refer to the "thousand" years that will follow the Savior's Second Coming (Revelation 20:4). If you are confused about those who are in Heaven now and those who will be on the millennial earth, or those who will be on the eternal Earth, please know that from the perspective of eternity, time and space are irrelevant. As it says in the Bible, *"one day is like a thousand years,"* and visa-versa (2 Peter 3:8).

I believe that based on what I beheld and what is recorded as Jacob's prophetic dream where he sees a ladder or stairway stretching from Heaven to earth, the connection between God and humankind will be forever. I also believe that after the Last Judgment when God forever seals satan and his minions, there will be a new Heaven and a new Earth, where we will love with and live in our resurrected bodies. In accordance with what I beheld, the heavenly Jerusalem will come down from Heaven to reside on earth. Heaven and earth will become enjoined forever, and we will "tabernacle" with God, just as I witnessed.

When I was in Heaven, I desired no food or drink, as noted in Scripture which says, *"Never again will they hunger; never again will they thirst"* (Revelation 7:16 NIV). But the *"wedding supper"* of Scripture describes a celebration that involves dining with the Lord, which I believe I also witnessed taking place on the new Earth (Revelation 19:9 NIV). All of these events will occur in our future.

I would like you to know that the events I beheld at the altar of God's Throne Room is not to be considered as equal to the accounts in the Bible, which is the spoken Word of God. The Bible is sacred. My account is only my witness that contains my observations, but I believe that my witness confirms the Scripture and certainly does not add to it.

I spoke with Jesus and the Holy Spirit. In a similar way, you too can speak with Him during your prayers and as you contemplate God's truth in His Word. I am not special, except in the very same way that you are special to God. He loves you beyond all measure—and of this, I am certain.

When Jesus revealed my life in review (as He does for most, if not all, afterlife survivors), He singled out the events that elucidated a common thread of how God was drawing me toward Him all the days of my life, even when I did not even consider God as anyone other than a name. He has done the same for you. Each moment of your life means something to God, because He watches over you 24/7. Nothing goes to waste. So, when you are at the effect of the

Storm, remember that all your days have led up to this point. We live in exciting times. God has chosen you for this period in history for a reason.

The Storm is coming.

26

"TELL THEM"

For whoever is ashamed of me and my words, of him
will the Son of Man be ashamed when he comes in his
glory and the glory of the Father and of the holy angels.
—LUKE 9:26 ESV

In nature, storms are caused by differences in air pressure, so it is perfectly possible to be able to feel a coming storm. But in my "super nature" (my spirit), I felt Heaven's Storm in my blood. My *spiritual* blood coursed through me from Jesus and provided me with life. Just as a person whose flesh and blood is whole feels healthy, likewise my spiritual blood made whole through Christ transfused joy.

When the Storm began, all of Heaven went silent. At that moment, I felt the gravity of the crucifixion. For the first time, the ease of being in Heaven felt heavy, like the sudden rush of a cold wind on a balmy day. While in Heaven, I vicariously felt the experience of the cross through Jesus when the sky became dark, as recorded in the Bible: *"It was now about noon, and darkness came over the whole land until three in the afternoon, for the sun stopped shining"* (Luke 23:44 NIV).

A vivid scene ensued when the finely-woven curtain hanging at the heart of the house of worship that separated the Holy Place from the Most Holy Place (Holy of Holies) was torn in two. This signaled the "Age of Grace," when no longer would the Holy Spirit breathe in a place separated from humankind. Now He would indwell those who confessed Jesus the Messiah as their Lord and Savior. The new Temple now *indwelled the believer* in Jesus Christ.

That was You, wasn't it? I asked the Holy Spirit.

Yes, He responded. *I tore the curtain so that no separation would exist between Me and those who are Mine.*

God and I often had these types of casual conversations, even beyond my time in Heaven. We no longer talked as mythic strangers but as intimate friends. He was no longer just the God I knew about. He is the God I know. I also know that knowing God as the *Koinonia,* the most intimate One, should be the most common relationship every believer experiences.

Heaven also left a sense of urgency in my soul. Our ministry continued to grow. We reached millions of souls but God sees every soul as the most precious one in His sight. My Comforter, the Holy Spirit, the voice of Jesus, imputed prophecies in my dreams and visions. It felt like a mosaic was being painted before me of what I beheld in Heaven and what I saw was being imprinted on earth.

After sharing the revelations I gleaned from Heaven, I felt another release birthing within me. At first, it felt like mine alone without the need to share the insights with others. But then the same conviction I felt from the Holy Spirit on that flight from Florida, again impressed upon my heart:

Tell them about the Storm, beloved, the Holy Spirit said.

"Oh Jesus, is this chapter coming to a close?" I audibly replied.

Did I not tell you to look for the signs, My beloved? He said.

The Storm…the Storm I saw in Heaven with You is now? I asked.

I speak not as in your spirit as we did in Heaven, beloved. Now I speak within your reasoning mind, He said. *You feel the Storm brewing in your soul like a mother giving birth to a message. For forty weeks have you dwelled on what you beheld from My Throne.*

A different tonality resonated within my soul. What I heard now came from the Father. Father God had decreed a release from His Throne. Only when the Father speaks a Word is it established on earth from Heaven. Only when the Father speaks and the Son agrees, can what Heaven establishes be poured upon the earth; then the Holy Spirit declares it on earth and it is done.

I thought back forty weeks earlier or nine months before this decree entered my soul, to recall what had happened. I asked the Holy Spirit to reveal the conception of God's decree to me. I thought, *What happened nine months ago* (40 weeks) *that was significant in my life?* Then I prayed:

"God, reveal the point at which You birthed the time in which You conceived this message—this appointed time for people to know the forthcoming beginning of the end."

I waited. For days, I waited and prayed and sought the answer. I looked at my calendar. I tried to deduce some significant event in my life as the starting point—the birthing of an idea or a compulsion to share what I previously felt was only consecrated unto God. But I didn't even understand the fullness of the events I had witnessed from the Throne Room. I thought and nearly pleaded:

Oh God, tell me what You birthed within me months ago that simmered within me before You released me to write this book. What? When did You plant the release of this prophetic Word? I am not a prophet!

Says who? The Holy Spirit answered, in an almost irritated way.

I did not go to seminary. I tried to disprove You when I took theological courses. I was a businessman, a lay person. I know Your Word, but I am not a scholar. I am not worthy to bring the weight of what You have to say.

You say you know My Word, but you pretend not to understand the ones I chose to share it with. They are ones like you. Beloved, I have not chosen you to author My Word. I have chosen you to share My Word for such a time as this—to declare that which I have already revealed to you.

But the cost of falsely stating...no one knows the time or day. I felt chills.

Beloved, this is true, but they must know the season. Tell them.

On a casual Saturday morning, God gave me my answer. It did not come with a loud voice. It did not even come during prayer. It happened while I used one of my respiratory treatments that I use each day to clear my damaged lungs.

Renee walked into the family room and said:

"It's been almost nine months since you started the YouTube channel and a lot of people are being touched—look at these comments..."

I began reading the comments from our RandyKay.org website and from our various social media outlets. I started tearing up while reading some of the comments:

- "I was at the point of taking my life and I came across your channel..."
- "These (near-death experience) stories have given me hope for the first time..."
- "I met Jesus while listening to your interviews..."
- "I've been an invalid and lost my husband, but for the first time I know my purpose..."
- "I was healed of cancer..."
- "I was healed of drug addiction..."
- "Thank you so much for your teaching and others— I know Jesus now..."

- "For the first time I am at peace after my son committed suicide…"
- "It all makes sense to me now…"
- "You've made Heaven real to me…"
- "I broke down knowing that God isn't angry with me…"
- "I used to believe in a bunch of other things but now I believe in Jesus…"

The messages went on and on and there were hundreds of them. For the first time, what God was doing sank into my soul. God was bringing Heaven to earth, and He started our ministry *nine months (40 weeks)* before the day of Renee's comment. The seemingly trivial moments in life can define the most momentous occasions of God's declarations. God had planted an answer in an undeniably simple way, and that registered within my soul as truth. God does this for so many of us and we can miss the nuances of God's messages as we piece together the puzzles of our lives.

That was the day I began to write *Heaven Stormed*. I didn't know all that God would reveal to me but I trusted that the Holy Spirit would inspire me with the truth of what to share. Clearly, God wanted me to share when *Heaven Stormed* and the other prophetic insights for today.

I thought that the proverbial writing was on the wall as I looked out the window and into the sky. Behold, just as the North Star pointed the wise men in the direction of baby Jesus, the heavens were pointing me toward the end of the earth and the birth of a new one.

27

LOOK UP

Now when these things begin to take place,
straighten up and raise your heads, because
your redemption is drawing near.
—LUKE 21:28 ESV

David scribed this beautiful prose: *"The heavens declare the glory of God; the skies proclaim the work of his hands"* (Psalm 19:1 NIV).

After flatlining, when the light of Jesus first tugged at my spirit body, I rose through an orbit of planets and atmospheres I can only ascribe to the galaxies of the universe. Make no mistake. These galaxies did not speak as god, they declared His Glory and majesty. Immediately after my death, I traveled through the second heaven and witnessed the spiritual warfare that surrounds every person's life. Angels and demons battle over the rights to whisper either truths or lies into our souls, depending on which side wins.

Of particular importance is that the prayers of God's children provide the angels with strength, in ways similar to how carbohydrates provide our body's main source of energy. Godly devotion grants a license for God's angels to speak His truths to us, but sin gives demons their energy to prevail. Just as toxins cause death, sin gives license to demons to speak lies within our soul (mind, will, emotions).

This battle involves a spiritual dynamic as mysterious as the inner workings of the human body. Our body can produce cancerous cells, which were once healthy cells that have been influenced by toxins, stress, and unhealthy lifestyles—but foremost because we mistrust God. Demons impart oppression and depression, whereas God's angels impart wisdom and joy. God works in mysterious ways that become ever so clear from a heavenly perspective.

My experiences in Heaven and my intimate reunion with Jesus in Lake Tahoe awakened my conviction in the supernatural. So once I returned from Heaven, I began seeking answers in unexpected places, including the galaxies noted by King David, and the stars of biblical times when the Magi watched the night sky for signs of the coming Messiah. I thought that perhaps the sign of the coming Storm that Jesus told me to look for would be revealed in a similar manner.

According to the prophet Daniel, the wise men could have calculated the time of the appearance of "Messiah the Prince," Jesus. The divine provision of a star would thus confirm that the Messiah's time had come (Daniel 9:24-27). The Bible account says that the star led the wise men from Jerusalem to Bethlehem. They knew where to go in response to the star, since this sign was for the King of the Jews and Jerusalem was the "capital" of Jewry.

A Bible passage that guided them is found in the book of Numbers, where the prophet Balaam prophesied Jesus Messiah's future coming as the "Star" out of Jacob and the "Scepter" who would rise out of Israel (Numbers 24:17 NKJV). "Star" means

"King," while the full phrase "Star of Jacob" refers to the "Son of David." The word "scepter" thus interprets as the Messiah. Jesus fulfills Scripture by first arriving as the Star and Scepter to redeem and deliver His people from sin. He will come again to reclaim His people at the end of this age to conquer God's spiritual enemies, leading to Israel's ultimate redemption.

The Magi, who brought gifts for the baby Jesus, were not astrologers but *astronomers*. Astrology looks for answers based on the formation of galactic bodies and is based on superstition. Astronomy is the study of God's handiwork outside of the planet Earth's atmosphere as a science. I reasoned, *Why would God not provide a similar sign for the second coming of Jesus?*

I can only believe that God implanted such questions in my mind as I wrote this book, as I felt prompted to reach out to a long-lost mutual friend of mine and Renee's. Renee called Stacey Mueller, whom she knew had been studying and teaching about the Hebrew calendar—one based on ancient astronomy and mathematics. Stacey would share about the *Feast of Tabernacles*, a Jewish holiday held in the fall, to celebrate the gathering of the harvest and the Jewish exodus out of Egypt. I knew the importance of the Jewish customs from my relationship with Sid Roth and his Messianic Vision ministry. Stacey mentioned that Jacob received covenantal promises from God.

Abraham, the father of faith, his son Isaac, and Isaac's son Jacob were the first Hebrew fathers who observed the covenant given by God in their day. (Jacob was the progenitor of the twelve tribes of Israel.) For over twenty years, Jacob's son Joseph suffered in an Egyptian prison because of a false accusation, until the time of Joseph's favor (Genesis 50:20).

In Genesis 22:4, God made a covenant of promise to Joseph's great-grandfather Abraham, that was *"afar off"* (NKJV) or *"in the distance"* (NIV) in Abraham's day. Abraham was sent to look for Canaan the Promised Land (later the Land of Israel) and saw Jesus's future arrival. Jesus later declared Himself the "I AM" and told the Jewish leaders that Abraham *"rejoiced at the thought of seeing my day"*—Jesus's arrival on earth (John 8:56-58).

God made the covenantal blessings conditional—by faith in His Word. The father of faith (Abraham) and generations thereafter that lived by faith in God's promises received God's blessings as long as they remained in faith—first under the Mosaic Law, then under the new (blood) covenant of faith in Jesus as Messiah (Hebrews 8:6). The Hebrew fathers remained faithful, as Joseph did throughout his imprisonment.

"What does this all have to do with the Feast of Tabernacles or how Joseph's life may be telling us about what is to come?" I asked Stacey.

Stacey explained that the Feast of Tabernacles and Joseph's blessings were in accordance with the Hebrew calendar, which demonstrated that the possession of God's favor is close at hand.

"The Ancient of Days favors the saints," she said.

The title "Ancient of Days" first appears in Daniel 7:9-10, when Daniel describes his vision of Heaven. Daniel references the Ancient of Days during a period when God is judge. That same description depicts God the Son judging the seven churches (Revelation 1:9-20). The title "Ancient of Days" is found only three times in Scripture. Each time it is in the book of Daniel and describes an ancient, or a venerable "Person," Jesus, who sits on a flaming throne with wheels of fire, and whose hair and clothing were white as snow (Daniel 7:9). The flaming throne is symbolic of judgment, while the white hair and title "Ancient" indicate that God exists before time began. In the prophetic sense, the "Ancient of Days" clearly refers to Jesus pronouncing judgment upon the world (Daniel 7:22).

These explanations did not just represent heavenly symbols to me. They describe exactly what I saw in Heaven. God exists in Heaven both in form and in the representation of His Word, as recorded in the Bible. This means that Daniel's vision and my experiences match both prophetically and visually. The Ancient of Days in the Bible clearly refers to Jesus, who is returning to pronounce judgment upon the world:

> until the Ancient of Days came and pronounced judgment in favor of the holy people of the Most High, and the time came when they possessed the kingdom (Daniel 7:22 NIV).

"Based on your study of the Hebrew calendar, where do you think we are in history?" I asked Stacey.

"I believe 2024 to be a year of cleansing and completion," she said.

"I have the same sense," I said. "I believe that the Joshua generation is living today and will enter the fullness of God's presence and Glory upon this earth. I believe we will see the greatest revival of all time, and we are living in the last days. Soon the seven-year Tribulation will come. The Millennials (those born between the early 1980s and the late 1990s) will experience the greatest overpowering sense of the Holy Spirit's presence."

Stacey noted an important prophetic marker as *"the Rosh Chodesh Nisan for the Hebrew Year 5784,"* which begins at sundown on Monday, 8 April 2024 and ends at nightfall the following day. In the Hebrew calendar, the month of *Nisan* is the first month of the Hebrew year, or *Rosh Chodesh*. The Hebrew calendar is one of the oldest and most accurate calendars on earth, because it is based on the rotation of the sun, moon, and earth.

Stacey explained what is called "the Nisan" in the book of Esther in the Talmud,[1] which it calls the New Year or *Rosh HaShana.*

The month of *Nisan* usually falls during March-April on the Gregorian calendar, and is a 30-day month that hosts the Jewish spring feasts. Each feast commemorates God's blessings and points to Jesus. Jesus was crucified during the feast of *Pesach* (Passover), buried on the day of *Unleavened Bread,* and raised on the day of *Firstfruits* (Leviticus 23:5-11). Then He sent His Holy Spirit on *Shavu'ot* (Feast of Weeks, the Christian Pentecost), seven weeks (fifty days) after Passover (Leviticus 23:17).

In 2024, the spring feasts take place in late April, always corresponding with the first (barley) harvest of the year and the later (wheat) harvest, which ripens fifty days later. *Shavu'ot* or Pentecost is the "day" (think 2 Peter 3:8) when God baptized 120 believers (and His disciples) in the upper room with His Holy Spirit and with fire (Acts 2:1-4).

If you study Matthew 13 and the parable of the tares of the field, you will see that the angels of the harvest are separating the wheat (righteous children of God) from the tares (children of satan) during the *wheat* harvest at the end of the world. The harvest is a *season* that points to late spring/early summer and the great outpouring at Pentecost that began in the upper room with the "120" and continues to this day until the Last Day (Matthew 13:36-43; John 7:37; Acts 1:15).

If we pay close attention, the number 120 is called in Scripture, "a hundred and twenty years" (Genesis 6:3). The Hebrew word for "hundred" is *mē'â*, meaning "an hundred fold"; and for "twenty" in Hebrew, the word is *eśrîm*, meaning "score." God said, "*...My Spirit will not contend with humans forever, for they are mortal; their days will be a hundred and twenty years*" (Genesis 6:3). The root of the word *contend* is the Hebrew word *dîn, which points to humanity's judgment* *during the end times, but it also may point to a timeframe of cycles and seasons of 120 days. One hundred and twenty days is four 30-day months on the Hebrew calendar, which may indeed point to the late spring-early summer (wheat) harvest season.*

The *month* of Nisan is in the spring and the name *Rosh HaShana* points to a future day when the Messiah returns to rescue the righteous and judge the wicked. This is also reflected in the Jewish fall feasts (i.e., fruit trees and vines…olives, grapes) that occur during the Hebrew month *Tishri*, (late September-October, Gregorian). The main fall feasts include *Rosh Hashanah* (Feast of Trumpets), *Yom Kippur* (Day of Atonement), *Sukkot* (Feast of Tabernacles), and *Shmini Atzeret* (The Eighth Day)—and all of these point to the end times.

The original prayer of *Rosh Hashanah* names Yeshua (Jesus) as the One who atones for our sins, yet contemporaries deleted the name "Yeshua" from the prayer. I believe that the Messiah Yeshua is and will continue to be revealed to Israel and the Jewish people so that during the fullness of God's Glory, the *Rosh Hashanah* prayer will return to its original text. Thereafter, many of God's chosen people *will bow* and their *tongues will confess* that Jesus is Lord (Isaiah 45:23; Romans 14:11).

As for heavenly signs, according to astronomers the next solar eclipses in 2024 will occur on 8 April, while the next lunar eclipses will be on 25 March and 18 September. I also learned that a solar storm (not a thunderstorm) is intensifying in 2024. NASA and the National Oceanic and Atmospheric Administration (NOAA) have issued warnings about solar storms, which have become more common during recent years. Apparently, the solar cycle will be at its peak in April 2024, per various models and projections made by scientists.

The question remains as to how signs and seasons prophetically fit our current day. God reminds us that no one knows the hour or the day of that last great day (Matthew 24:36-37). Referring to the end times, the Word says, *"as in the days of Noah,"* which is usually translated as the *conduct* of the times, not the actual *days*. Perhaps we have been remiss at looking at Noah's *days* (Genesis 8:6, 9:29; 1 Peter 3:20). In the Hebrew, *day is yôm, and may point to the fall feast of Yom Kippur or the Day of Atonement (Judgment)*. In the Greek, the word *day* is *hēmera,* which can be understood as a metaphor for abstaining from unrighteousness.

Astronomical signs frequently had Messianic significance in Scripture. Perhaps they will signal Christ's return or the Glory of God being manifested on earth. Remember how the Magi knew of Jesus's birth as recorded in the book of Matthew. They saw His star (in the east) and followed it so they could worship Him (Matthew 2:1-2). When I witnessed the release of God's presence upon the earth from my vantage point in Heaven, it appeared as shooting stars. Maybe these "stars" were the Light of Jesus fracturing through the atmosphere. Maybe they were angels breaking through the second heaven to release God's authority on earth. This I know—Jesus is coming, and His presence will cause all on earth to bow in awe.

Just as God sent a supernatural star to the Magi to mark Jesus's first coming, God may send a supernatural event in the heavens to signal His second coming. The prophetic voice of the cosmos is not astrological or superstitious. It is well documented in the Bible. The Bible is filled with references to the cosmos. King David the poet often wrote about the sun, moon, and stars as reflecting God's goodness and majesty. He wrote: *"The heavens declare the glory of God, and the sky above proclaims his handiwork"* (Psalm 19:1 ESV).

The prophet Isaiah speaks of God recreating the universe in the form of new heavens and a new Earth, a reality confirmed by Jesus and the apostles in several places within the New Testament. But

275

always God warned His people to be wary of astrology (not astronomy) and reminds us to worship the Creator—not the created. I believe these astronomical signs do not just spell the end of the world, they portend a pervasive sense of the Lord's presence creating a spiritual atmosphere over the entire world—but will it begin in 2024, or beyond? Only God knows.

I decided to seek God's revelation by taking a trip to my favorite spot that overlooks the ocean along the Carlsbad State Beach. It is where I bicycled at the start of my fatal journey that led to blood clots, the Emergency Room, death, and ultimately to Heaven. I felt a pull in my heart to return to the spot where I first felt the heavy pain in my calf. When I reached that very spot, I felt an ominous tug at my soul. That day, while sitting atop the rock that once served as my brief respite from the arduous trek sixteen years before, I became hypnotized by the rolling waves as they reflected the closing day's sunlight.

I closed my eyes as the sun settled into darkness. When I reopened them, darkness hovered over the ocean and hid the waves as the stars emerged in the night sky. One star in particular flashed above me so distinctly bright that it drew my attention as it appeared to wink at me with every twinkle. The ocean current now rolled softly with the gentle breeze. As I looked across the vastness of the darkened waters, I heard a soft voice speak within the whispering wind:

"I speak light into the darkness. Fear not."

"What?" I responded. "Lord, I don't fear the darkness anymore."

I listened silently, hoping for some audible sound but nothing followed. I waited, hoping to hear His voice whispering in the winds again, just as the Holy Spirit had spoken to me in Heaven, but I heard nothing. Then I realized something that I had known all along. In Heaven, God's voice sounds clear and bold; whereas in this world, He speaks in the silence—and even more profoundly through the heart. So, I listened to my heart, trusting that Jesus would unveil the truth of what He meant, and He did.

You seek answers in the stars, beloved, but you will find them in your heart. You seek the time of My return, but no one knows the time. You seek the truth. I AM the Truth.

"Yes," I whispered softly in return. "I knew the answer all along, Lord. You have sent Your messengers like me, from Heaven or hell, as a sign. You are coming for us, Lord. I feel it. I sense it. Why else would You reveal Heaven to the world, if not to prepare those in this world for Heaven?"

I could envision that smile again on His face—the smile in Heaven that told me I was right because His Spirit had revealed the answer to me.

"Trust Me," He had said when I first met Him. Indeed, I would trust Him to speak His truth to me. In the next moment, I knew the answer to the question—the Storm was happening now. The earth was in the beginning stages of the Storm. The Holy Spirit is showering His Glory upon the world and it will have a cascading effect that will begin in isolated places around the globe, before expanding in scope. God's greater Glory is being birthed upon the earth.

After an unprecedented move of God's Spirit in the world, the second phase of the Storm will begin. That will be the subsequent and terrible removal of God's presence. The contrast could not be more striking when this occurs. After that will be the period of great trials—and finally, the new Earth.

I sat on a rock in a stupor, overlooking the ocean as it was touched by the moonlight. After what seemed like hours, I stood up to enter my car that I had parked beside the rocky cliff. I knew without a doubt that the Joshua generation living on the earth today would not only see the greatest revelation of God's Glory the world has ever known, but that some people who are living today would never taste of death (Mark 9:1).

Note

1. The Talmud is a primary theological text of Rabbinic Judaism.

28

RETURNING HOME

I regarded home as a place I left behind in
order to come back to it afterward.
—ERNEST HEMINGWAY

The meeting in Philadelphia ended early, with hours before the departure of my return flight to San Diego, so I drove to Cherry Hill, New Jersey, where I had attended grade school and junior high. Our small ranch home wore the same green paint which peeled at the corners, and the red brick still surrounded the base of its façade. Suddenly I pictured little Casey running up to greet me, just as he did in Heaven. And I imagined my mother standing at the large picture window overlooking the sidewalk, where she watched to see that I walked safely to the school bus, without a clue how I loathed going to school, for fear of impending ridicule.

I got out of the car to touch the big spruce that my father and I had planted, when it stood nearly as tall as my then forty inch-plus frame. Now it towered at least fifty feet in height. A slew of memories flooded my mind as I thought of the period when I lost my innocence to a truckload of insecurities and feelings of worthlessness caused by the taunts of school bullies toward a shy, speech-impaired, and overweight boy.

"Why me, Lord?" I asked.

Why did this little boy, who grew up bearing a lifetime of self-doubt, experience an afterlife that would invite a mountain of ridicule? Ironically, such mockery came from people (who I was once like) who did not believe in near-death experiences. I used to think badly of "NDE people" who wrote books and appeared on shows. To me, they appeared as exhibitionists. After returning from my own near-death experience, of all people, I did not want the attention—testified to by the fact that it took fourteen years before I publicly shared my experience.

As I continued walking toward the backyard, I saw bricks that lined the side walkway, still stamped with the name "Keokuk." My dad and I had hand-placed the bricks he had found on one of our many trips to see Grandma Kay. I could vividly remember being a thirteen-year-old boy dressed in my football outfit ready for practice as my dad handed me each brick to lay it overtop the holes we had dug.

I entered the backyard, hoping the current occupants of 700 Covered Bridge Road would not be alarmed at my snooping around. There stood the old oak tree that the squirrel climbed after taunting little Casey, the dog who zipped to the end of his chain barking in frustration—until the day the chain broke, the squirrel froze in terror and both stood face to face, not knowing what to do.

"It seemed like yesterday," I said to God.

While reminiscing about my boyhood, I remembered my little Casey in Heaven and how gracious Jesus was to bring my lone childhood buddy to Heaven.

"See, I give you the desires of your heart," He said to me in Heaven.

I bent down and touched the leaf-covered ground, thinking of how I labored over years to rake all those leaves, how my friend

Jimmy and I played catch in the yard, and how no one remembered anymore about the past but me. By now, both my father and mother were in Heaven.

I remember, whispered the sweet voice of the Holy Spirit.

Oh God, You are the only One who remembers every second of my life.

No regrets? He asked.

No regrets, I answered, *how could I regret what You did for me?*

You've learned a valuable lesson, My beloved, He said.

Instantly, I remembered my favorite Bible verse: *"And we know that in all things God works for the good of those who love him, who have been called according to his purpose"* (Romans 8:28).

I began walking back to the car with each step flooding my mind with details of this boy's life. Then an epiphany came to me: *everybody's life is filled with stories to which only God can fully relate.* I stopped to look at the bus stop corner where my only boyhood friend was beaten, a terrible thing that caused his family to move away.

Most of the time we are consumed with the cares of the world—all the stuff that doesn't seem to mean anything. Why God?

I opened the car door and slid into my seat and sat there waiting for an answer. I would not leave without an answer, but none came for at least twenty minutes. Then I remembered what I needed to say:

"I am so sorry for doubting You. I should have trusted You."

I couldn't see His figure in the passenger's seat, but I knew Jesus sat there. I didn't imagine it.

I know He sat there smiling at me as He reached over to give me a hug. Then He leaned to the side and looked straight into my eyes.

Every moment of your life mattered to Me, He said, *and none of it was wasted.*

I leaned back in my seat knowing exactly what He meant. All those moments added up to who I am, and all of who I am is valuable to God.

Ah beloved, I AM.

Jesus explained Himself as "I AM," with metaphors that expressed His saving relationship toward the world—all of which were recorded in the book of John:

> *"I AM the Bread of Life."*
>
> *"I AM the Light of the World."*
>
> *"I AM the Door of the Sheep."*
>
> *"I AM the Good Shepherd."*
>
> *"I AM the Resurrection and the Life."*
>
> *"I AM the Way, the Truth, and the Life."*
>
> *"I AM the True Vine."*
>
> (John 6:35; 8:12, 10:1-11, 11:25, 14:6, 15:1)

The consummation of our life can be summed up in this statement: *All of who I am and all of what I've done is completed in Christ because "I AM" makes me who I am.* Knowing that our value rests in the value that God places upon you and me makes all the difference. Knowing that God is the only relationship that continues from birth to death to eternity, makes God the only One who truly knows us, and the One who loves us the most.

I asked Jesus one final question while sitting in my car, looking down the sidewalk of my childhood treks to school and walks with Casey:

"Wouldn't it have been easier if You just told me when the Storm would take place instead of me looking for a sign?"

As I waited for an answer, none arrived.

Then I remembered those first words that Jesus spoke to me in Heaven: *Trust Me.* That was my answer—and yours as well. I turned on the car's ignition to drive toward the airport from the place I once called home. As I drove away, I remembered all the other homes where I had lived.

Heaven is now my home, and that understanding will never leave me. Heaven is your home as well, if you know Jesus.

29

YOUR ASSIGNMENT
DURING THE END TIMES

*So, because you are lukewarm—neither hot nor
cold—I am about to spit you out of my mouth.*
—REVELATION 3:16 NIV

A few months ago, I gave a prophetic message about the Holy Spirit's winds blowing through the United Kingdom (UK) as the outpouring of God's Spirit during the end times. Recently, an artist by the name of Julie Ann Scott reached out to me, saying that she had been inspired to paint a series of artworks about the Storm from Heaven, without any prior knowledge about the Storm that I beheld in Heaven. She simply saw a video about my time in Heaven and felt called to contact me.

"Jules," as she prefers to be called, is not just any artist—she has been commissioned to create artwork for the UK's royal family, including portrayals of Windsor Castle. But now she is revealing a series of paintings about Heaven's Storm, completed long before our discussion.

When I told her about this book, about my prophecy concerning the UK, and how her artwork is "touched by the Hands of God," she repeatedly said, "Wow!" Jules is one of the most acclaimed painters in the world. When I first saw her paintings, all I could say in return was, "Wow!"

God weaves together our lives in unexpected ways. He connects the dots without our knowing the picture. As I shared earlier, my story began when I received an invitation from a friend (Rich Marshall) to talk about "thriving in life" during a GodTV production called *God@Work*. Then Sid Roth invited me to speak on his *It's Supernatural* program to discuss my book *Revelations from Heaven*. Next, Shaun Tabatt invited me to join him for a podcast called *Two Christian Dudes*. Then I launched a vodcast called *Revelations from Heaven* to an audience of about forty people, which grew to over fifteen million viewers.

I never wanted any attention to my story about Heaven. I simply wanted to be alone with my family, my books, and occasional baseball games during an easy "retirement," but God had different plans. Maybe your personal assignment is not on the world's stage—Lord knows I never yearned for that. Maybe your assignment begins with taking flowers to senior centers and spending weeks praying with the residents. Or, your talent could blossom into masterpieces as with Julie Ann Scott—if not on earth, then certainly to the utmost in Heaven. Whatever your assignment, you must do it and you must do it now.

Think moments, not years. Think that God will claim you at any time, not sometime in the future. Think that if you do not share the "Great News" of Jesus Christ through your kindness, talents, and boldness, that lives may end up in hell and your lost purpose will fade into the abyss of "lost dreams" I witnessed from Heaven.

During these last days, God will accelerate your influence and abilities, just as He has done with me. Do not be surprised if like me, you will be asked to do something apparently small but God blows it up. These last days are a time of "purposeful acceleration," wherein we must answer ministry opportunities with a resounding "yes," so that God can open the door to a multi-fold expansion of our abilities and scope of the ministry impacts we will make.

Don't be surprised if you face persecution—know that Jesus rescues you to make you a closely relied upon servant of Jesus, as Mary Magdalene became after she lay on the verge of being stoned. Don't be surprised if, like David, you work at a seemingly menial job and you suddenly find that your calling is to lead thousands. And don't be surprised if you pray for God to "show up" the way Elijah did, and God pours fire down from Heaven for you before ushering you into Heaven without you having to die first.

Beloved, now is the time of acceleration of your influence, reach, and ability to serve God. You can receive this blessing by first saying "yes" to the opportunities God sets before you. Then you must rely upon God to work miracles through you. Perhaps never before in the flow of all of history has such a magnificent calling been placed upon all our lives—to be fully prepared (2 Timothy 4:2). God has anointed you to do far more than you ever imagined. All you need to do is say "yes." Then, as I learned in Heaven, you simply trust Jesus to do the impossible.

Now is your time of influence—NOW, not tomorrow. If you have placed a ministry dream on the proverbial backburner, take it off and serve that dish. Nothing is too small for God to blow up into the size of a giant blimp so that you can soar above every one of your limitations.

Beloved, the Storm is not only coming, it is here. We are witnessing revivals scattering throughout the world. The outpouring of God's Spirit is causing people to fall prostrate in worship, confession, and repentance, in like manner to what I experienced in Lake Tahoe. This may sound cliché, but if you don't answer the call, who will? The answer, dear child of God, is NO ONE.

We now live in the "calm phase of God's Storm." God is cleansing the spiritual air from powers, principalities, and spirits of darkness, to leave an open portal to His angels, and of course, His Spirit. Soon, as with my own personal life, the floodgates of your works will pour out like never before. And you will be Godsmacked that He could use you in such powerful ways.

Perhaps the best part is that you will see the fruits of your labor in Heaven. People in Heaven will say "Thank you" to you because of what you did here—sometimes unwittingly—to bless them—and in some cases, to save them.

During these end times, God will no longer tolerate "pew warmers" or "seekers." The most guttural Scripture in the Bible says: *"So, because you are lukewarm—neither hot nor cold—I am about to spit you out of my mouth"* (Revelation 3:16 NIV).

I often had to pray for my own personal revelation about that verse.

"God, does taking You for granted really upset You that much?" I asked.

The answer recently came on a sun-kissed day on a grassy knoll by the marina in downtown San Diego, while I listened to the flapping of sails and waves slapping the boats in dock and walked my little Maltese dog, Buddy. Along the gravel pathway, I got close to the edge of the rocks that shield the Bay waters, just as a large wave crashed against the rocks and sprayed trickles of water over me.

"How does that feel?" asked the Holy Spirit.

"Did You just spit on me?" I giggled.

I could envision Jesus laughing in response, just as He did while holding my tears in Heaven.

"I just anointed you," answered the Holy Spirit. *"Go."*

Conviction overtook me, not to start writing a book or to witness to the next person I met. No, I just started praying for everyone within my line of sight. I prayed that the Holy Spirit would touch down on people dining at restaurants, on joggers, homeless people camping out, and boaters on the Bay. Then I prayed a prayer just for me:

"Lord, never let my soul run dry."

Tears swelled in my eyes and I began confessing the many times I ignored God and consumed myself with the ways of the world.

"I'm sorry, Lord." I meant it.

A flood of my personal failings crossed my mind and I ticked off each one with an ensuing petition for God to forgive me. Then I shook my head and sat upon a cement bench, with slouched shoulders and an even more contrite soul.

"I can't possibly justify myself," I said.

Aha, the Holy Spirit said. *That is the beginning of wisdom.*

So, You're not going to spew me out of Your mouth? I asked.

An alarming stillness filled my space. I just waited, hoping for a response, wishing for a Holy Spirit chuckle.

There was nothing but silence.

Then a homeless man came up to me and asked me for some change. I turned my glistening eyes toward him and fumbled for a five-dollar bill in my wallet before giving it to him. As he began to walk away, I heard:

I'm starting to spew… came that still small voice.

So, I stood up and said to the man, who was now about six feet away:

"Do you know Jesus?"

"Huh?" he replied.

"May I pray for you?" I asked. Then I prayed over the man.

Still spewing, came that still voice.

"Would you like to have lunch with me?" I asked.

"Huh? Me?" the man asked, as surprised as I was.

We traveled to a nearby takeout place and sat at a cement table and munched on fish and chips as we talked about his life and his losses and finally, about Jesus.

Beloved, when you invited that man to lunch with you, you invited Me to lunch with you, the still voice said.

Immediately thereafter, I remembered the formerly homeless man I had met in Heaven. I wondered if somehow, someway, the man I saw in Heaven could possibly be this same homeless man with whom I was now eating lunch. I had heard from other afterlife survivors about seeing their loved ones in Heaven before they died. At this point, I could never rule out the impossible concerning God, who lives in our future. My next thought was:

Oh my, how small and yet how grand are the ways of God!

Beloved of the Lord Jesus, this I know for sure—you have grossly underestimated God's love for you, so let us please stop underestimating our capacity to love others. God's purpose for us lives in the moments of our lives, kissed by Jesus, empowered by the Holy Spirit, and made everlastingly creative by the Father who creates the new in our lives, from His Throne.

The simplicity of pleasing God strikes me most—doing good works as God presents the opportunities. Look in unexpected places and even unwanted places. Smile first when meeting someone. Don't just follow someone else's smile. Be steeped in God's presence and confess, ask forgiveness, and thank God—profusely.

Just like that homeless man I met in the park, all I did was give him food and companionship. Yet something far greater invariably lies in wait—and that something will be born forth in those who have the courage to trust God. It was at that humble luncheon, beloved, that I heard within the silence of my heart, the thunder of my soul. And that thunder was God finally releasing me to write this book.

Why is it so increasingly important during these last days to do the good works that God asks of us when those opportunities present themselves? Because God wants to save all who can be saved and He needs us to shine brightest in an increasingly ominous world that shields His light.

God's light shines the brightest when we confront oppression in the world. That means we need to look under "spiritual rocks," in the unexpected places, like the homeless man who didn't need money as much as companionship—the kind that opened the door to his salvation as we prayed together—and all of Heaven celebrated in response.

Do you remember the butterfly I met in Heaven? It represented the voice of wisdom telling me what to do. Do you also remember what Jesus said to me during this revelation? He told me that "moment by moment He would reveal His purpose to me." I wanted a grandiose scheme or ten-year plan for my life. Jesus wanted me to be still and listen to Him—softly, quietly, humbled.

Right now, God offers opportunities to feed the deepest needs of people so that *"Whatever you do, do your work heartily, as for the Lord…* (Colossians 3:23 NASB). Does that require sacrifice?

Here is my takeaway from having lunch with a foul-smelling homeless man whose breath smelled like a brewery—it was one of the most satisfying meals of my life. That is your answer, beloved. Sacrifices unto God are always the most satisfying.

Back when I flew from Philadelphia to my current home in San Diego, a new confidence rested in my soul. It would be years before I would feel the need to share my story in Heaven, and I did—but not about the Storm, until today.

Now, a sense of urgency brews within my soul. What I beheld in Heaven had already been established and is only beginning to manifest as a global revival that will culminate in the fullness of God's Glory on earth. When that happens, this world will never be the same, and all who refuse God's last invitation will be entirely left without excuse.

God forewarns His beloved of what will come to earth, but Heaven knows it right now. Heaven is the incubator of all things good. Many people look forward to the outpouring of God's Glory and His reclamation of His children, but few, if any, look forward to His Judgment. Sadly, despair will reign for those who are left behind without Christ—and they will be lost without Him during the cruelest period of earth's history. There will still be hope, but not much. This world will be a wasteland, and those who remain in it will waste along with it—unless they repent and acknowledge Jesus as their Lord and Savior.

Those who come to know Jesus as their Lord during the Tribulation period will not experience the same intimacy that believers such as you and I enjoy today with the Holy Spirit. For them, it will be like the ancient times when God spoke mainly through the prophets and priests. Sadly, many people will nevertheless continue to wallow in self-righteousness and some will even blame God for being "negligent."

Beloved of the Lord, if you have not done so, will you please confess Jesus as your Lord and Savior right now? Your time to draw unto the Lord Jesus Christ is *today*. Let us no longer ignore Him, as Jesus admonished me to say when I was in Lake Tahoe. We have been taking God for granted for far too long. Like a faded mist, our life on this earth will come to an end. Soon you will see the things that I saw in the afterlife. Meanwhile, know this very important truth—YOU mean *everything* to God.

ABOUT RANDY KAY

Randy Kay, an ordained minister, founded Randy Kay Ministries to bring the "Great News" of Jesus Christ to the world through inspiring stories and messages, including Christ-centered after-life experiences. Randy's work can be found in his *Revelations from Heaven* vodcast, the *Heaven Encounters* TV show on Sid Roth's ISN Network, the *Two Christian Dudes* podcast with his co-host Shaun Tabatt, the *Heaven on Earth* vodcast with co-host Taylor Jensen, and several other podcasts, media presentations, livestreams, prayer rooms, counseling sessions, and events, including the first Christian Afterlife Conference.

Prior to his ministry, Randy was an executive in the healthcare industry, having led operations for the fastest-growing neuro-bio-pharmaceutical company in the world. He was CEO of a biotech company, marketing and clinical director for two cardiovascular companies, and training director or consultant for ministries and fortune 100 companies. He also developed the first validated course for thriving in life.

Randy and his wife, Renee, live in the San Diego area and have two grown children and two grandchildren.

THE *REAL NEAR DEATH EXPERIENCE STORIES* SERIES

Stories of Heaven
and the Afterlife
9780768471816

Heaven Stormed
9780768473308

Visiting Heaven
9780768463347

Real Near Death
Experience Stories
9780768464054

A Message
from God
9780768464320

A Rabbi's Journey
to Heaven
9780768461442

A Rabbi Looks at
the Afterlife
9780768404104

Revelations from
Heaven
9780768459371

Heaven is Beyond
Your Wildest
Expectations
9780768402865

A Journey to Hell,
Heaven and Back
9780768458350

From

Sid Roth

So this is Heaven!

These true stories are your unique, personal opportunities to enjoy a taste of Heaven here on earth. *Heaven Is Beyond Your Wildest Expectations* shares the testimonies of ten ordinary people who have been to Heaven—having died and returned, or in a vision or dream.

These real-life, modern-day stories inspire faith that, no matter what happens here on earth, all troubles are momentary, light afflictions compared to the glory that awaits you in Heaven. *For momentary, light affliction is producing for us an eternal weight of glory far beyond all comparison* (2 Corinthians 4:17).

When you see God's love permeating all of Heaven and realize that He reaches down to you right where you are, your heart will come to rest in Him—knowing He is watching over you and that His angels will minister to you in every moment of need. When you know that Heaven's splendor and glory are your eternal destiny, you can endure whatever you must while patiently waiting for the day when you will enter Heaven and your eternal joy in the presence of the Lord.

Purchase your copy wherever books are sold.

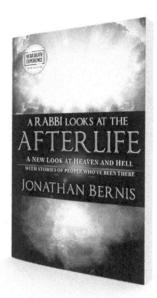

From
RETHA MCPHERSON

When Aldo McPherson was 12 years old, a car accident left him in a coma. While in the coma, he had a supernatural experience where he went to heaven, saw God, angels, Moses, and Abraham. Aldo came back with one message: "Jesus is alive!" This book challenges the complacent. Is God still your first love? Are you sold out for Him?

Filled with Scripture references and direct quotes from the Bible, *A Message from God* will ignite the sparks of the Holy Spirit in your life and bring you closer to God, while Aldo's letters in his own handwriting give a sense of authenticity not often found in miracle stories.

Purchase your copy wherever books are sold

From
FELIX HALPERN

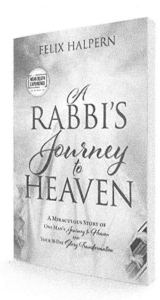

A Rabbi's Journey to Heaven

It all happened suddenly. In a twinkling of an eye, Rabbi Felix died, left his body, and crossed over into Heaven. Amazed, he experienced the glories of Heaven that he always read, pondered, and dreamt about. He also saw the lower realm—the second heaven where demons dwell.

Three days after returning from Heaven, God also gave Rabbi Felix a gift called "the heavenly soul cleanse" which holds the keys to a transformational prayer life that turns our current prayer culture upside down. Rabbi Felix now lives from an open heaven, and as he shares these heavenly keys with you in this book, so will you. Imagine saturating your soul in heavenly glory and starving your soul from the natural order. As you do, God will heal your soul, and you will be launched into an entirely new operating system.

Take this journey with Rabbi Felix and experience this heavenly transformation. True freedom awaits you, and you will never be the same!

Purchase your copy wherever books are sold

YOUR
Prophetic
COMMUNITY

In the Right Hands, This Book Will Change Lives!

Most of the people who need this message will not be looking for this book. To change their lives, you need to **put a copy of this book in their hands.**

Our ministry is constantly seeking methods to find the people who need this anointed message to change their lives. **Will you help us reach these people?**

Extend this ministry by sowing three, five, ten, or *even more* books today and change people's lives for the better! Your generosity will be part of catalyzing the Great Awakening that many have been prophesying and praying for.